PRAISE FOR
TOO CLOSE FOR COMFORT?

"*Too Close for Comfort?* takes a new and close look at the mother–adult daughter relationship. Gordon and Shaffer provide insight, humor, and practical advice on one of the most significant relationships in a young woman's life. Whether you are a mother or a daughter, this book will resonate."

—Dr. Michele Borba, author of *The Big Book of Parenting Solutions: 101 Answers to Your Everyday Challenges and Wildest Worries*

"At last, a parenting book that starts where the other ones end! *Too Close for Comfort?* provides mothers with the understanding, strategies, and tools to help them successfully parent emotionally healthy adult daughters. Gordon and Shaffer offer practical advice to help readers of both generations recognize and resolve the opportunities—as well as the inherent land mines—that crop up when the roles of 'mother' and 'friend' are paired."

—Irene S. Levine, PhD, professor of psychiatry, NYU School of Medicine, and author of *Best Friends Forever: Surviving a Breakup with Your Best Friend*

TOO CLOSE FOR COMFORT?

Questioning the Intimacy of Today's New Mother-Daughter Relationship

LINDA PERLMAN GORDON and
SUSAN MORRIS SHAFFER

BERKLEY BOOKS, NEW YORK

THE BERKLEY PUBLISHING GROUP
Published by the Penguin Group
Penguin Group (USA) Inc.
375 Hudson Street, New York, New York 10014, USA
Penguin Group (Canada), 90 Eglinton Avenue East, Suite 700, Toronto, Ontario M4P 2Y3, Canada
(a division of Pearson Penguin Canada Inc.)
Penguin Books Ltd., 80 Strand, London WC2R 0RL, England
Penguin Group Ireland, 25 St. Stephen's Green, Dublin 2, Ireland (a division of Penguin Books Ltd.)
Penguin Group (Australia), 250 Camberwell Road, Camberwell, Victoria 3124, Australia
(a division of Pearson Australia Group Pty. Ltd.)
Penguin Books India Pvt. Ltd., 11 Community Centre, Panchsheel Park, New Delhi—110 017, India
Penguin Group (NZ), 67 Apollo Drive, Rosedale, North Shore, 0632, New Zealand
(a division of Pearson New Zealand Ltd.)
Penguin Books (South Africa) (Pty.) Ltd., 24 Sturdee Avenue, Rosebank, Johannesburg 2196,
South Africa

Penguin Books Ltd., Registered Offices: 80 Strand, London WC2R 0RL, England

Cover design by Annette Fiore Defex
Cover photo: plainpicture/amanaimages
Book design by Tiffany Estreicher

PRINTING HISTORY
Berkley trade paperback edition / September 2009

Library of Congress Cataloging-in-Publication Data

Shaffer, Susan Morris.
Too close for comfort : questioning the intimacy of today's new mother-daughter relationship / Susan Shaffer and Linda Perlman Gordon.
p. cm.
Includes bibliographical references and index.
ISBN 978-0-425-22960-6
1. Mothers and daughters. 2. Adult children—Family relationships. 3. Intimacy (Psychology) I. Gordon, Linda Perlman. II. Title.
HQ755.85.S494 2009
306.874'3—dc22

2009006407

PRINTED IN THE UNITED STATES OF AMERICA

10 9 8 7 6 5 4 3 2 1

To our daughters, Emily and Elizabeth

We hope we have given you both the ability to grow into strong, loving, and compassionate women with the freedom to make your own choices no matter how close we are or how far away.

To our mothers, Jeanette and Jeanne

We wish you could have shared the last two decades with us. We miss your humor, wisdom, and irreverence. You both would have loved knowing your grandchildren as adults.

If a girl never learns how to be a daughter, she can't never know how to be a woman . . . A daughter is a woman that cares about where she came from and takes care of them that took care of her . . .

—Toni Morrison

ACKNOWLEDGMENTS

We want to give particular thanks to all the mothers and daughters in our focus groups for sharing their personal stories with sensitivity, honesty, and humor.

To Mark: chief chef, reader, and editor, with thanks and love.

To Arnie: for support and patience when I wasn't available and for making all the plans for fun when I was.

To Sue Wechsler (from Susan): Without you, parenting our daughters into adulthood doesn't seem possible.

To Judi Deutsch (from Linda): Your parenting and grandparenting wisdom is always reassuring.

To Paulette Hurwitz, Kimberly Kol, Sue Wechsler, Mickie Simon: for your invaluable counsel and psychological expertise.

To our agent, Joelle Delbourgo: For your insightful guidance, enthusiastic advocacy and interesting conversations, which motivate us to further exploration.

To our editor at Berkely Books, Emily Rapoport: for believing in our ability to investigate the complex relationships between mothers and adult daughters and tell their stories.

To our copyeditors for your assistance and attention to detail.

To our sons, Zach and Seth: for having a deep and sympathetic understanding of the complexities of human relationships and for always being interested in what we do.

To our public relations team from Berkley Books: Craig Burke, Julia Fleischaker, and Jennifer Bernard for your creativity and enthusiasm.

We are grateful for the encouragement, personal stories, and support of so many mothers and daughters who made this book possible.

CONTENTS

Introduction: Can a Mother Be a Daughter's Best Friend? 1

1. Catch and Release 7
2. A Paradigm Shift: Where's the Gap? 20
3. Attachment vs. Individuation: Like Mother, Like Daughter 41
4. Differences Between Supporting and Enabling: She's a Young Thing and Cannot Leave Her Mother 67
5. Characteristics of Friendship: "You've Got a Friend" 96
6. Archetypes: Mother Superior . . . My Mom Is Running My Life from Across State Lines 122
7. Marriage, Motherhood, and Divorce: From Here to Maternity 164
8. Boundaries: Staying Close Is Hard to Do 204
9. Tyranny of Beauty: "Mirror, Mirror, on the Wall . . ." 221

10. Lessons Learned: Close Encounters . . . of the Mothering Kind 235

11. Strategies: Strengthening Healthy Connections 253

Notes 269

Bibliography 277

Index 285

INTRODUCTION

Can a Mother Be a Daughter's Best Friend?

One generation plants the trees; another gets the shade.

—Chinese Proverb

The following statements are testaments to the complicated, dynamic, and changing relationship between a mother and her adult daughter. The energy of motherhood sustains and nurtures both mother and child. But this relationship engenders a wider range of emotions. A mother loves having the opportunity to be close to her daughter, but sometimes feels taken advantage of by the expectations of the relationship. A mother loves feeling needed and sharing intimacy with her daughter, but also feels overwhelmed by her daughter's extended dependence. A mother feels appreciated one moment, neglected the next. A mother is thrilled to see her daughter become a good mother, but takes

"My daughter is the joy of my life and the bane of my existence."

"I put my daughter in the way back of our station wagon in 1975, and now I need a police officer to certify the installation of my grandson's car seat in my Honda before my daughter will allow me to drive him."

"She tells me everything—some details I would rather not know!"

"I've held my tongue so much, it's a surprise I haven't bitten it off."

"I feel like the character from the book The Giving Tree*—my daughter climbed on my trunk, swung from my branches, ate my apples, and someday she'll sit down when all I have left to give is the comfort of my stump."*

"My daughter makes more money than me, so why in the world do I feel guilty if we go shopping and I don't pay for her Coach bag?"

"When I was single, my daughter and I were much closer. I spoke to her every day. Now that I am remarried, I feel she doesn't think that I need as much attention."

"Often it's hard for me to know where my daughter ends and where I begin."

some small and hidden pleasure to see her daughter pulling her own hair out when she can't control her child.

As we discovered when writing our previous book about parenting twentysomethings, there are few books exploring the relationship between parents and adult children at any age. Therefore, we were not surprised when mothers in our focus groups were very enthusiastic about discussing their relationships with their daughters. They confirmed our belief that there is little conventional wisdom and no road map to guide them.

Daughters told us stories about their frustrations with their mothers, and also shared stories about how satisfying they find their adult relationship. Daughters feel blessed and lucky to have a strong support system, and yet worry about being too dependent or less competent, and become irritated by a lack of boundaries. Some are disappointed that their mothers aren't what they want them to be. Others are fearful that they can't be as selfless as they perceived their mothers were when they were growing up. Fortunately, many daughters do find peace with their less-than-ideal mothers and selves.

Some daughters describe their relationship with their mothers as being best friends. Very few mothers described their relationship with their daughters as such. Uniformly, mothers had a visceral reaction to the idea of being their daughter's best friend. Most mothers we spoke with had an innate sense that there was something that didn't quite resonate with them about being best friends with their daughters. While many of their relationships include aspects of friendship, such as intimacy, advice, listening, and sharing good times, they bristled at the idea of *best friendship* with their daughters.

As mothers of adult daughters, we were curious about whether adult daughters and mothers could achieve what might be considered the closest of friendships: best friends. But from our interviews and research we have come to believe that these daughters are not really describing a best friendship. The mother-daughter relationship is much more comprehensive than even a best friendship. Mothers never stop being mothers, which includes frequently wanting to protect their daughters and often feeling responsible for their happiness.

Mothers want to support their daughters and offer the perspective of their accumulated life lessons and wisdom. Many mothers say, "We want to give our daughters the benefit of our experiences." While selflessness is an essential component of motherhood, it poses some pitfalls for the mother–adult daughter relationship. Regardless of the strong emotions, hurt feelings, and immense joy that accompany the mother-daughter relationship, we see their continuing connection as a source of great strength.

A parent's job is never over, it just changes. A mother must adjust to her daughter's developmental stages over a lifetime. Her role is to model and confirm the joy of the positive, teach empathy, and instill the resolve needed to address adversity. Young adulthood is the time to develop mutually beneficial boundaries and respectful interdependence.

What's It All About?

In writing this book we came to believe that the parent-child bond defines the relationship in which a mother is always a mother and the daughter remains the child. This is a relationship that is not replaceable by any other. This bond doesn't mean that when daughters mature they can't assume more responsibilities and give back to their mothers, but the very nature of the relationship is never equal, nor is it supposed to be. Mother always "trumps" friend.

Although we have written this book from a mother's perspective, we include the voices of both mothers and daughters throughout. Navigating a relationship with daughters when mothers are in midlife is complicated. Cultural issues and contemporary social developments have created new opportunities for friendship. Have those opportunities been a result of a sociological shift, and/or are mothers and daughters closer now than in the past? What are the psychological dynamics of the mother-daughter relationship? We will discuss gender role expectations, and how to achieve a successful balance between attachment and individuation.

Many mothers are unsure about when to expect adult behavior from their daughters because the old markers of adulthood no longer apply. They are marrying and having children later in life and often remain economically dependent even after college graduation. Mothers are searching for ways to provide appropriate support that contributes to self-confidence and maturity while preserving a strong connection. How much support is helpful, and how much is hindering?

For purposes of discussion, we have identified mother classifications and archetypes that impact the close mother-daughter relationship and potential for a best friendship. Some of them may be broader than we would like, but when you examine them closely, in many cases you will see characteristics of yourself. And it is likely that you will find aspects of yourself in more than one archetype.

Potentially damaging behaviors need to be identified and understood in order to create healthy adult relationships between mothers and daughters. The behavioral characteristics offered will provide you with helpful guideposts for parenting adult daughters.

We will explore our daughters' significant life cycle events: marriage and/or committed relationship, motherhood, and divorce. With these changing events, how do we work to negotiate and maintain boundaries that allow for individuality and closeness? We evaluate how mothers and daughters create limits that work for both, while staying connected; what happens when boundaries aren't set; how boundaries enable daughters to become self-reliant; and the ways in which healthy boundaries protect feelings and create positive adult relationships. We also explain the preoccupation of impossible standards of beauty on mothers and daughters.

We provide basic principles for parenting adult daughters based on our personal and professional experience, research, and the wisdom offered by the mothers and daughters in our focus groups. To implement these principles, we have created a "Baker's Dozen" of strategies to guide your parenting of adult daughters. We believe these strategies can help you to develop and sustain a positive and rewarding relationship with your adult daughter.

Exploring the circumstances and responses of today's mothers and daughters helps us to understand more about their lives and identifies opportunities to nurture healthy connections. A daughter's reliance on her mother need not be a "dependent" one in which she fails to achieve capacity for independent action and thought. We hope you will take away from this book a new understanding and some additional tools to strengthen your relationship with your daughter.

1

Catch and Release

What I wanted most for my daughter was that she be able to soar confidently in her own sky, whatever that may be.

—Helen Claes

More Than Words

The mother-daughter bond is inherently a complex relationship, mixed with love and affection, pleasure, conflict, judgment, responsibility, reassurance, guilt, and perhaps most important, connection. A mother intuitively understands that her intense connection to her daughter's life is normal. Elizabeth Edwards, wife of former Senator John Edwards, describes her relationship with her adult daughter, Cate, in thinking about the possibility of her early death from breast cancer. She says, "I want her [Cate] to thrive when the part of her grapevine that is entwined with mine is pulled apart. I want her to hold on to pieces of my vine, and I know she will." Even in death the connection between a mother and daughter is strong. A daughter's relationship with her mother has a lifelong impact on her sense of self and well-being. Adult daughters and mothers have more avenues for closeness and more access to each other than ever before because of sociological trends and new technology.

The popular press has sometimes suggested, and we have heard daughters say, "My mother is my best friend." As we did in our other studies of the parent-child relationship, we began by conducting literature reviews and research and used this information to facilitate focus groups throughout the country with mothers and daughters both separate and together. We looked to them to answer the question, "Can mothers and daughters be best friends?" In our inquiry, it became clear that daughters and their mothers had a very different perception about the possibility of friendship, let alone best friendship. In order to answer this question, in this chapter we discuss the impact of culture and contemporary times on the mother-daughter relationship; we explore why some mothers and daughters are not close and whether some are too close.

Bonnie says, "There is a mother presence of white noise when it comes to my daughter. Everything is vetted through my mother ears. We certainly share girlfriend-like experiences, but the overarching relationship is: I am her mother, and Monique is my daughter. I want to be her mother more than her friend, and I want Monique to have her own best friends. I'm glad she has them."

Kathy, the mother of Leah, says, "I've heard my daughter say that I am her best friend and it makes me uncomfortable." Another mother says, "I'm not sure I'd say my daughter is my best friend, although I love to be with her. I think she needs best friends her own age, with whom she can be free to talk about anything.

Sometimes, she will tell me things I'd think I'd really rather not know. I think to myself, 'Way too much information.' Sometimes I tell her 'Please, honey, tell someone your own age.'" We believe that this sentiment is best expressed by one mother, who says, "We share best-friend moments, but she is not my best friend, that would rob her of what we really cherish—which is that I am and remain her mother." What we have learned is that being a mother supersedes all other aspects of the relationship, including friendship.

Seizing the Moment

These days, daughters are delaying the traditional markers of adulthood and independence. Because marriage, career, and motherhood now typically come later in life, the time during the daughter's twenties offers an opportunity for mothers and their adult daughters to develop a friendship after the turbulence of the teenage years—time that former generations did not share. One mother says, "I find myself telling my daughter things that I used to tell only my women friends."

This sociological shift has taken place for many reasons. These days, the journey to adulthood is often more circuitous than it was in previous generations. This journey is not as fast, nor is the path as clear, as it was when today's parents were young. Our research initially looked at a quantitative comparison. The average age for first marriages is now closer to 30 than to 20, and many young adults delay having their own children until they're in their mid-thirties. Satisfying career-track jobs are also more difficult to find, and changing jobs is more common. According to the Bureau of Labor Statistics (2000), the average person now holds 9.2 jobs between the ages of 18 and 34.

In 1960, only 40 percent of women ages 25–54 were in the labor force; by 2000, 70 percent of women that age were employed. For married women with children ages 6 through 17, employment rates increased from 40 percent in 1960 to a peak of almost 80 percent by the new millennium. Sixty percent of married women with school-age children now work for pay, compared to less than 20 percent in 1960. Mothers are still more likely than fathers to work part-time, but they are less likely to do so than they were in the past. Wives now work for pay 80 percent of the hours their husbands do, a huge increase since the 1960s.

Most of us were not single for an extended period of time after college. And, for many of us who grew up in the 1960s and 1970s, the generational divide between our world and our mothers' was too large for us ever to feel like friends. Sydney, mother of three adult daughters, says, "My mother wore perfectly ironed blouses and changed into a fitted housedress when she came home. She didn't go to college and stayed home to raise my brother and me, not because she wanted to, but because that was what was expected. Until my children were born, my mother and I shared few experiences. My daughters and I, however, have been crisscrossing paths for years." Another mother, Ellie, says, "I didn't have the experience of being single in my twenties. I was married at twenty-two and had my family. I didn't have time to go to a yoga class with my mom."

Today we have more time to cultivate and enjoy a friendship with our daughters. Dr. Karen Fingerman, Professor of Sociology at Purdue University and researcher on mothers and daughters, said in a personal interview that she believes that relationships have changed because of mothers' increased life spans. Thanks to rising life-expectancy rates, a mother is in her daughter's life longer than ever before. Centers for Disease Control and Prevention data show that baby-boomer moms, who had children in their early twenties and may live into their eighties, will be in their children's lives for more than fifty years, almost ten years longer than their own mothers had with them.

Painful Truths

While many mothers and daughters have found a comfortable relationship balance between parent-child and friends, many others are frustrated with one another and in pain. Several researchers report that some mothers are being hurt by and shut out of their daughters' lives, and some daughters say they keep their mothers at a distance because they often feel criticized and can't do anything right.

Donna, mother of 26-year-old Tara, says, "In the last six months, Tara has distanced herself from me. We used to have lunch a few times a month, but now we don't even do that. She blames me because her dad wasn't involved in her childhood. We were divorced by the time she was six years old, and he moved out of town. I tried to do my best, but he remarried and had two more children with his second wife. It hurts me to think that I couldn't protect her from the loss of her dad when she was young, and now I'm being cut off and blamed for his disinterest."

Less-than-perfect relationships don't have to stay that way.

With diligent effort, they often can be repaired. For purposes of our research, we have targeted mothers and daughters who have some degree of closeness and a desire to stay connected. We won't address relationships where the mother suffers from a personality disorder such as narcissism or borderline personality. These mothers require a much different conversation. We are sensitive to the reality that many mothers and daughters are not in satisfying relationships. For those of you who fall into this category, just know that you are not alone.

We can identify more readily the harm caused by an abusive or abandoning mother. However, there are insidious ways in which the relationship can cause anguish and confusion and leave lifelong scars. Leo Tolstoy famously wrote, "All happy families are happy in the same way, whereas unhappy families are all unhappy in their own way." We believe Tolstoy's observation applies to mothers and daughters as well. Troubled mother-daughter relationships have their own dynamics with their own recurring dysfunctional dance.

Because it is normal for mothers and daughters to butt heads and have conflict, particularly during adolescence, it is not surprising that many of them continue to have difficulty addressing these conflicts as the relationship matures. Resolving conflicts depends on their skills and their desire to heal the relationship enough to become close. Leah, a 32-year-old daughter, says, "My mother still tries to control my life from six states away. And now she has just learned how to text message. So now when I don't answer my cell phone, Mom text messages me six to seven times until I respond. My life is over as I knew it!" Harassing your daughter probably will not bring the desired effect. Daughters who ignore boundaries without consideration of their mothers' feelings may also inhibit the possibility of developing a positive relationship. The extended period for young women without family responsibilities is potentially a time for self-absorption. Brenda, mother of 30-year-old Marissa, says, "I wouldn't enter my daughter's apartment unannounced, yet she borrows my shoes without my knowing, and half the time they don't come back." Developing an adult relationship must come not only from love, but also from a place of mutual respect.

Caught in the Web

Some mental health professionals express the concern that a lack of boundaries and/or a symbiotic relationship may prevent a daughter from separating from her mother, becoming independent, and learning to take care of herself. With the start of the 2008–2009 school year, colleges openly expressed their concern with what they call "helicopter parents," those who hover and are hyperinvolved in their children's lives. A recent study of sixty public universities and colleges, conducted by Patricia Somers, Associate Professor at the University of Texas, Austin, found that 40 percent to 60 percent of parents engage in this "stealth parenting" behavior, helping with assignments, daily e-mails and phone calls, and laundry service, and 10 percent admitted to writing their child's papers. Campuses across the country have set up videophones so moms can see and talk to their children.

Employers also are concerned about this hyperparenting. Paul Levy, CEO of Beth Israel, a Boston hospital, has observed that "helicopter" or "stealth fighter" parents actually write thank-you notes to their child's first post-college job interviewers. According to a recruiter for a Fortune 500 company, "Parents want to discuss offer letters and benefits, or information about 'work-life balance.'" Some parents will go so far as to ask whether their daughter will be able to take time off work to come home for the family's traditional Christmas.

Mothers seem to feel responsible for everything that happens to their daughters. They feel their daughters' pain to the extent that they try to manage their frustrations and disappointments. Lyla, 27, tells us, "I applied for my dream job and was one of three finalists. When I didn't get the job, I realized I was most worried about telling my mom because of how bad I knew she would feel. I prepared myself to tell her, masking my own feelings in order to protect her, but my mother teared up anyway. My mom always feels that she can arrange or fix everything, and when she can't it drives her crazy."

Some mothers feel they are clairvoyant and capable of preventing all negative experiences. They "should have known better" or "warned" their daughters of unanticipated events! To prepare girls for life, mothers report, they should anticipate as many experiences as possible that their daughters will encounter. It's as if these mothers are their daughters' personal red or orange danger alert. Daughters report that this hypervigilance increases their anxiety, eliciting exactly the opposite of their mothers' intent. Melissa, 29, says, "My boyfriend, Jesse, forgot my birthday, and even though I was furious at first, we talked it over and I feel like we worked it out to my satisfaction. Unfortunately, when I was first angry at Jesse, I told my mother and she had a lot to say about his transgression. From the comments she made to me, it is clear she believes that forgetting my birthday is a giant red flag for the future, and this caused me to doubt my own feelings."

Common Ground

Adult daughters in our focus groups talk about how many of them enjoy the benefits of a close relationship with their mothers. Kimberly, a 30-year-old mother of 2-year-old Emma, says, "I persuaded my husband to settle in the city near my parents. Once I had Emma, I knew that living near my mother would provide built-in support, physically and emotionally, for my family and me. My friends would tease me about how many hours I could spend at the kitchen table with my mom, like *The Golden Girls*. I don't want to miss that connection, and I want Emma to benefit from having a close relationship with her grandma."

Many mothers respond in kind. One mother of two adult daughters (ages 31 and 33) shares, "My greatest reward is sharing the bond of friendship—trusting their advice, counsel, and perspective, and knowing they trust mine. It's nurtured through mutual respect."

Unlike the cultures of previous generations, today's culture provides many opportunities for friendship and enjoyment of common interests. Mothers and daughters share the same love of work, fitness, media, fashion, and youthful orientation. Some have labeled this lack of a generation gap, "the generation overlap." These mutual interests enable us to enjoy a greater level of comfort with our adult daughters.

Laurie and her 25-year-old daughter, Alix, are training together for a triathlon. Laurie says, "If you [had] told me twenty years ago that I would own a heart-rate monitor, a bike helmet, and Speedo goggles with my prescription, I would have said you're on crack! Training together gives us countless opportunities to talk and work toward a common goal." Daughters also see their mothers, as they see themselves, as being part of the workforce. This allows daughters to observe their mothers in more than one role. Seeing their mothers as competent in many different spheres creates opportunities for new and different kinds of relationships.

A Cultural Approach

According to Professor and Chair of the Department of Gender Studies at Indiana University, Suzanna Walters, "We cannot tell one story of mothers and daughters. No single narrative, no unified discourse, can possibly flesh out the complexities and contradictions in mother/daughter relationships. The variations of class, race, ethnicity, national identity, sexual preference . . . all help create a multitude of possible narratives."

American mainstream culture looks at closeness between adult daughters and mothers with suspicion. In other cultures, connection is valued, and, in most other cultures, it is common for multiple generations to live together and support one another. One Latino mother says, "When I got married, we moved in with my parents. We purchased a three-story duplex. My father still lives on the top floor, and my brother's family lives on the bottom floor. Our family lives in between. My twenty-five-year-old daughter,

Maria, still lives with us and we wouldn't have it any other way." In increasing numbers, adult children in the United States are moving back to live with their parents after college or between jobs. Today more than 60 percent of twentysomethings live with their parents for some period of time. As our society becomes more multicultural, other cultures may contribute to normalizing this new phenomenon for mainstream culture. Or is this a maturation of American culture that has existed in other cultures for years?

Playing for Keeps

During all of these different stages, mothers offer wisdom, unconditional love, advice, protection, and support. Only when mothers accept this altruistic role can they truly experience the rewards of parenting and the possibilities and benefits of creating friendships with their adult daughters. Just as in Shel Silverstein's *The Giving Tree*, mothers give until they have nothing left to give. This is especially true when grandchildren are involved.

Today mothers who are also grandmothers are helping their daughters to balance their work and home lives. They are taking time off from their own work, retiring early, or moving to be closer to their grandchildren. This extensive involvement stems from a variety of reasons: the closeness we have established with our daughters, the high cost of child care, and the anxiety involved in finding a good provider. Even President Barack Obama and First Lady Michelle Obama asked Michelle's mother to leave her job to care for their two young daughters while they campaigned for the presidency. Since her son-in-law's election, Marian Robinson has made headlines on her own as a new kind of role model for grandmothers; along with her daughter, son-in-law, and granddaughters, Mrs. Robinson moved into the White House to continue to help with the children and provide continuity.

"A young woman with a new baby and a professional life is under much greater pressure than her mother ever was," says Sylvia Ann Hewlett, author of *Creating a Life: Professional Women and the Quest for Children*. She and her mother have "a very affectionate, dutiful relationship, but not a whole lot in common." She says longer workweeks and global competition have changed the professional landscape. "Women have these templates of superaccomplished moms, and it's very hard for them to measure up." Most mothers are only too happy to help out, but a balance must be maintained so daughters can develop the same competence they see their mothers have and so mothers are able to continue with their own lives. This balance creates a new opportunity to offer support and friendship.

While mothers and daughters can be friends, and their relationship at times may appear to be democratic, it is not egalitarian. One mother laughingly says, "If my best friend took my moisturizing lotion without asking me and in its place left a half-filled hotel sample of perfume-filled lotion (I'm allergic to fragrances, which she knows), I would be angry—but with my daughter, I laugh and say, 'That's my girl!' "

Currently, there are no long-term studies of whether closeness between mothers and daughters is detrimental to our daughters' ability to become self-sufficient and create positive adult relationships. However, it is commonly accepted that a daughter builds her sense of self by identifying with her mother, usually the first attachment figure in her life. A daughter doesn't have to form an identity in opposition to her mother because they share the same gender. This makes the process of individuation for girls very different from the one for boys, who have to assume a gender identity that is not female.

While they are changing, the expectations many parents and society have about girls' versus boys' adolescence can still be very different. Society encourages parents to help boys become men by pushing them away so they can learn to resolve issues on their own. At the same time, our culture gives us permission to maintain a deep connection with our daughters. While sex-role expectations are changing, we still value protecting our daughters and keeping them close. These sex-role expectations influence parenting throughout childhood and create a lifetime of interactions that influence the way our daughters feel about themselves and how they relate to the world.

By keeping our daughters close we create opportunities for both intimacy and conflict. Unlike with mothers, a father and daughter often seem to have fewer everyday struggles, because a daughter is not trying to establish her independence from him. Their relationship is often less stormy because a father has a built-in ability to differentiate and separate from his daughter. Unlike her relationship with her mom, a daughter doesn't share the same familiar buttons with her father. Psychologically, gender impacts how we parent our daughter, which then affects how she feels about herself. The strict sex-role distinctions have certainly changed, but the shared biology and culture of women will always profoundly influence the mother-daughter relationship.

2

A Paradigm Shift: Where's the Gap?

You come from a tribe of feisty foremothers. It's up to you to walk in their footsteps and continue their journey.

—**Letty Cottin Pogrebin, *Family Politics***

Family Album

It has been said that along with air travel and the microchip, the women's movement was a defining event of the twentieth century, with benefits increasing during the last three decades. The resulting social changes are still so fresh that adult women and their daughters continue to adapt to the transformation in roles and increased opportunities and challenges. Our focus groups reveal that many mothers still struggle to manage their own independence, while simultaneously trying to be useful role models for and providing guidance to their daughters.

Daughters who need direction may find their mothers' preoccupation with their own struggles to be a source of loss, disappointment, and resentment. Admiration for their mothers' accomplishments often comes later, when daughters begin to see their mothers as human beings separate from themselves. For daughters whose mothers overidentify with them, their mothers' independence may be a welcome relief.

Mothers who actively pursue their own lives may have less emotional energy for their children. Regardless, communication and connection are vital. This communication should include helping our daughters see their own struggle for independence from a historical and a contemporary perspective.

In earlier times, when grandmothers, mothers, and daughters lived under the same roof, traditions and history were more accessible and obvious. In contemporary society, we are less likely to take the time to pass on this cultural information and knowledge. Over the last forty years, daily activities have changed, affecting our daughters' perceptions of their social roles and life expectations. Today they perceive their choices as being different from ours when we were their age. Mothers can best assist their daughters to understand and manage their lives by providing a historical context.

Contemporary culture presents a challenge to our daughters' abilities to maintain self-respect, build personal responsibility, and sustain close relationships with us. Technological advances increase access to information and facilitate communication while at the same time depersonalizing relationships. One mother said, "I hear from my daughter more often than I spoke with my mother, but these contacts don't feel like real, interactive conversations." Communication today often is reduced to task management.

One thing remains the same; mothers are still ultimately responsible for maintaining "kinship" within their family. Sheila states, "No matter what changes we have been able to affect, and how involved dads are in the lives of their children, having a child still has some traditional expectations for the mother." Julie, a new mother, said, "Does it bother you when everyone thinks your husband is a doll when he does more than the minimum child care? He is considered a saint because he takes care of his own child. Me, I'm the mother; anything less would be irresponsible and unloving."

There have always been friendships between mothers and daughters. Today, because of the lack of a generation gap and the overlap in clothing, books, music, and movie tastes, mother-daughter friendships may appear to be more common. However, the primary responsibility of a mother to be a role model and source of advice for and comfort to her daughter remains the same. In this chapter, we explore the recent history of the mother-daughter relationship and the impact of technology, contemporary culture, and the new characteristics of adulthood our daughters will need in the twenty-first century.

The Last Hundred Years

At the end of the nineteenth century, parenting began to change with the identification of adolescence as a unique developmental stage. Motherhood was perceived as an expertise to be acquired and developed by absorbing a new body of knowledge. Family characteristics, such as moody daughters or impatient mothers, were seen as potential problems and blamed on the mother. Magazine articles and books contributed to this changing perception by focusing extensively on mother-daughter issues.

Popular magazines emphasized mother-daughter conflict and focused on communication difficulties revolving around mothers' reluctance to answer questions about their daughters' bodies, religion, and intellect. The Victorian view of sexuality was still prevalent, which caused a generation gap that separated young women from their mothers. For the first time, young women began to attend college, and literacy became more widespread for middle-class white women. Young women were reading books and magazines that contributed to a heightened tension between daughters and mothers. An example of the writing that reflects this schism appeared in the following excerpt from a 1917 issue of *Good Housekeeping*:

> *In the lifetime of girls even twenty years old, the tradition of what girls should be and do in the world has changed as much as heretofore in a century. It used to be that girls looked forward with confidence to domestic life as their destiny. That is still the destiny of most of them, but it is a destiny that in this generation seems to be modified for all, and avoided by very many . . . The mothers of these modern girls are very much like they have hatched out ducks. Whether they believe in current feminine aspirations or not makes not very much difference . . .*
>
> *Separated by this generation gap, mothers were nonetheless expected to continue to be primarily responsible for facilitating and maintaining open communication with their*

daughters. They were urged to discuss with their daughters the books they read and about decorating homes, while taking their daughters' interests seriously. A mother's responsibility was clear: There should be no one upon earth to whom that daughter should feel so ready to go with every thought, every hope, every plan. If she does not, it is her mother's fault.

The gap between Victorian mothers and their more modern suffragist daughters is mirrored by the gap between today's Vietnam/Watergate–era mothers and their adult daughters. Think of Donna Reed and Harriet Nelson, compared to Gloria Steinem and Hillary Rodham Clinton. Generational values change and they are always different. The consistent message across the generations is that it is the mother's duty to bridge these differences. Communication and connection is the mother's domain. One advantage contemporary mothers have over our predecessors is that few topics are off limits.

THE LAST FIFTY YEARS

The next major change in parenting practices occurred after World War II. One of the strongest influences for change was *Dr. Spock's Baby and Childcare*, published in 1946—the most popular parenting book of its era. While the subsequent baby-boomer generation and its excesses were blamed on Dr. Spock's revolutionary methods, it took a while for his philosophies to become mainstream. Dr. Spock gave parents permission to comfort their children on demand. His views represented a radical departure from the prevailing opinion that feeding and sleep should be rigidly scheduled and pacifiers avoided.

Arlene, a 58-year-old mother of two adult children, remembers: "My mother was amazed at the freedom I had to comfort my daughter in 1973." When Arlene's mother had babies in the post–World War II baby boom she was told not to pick them up when they cried; she hadn't read Dr. Spock in time for her new baby. She wanted to give her daughter a pacifier, and her doctor told her not to. Arlene's mother felt sad that she couldn't comfort her children, especially since one of them had been colicky and cried all the time. She always marveled at how confident her daughter was in soothing her own daughter whenever the baby was upset.

As late as the 1960s only 10 percent of children under age 5 went to nursery school; those were the days when Mom plopped the baby in the playpen. Kids had more opportunity to be independent, play outdoors, and go to a friend's house without a predetermined play date. Children had the freedom to walk home from their friends' houses; they participated in fewer extracurricular activities. Moms did not have the option of choosing activities such as Suzuki violin and movement classes for their children.

At the same time, boomer mothers were raised to believe that the world was their oyster. The 1960s slogans "Do your own thing" and "We shall overcome" express our belief that we could correct past wrongs and we had the self-confidence to believe we should follow our personal dreams, rather than the existing cultural norms.

As mothers of today's adult daughters, we extended our core beliefs and so-called counterculture values to our parenting. If the world really was our oyster, we raised our children to feel as if they were the pearls. Even though Dr. Spock gave our parents permission to comfort us on demand, they still required that we, not they, be primarily responsible for our lives.

Lydia, a 59-year-old mother, tells how she applied to college without any outside guidance. What a concept! She did things on her own. Lydia's experience is in stark contrast to how overly involved contemporary parents are, for example, in the college admissions process. In Lydia's words, "We've been programming our children for years."

Lydia's parents, like many of her peers' parents, are the children of immigrants. They are first-generation Americans who believed that going to college would ensure their daughters' success. When Lydia's mother was young and money was scarce, her uncle went to college, not her mother. Daughters worked and/or got married. Lydia's parents begged her to go to a local state school and even offered her a car if she would do so. She didn't take any SAT prep courses and didn't receive help with any of her essays. When it was time to leave for school, Lydia packed her own trunk, made her reservations, and flew, for the first time in her life, alone, to college.

Lydia often compares this experience with how closely she guided the education of her two daughters. From early in their high school years, she and her husband did everything possible to help her children stand out from the others when applying to college. Lydia remembers, "We made sure our kids took every damn advanced class, went to every museum, and participated in every extracurricular activity we could squeeze into our schedules." They opened doors that Lydia never knew existed and never thought about when she was a young adult. The family took college trips to decide what kind of environment best fit their daughters. Lydia said she wanted to give her children the benefit of her knowledge of how the world works.

Lydia is not unique. Many of the mothers in our focus groups are proud and happy to have given such guidance to their daughters. However, they are also aware that such extensive involvement has created a very different young adult who feels dependent on her parents' skills to navigate the adult world. Today's parents obsess over exposing their children to as many opportunities as possible. While the goals of academic achievement and financial security are the same among these generations, how they are implemented is very different.

Baby-boomer mothers report they learned to be resilient because they were less coddled. Yet, these same mothers say they responded to everything their children did by saying, "Good job!" With this constant praise, they unwittingly gave their daughters unrealistic expectations of how the world should treat them; they neglected to give them a reality-based notion of their role in the world. This unrealistic estimation of their own importance sometimes adversely affects both young men's and women's ability to juggle the complexities of modern life. However, this may also affect the mother-daughter relationship in unique ways. As one mother said, "I struggle with getting all the details of my own life under control, yet I serve as my daughter's personal concierge."

Sisterhood Is Powerful

Both generations talk about gender and racial equality, but our shared language does not necessarily reflect either a universal understanding of that language or a common lesson derived from it. Our generation grew up at a time when women had few options, and people of color were expected to "know their place." We devoted much of our youthful energies to addressing these inequities. Many young women, however, seem unaware of this history. Linda Shevitz, who works for the Maryland State Department of Education as an educational equity specialist, was talking to one of her daughter's friends about celebrating the 35th anniversary of Title IX. The young woman responded, "I know about Title IX. It gave girls the right to participate in sports, just like the boys." Linda explained that Title IX encompasses much more than just athletics. To make her point, Linda asked the young woman how many women were in her medical school class. The young woman answered, "Sixty percent." Linda smiled and reminded her that this transformation also was the result of Title IX and the struggle for gender equity.

When baby boomers were in their twenties, feminism of the late 1960s and early 1970s profoundly transformed the lives of women in the United States. This struggle brought about upheavals in both law and the customs of everyday life and altered women's consciousness. The women's movement redefined roles, attitudes, and values, because the traditional definitions of men and women were so at odds with women's actual experience. Women no longer would be confined to girdles and poodle skirts, and stymied by a "Men Only" economy.

The feminist movement changed the role of women in society and the expectations that girls could have for their lives. Even when our daughters acknowledge the benefits of the women's movement, many still don't want to be associated with it. What is hard to appreciate now is that even the smallest changes required hard-fought battles.

Most young women know little about the history of the women's movement, or of the restrictions on women's lives a mere generation ago. Suzanne, mother of Jody, told us about an unexpected conversation she had with her daughter: "My mouth fell open when I heard my daughter, Jody, say, 'I hate the word *feminist*.' After I slammed my foot on the brakes, I said, 'Oh, really. Is it too strident for you? Why do you think you can apply for a soccer scholarship at UNC [University of North Carolina]? It wasn't always this way. Jody, feminists are really just women who struggle together for women's rights. That includes you and you have to realize the benefits you have because of the women who called themselves feminists."

Many mothers remember what it was like for them when they were younger. Lucy recalls, "In an all-girl dorm we couldn't go downstairs to the dining hall without wearing a skirt." Charlotte, a 61-year-old mother, tells us, "I shudder when I remember how cold I was walking to high school in my pleated wool skirt and knee-high socks. The cold air would blow under my skirt, and my knees would be chapped and frozen. The only time girls could wear pants to school was to football and basketball games. What was that about? We had no say and no power to make life a little more comfortable for ourselves."

According to Sherry, "It was just a given that girls would wear bathing caps in swimming pools and skirts in school. I always wondered why boys didn't wear bathing caps in the late sixties, when their hair was every bit as long as girls'. Was the pool drain particularly sensitive to girl hair?" Another mother remembers participating in a lawsuit to establish her right to continue teaching while she was pregnant. Our daughters may dismiss feminism as strident and unfeminine because they take for granted so many of the benefits they have. They don't understand that the women's movement was a century-long struggle in which the same gains had to be won again and again.

Protected Class

We want to make sure our daughters don't experience some of the same disappointments we did at their age. Yet, new opportunities and greater expectations can create conflicts for mothers and daughters. We still don't have all the answers, and not all women have choices. Our daughters came of age during a socially conservative period when many wanted to reverse the gains of the women's movement. This backlash upsets many mothers who fought for women's equality.

Beverly remembers telling her daughter how much she wanted a particular job her first year out of college when she was newly married. It was a job in a contract furniture showroom, for which she felt well equipped. During her interview, the owner said, "I'm sorry. If you were a man, I would hire you, but I'm worried that after all the training, you'll leave and have a baby." Her daughter was shocked and asked, "Why didn't you turn him in, Mom? You could have sued for discrimination!" Beverly laughed and said, "Sue, no way. In those days I couldn't get a credit card in my own name."

Mothers offer daughters a safe place to address workplace and social issues. We understand from our own experience that many of our daughters trust us, even if they do argue about the term *feminism*. Because of our closeness to the issue as well as to our daughters, we are able to understand their frustrations and disappointments and provide perspective.

Our generation became engaged in a common struggle to carve out a place for ourselves in a society that left many of us feeling, at worst, stranded and, at best, disillusioned. We wanted to connect with one another through friendship and family relationships and to be of consequence in the world. Our children watched us trying to have it all, and they did not see a pretty picture. Brenda, a 28-year-old department store buyer, said, "I watched my mother struggle raising me and my two brothers while juggling the stress of her more than nine-to-five job. I don't want that same amount of stress. I know when I decide to have children I'm going to have to give up something. I am going to have to find a better balance."

Rebecca, a 32-year-old physical therapist, said, "For my mother's generation, even if they finally got to where they wanted to go, it was so much harder for them to get there. They had to fight for everything. I remember when my mom went back to get her Ph.D., her mom, my grandmother, was so angry with her. My grandmother actually asked my mother, 'Graduate school, what could you be thinking? You already have children. Isn't that everything?' "

Mothers and their adult daughters share a common history and some common experiences, but they often lack a common understanding. To bridge these differences, mothers should tell their history and stories to their daughters to help them gain perspective and negotiate their world. While friends offer similar stories, they speak as peers, rather than someone who speaks with the life experience of a mother.

Supermom Replaces Perfect Mom

In the post–World War II era, moms were expected to run the perfect household. Dinner was on the table at 5:30 every evening, the house was immaculate, school lunches were made, and Mom wore an apron and pearls. June Cleaver, Mrs. Stone, Harriet Nelson, Mrs. Brady, and even Aunt Bea were cultural icons, and the households they ran determined these women's value.

Despite their juggling work and family, many women are able to spend more time with their children today than were the mothers in the mythical family of the 1950s. This extra time is the result of less housework, better appliances, polyester, prepared meals, the microwave oven, and fewer expectations of a perfect home. Wrinkle-free shirts and jersey sheets have replaced starched sheets, collars, and underwear that needed ironing. The era of the mangle (linen presser) is over. Beginning in the 1980s, more mothers began to gauge their self-esteem on the basis of their ability to multitask. We operated in hyper mode, attempting to maintain work and home in a society that still questioned whether women could be mothers and workers at the same time and without the full support of our husbands. We gave our daughters the message that women didn't have to give up home responsibilities or professional opportunities. The Supermom was officially launched.

We replaced homemaking perfection with parenting perfection. Frozen waffles became good enough for our daughters' birthday parties. We had to give up the notion of domestic perfection; we were not domestic goddesses. According to Judith Warner, author of *Perfect Madness: Motherhood in the Age of Anxiety*, we became mothering perfectionists instead. We wanted to be everything to our children, but often "good" did not feel good enough. Diana tells us about her mother's reaction to Diana's putting her daughters in daycare when she went back to graduate school. One day her mother's telephone greeting was, "How are my little orphans doing?" Even though Diana knew this comment was ridiculous, it still stung.

As working parents, our time was more limited, but our job expanded. We became soccer moms, working moms, chauffeurs, party planners, chore completers, and bail-out specialists. This new level of overinvolvement, once thought of as odd, was now considered normal. Moms who didn't perform were often wracked with guilt.

For Supermom, the bar was raised very high for career and traditional women's skills, and being proficient in one skill didn't necessarily make up for not having the other skill. Linda recalls, "I can sew a sport jacket from scratch. I can do drywall. And I can give a keynote speech in front of hundreds of people. But none of these counts when I compare myself to the other Supermothers. I thought I could keep my inadequacies in the kitchen to myself until my daughter inadvertently exposed my lack of culinary skills during a Girl Scout troop meeting. The girls were asked to contribute to a recipe book, and my daughter's recipe was so simple that everyone knew how little she had learned in the kitchen at her mommy's feet. Her recipe began, 'First you buy a box from the store and then you open it.' I know that this is silly, but I felt so embarrassed that mothers reading the book would feel bad for my daughter's lack of skills."

Many focus group mothers share stories of how their daughters asked other mothers how to make tuna fish, or how their daughters marveled at seeing real potatoes being mashed for the first time; or how they sprinkled a cake with baking powder instead of powdered sugar. Somehow all of our competencies in areas other than the kitchen don't matter if we fail to excel in traditional female skills. Once again we don't measure up. According to physician Nancy Snyderman, "The cultural vision of superwoman—with all of its problems and contradictions—has filtered down to a new generation of girls."

Where's the Gap?

Generational conflicts in the American past emerged as a phenomenon during the age of immigration, when parent and child embodied real collisions between the values of the old and new worlds. For new immigrants, this may remain an issue. Sally, a 56-year-old mother, remembers, "I always felt like my parents were kind of remote figures. They didn't really relate all that well to me, and they sure didn't have a clue as to what I was thinking. I think it's because of the way they grew up. Life was tougher for my folks; they didn't have money, and they lived through the Depression and World War II. My parents were the ones that had to learn the ropes, because my grandparents' cultural context was entirely outmoded. I feel like my kids are more in touch with me, and I'm more in touch with them. I definitely feel less of a generation gap than I did with my parents."

Phyllis, a 59-year-old mother of three adult daughters, reflects,

"We are so tied into our children. Maybe our parents were not as involved with us in the same way because their life experience was so different from ours. The differences gave us something to rebel against, something to walk away from, not to want to be like. This increased our independence. It's harder to walk away from us. Our children look at our lives, and they look pretty good. It's harder for both of us to separate, and more difficult for our children to create an identity separate from ours."

As a result of the reduced generation gap, children are less likely to rebel against their parents by becoming alienated and rejecting their families. Boomer parents help to alleviate this potential conflict by staying young. One mother says, "I made myself learn how to text message and then BlackBerry message my daughter. I don't want to be left behind." Our parents gave themselves permission to accept what was and didn't fight change or aging in the same way we do. It isn't that our parents weren't interested or loved us any less; it's that they were satisfied to hear about our lives, whereas we want to experience things with our daughters firsthand. We fight to stay in the game.

Today, commonality and companionship are both possible. The similarities we share with our daughters help to sustain connection. The cultural and political rebellion, so common to baby boomers' experience, seems to be missing from the experiences of the daughters we interviewed. However, in many ways, they share similar interests and aspirations with their mothers. We live in a time when mothers and daughters shop for the same clothes, and Madison Avenue still uses Beatles music to sell Nikes and cars.

Both boomer parents and their adult daughters watch *Lost*,

Grey's Anatomy, *30 Rock*, and many reality shows. Hallmark sells cards inscribed, "To my mother, my best friend." Most young-adult daughters can come home with a tattoo, blue hair, or a modest piercing without fearing a nuclear parental explosion. Nowadays, the lines delineating a distinct youth culture from the prevailing adult culture are disappearing, and families have experienced a continuing power shift from parent to children. This democratization of the family has contributed to intergenerational closeness.

Although the two generations have much in common, we have grown up in different times. Therefore, we wrestle with different issues. Mothers of adult daughters are a hybrid generation, somewhat traditional and somewhat experimental. Our daughters are a generation that lives in a world that offers greater options for exploration, but at the same time engenders caution due to greater risk. This caution is most apparent in current overprotective child-rearing practices. We took our kids out to dinner in plastic infant seats at two weeks old. Our daughters slept with bumpers and blankets in their cribs. Today, mothers who have not washed their hands with Purell can't touch children. We fed our children peanut butter at six months old. Today's young parents do not allow their children to eat all foods until they are five years old. We fed our kids food that fell on the floor based on the "five-second rule." Today there are specially made airplane-tray placemats. We carted our kids around in fifteen-dollar umbrella strollers. They chauffeur their children in strollers the size and price of a Smart car.

These minor distinctions aside, both generations hold themselves accountable for their children's achievements, happiness, well-being, and psychological health. Escalating fear for child safety, concern that our children avoid boredom, desire to build their self-esteem, and two working parents foster greater parental anxiety.

Parallel Universe

It may be that baby boomers' difficulty in accepting their age also has something to do with compatibility with their children. Baby boomers prize youth and continue to define themselves by embracing change and making an effort to stay current. Our orientation toward youthfulness creates a comfort level with our own children. It gives our daughters the confidence that they can rely on us for opinions about relationships, work, a movie, concert, or cultural event. Our adult daughters assume we can connect with them and talk happily with us about their experiences.

Judy, a 55-year-old mother from Norfolk, Virginia, said, "I can't imagine calling my mother and father at midnight to ask if they saw *Juno*, but my daughter needed to connect with me immediately after she saw the movie. Oddly enough, or maybe not oddly, I had just seen the movie and knew how she felt!" Jane, a 25-year-old accountant, calls her parents Sunday night, right after *Mad Men*, to discuss the nuances of the show. In response to this ritual, Jane's mom said, "I had no desire to call my parents to discuss the characters in *The Godfather* thirty years ago." There is almost no time that "we are off the clock."

Susan, the mother of 23-year-old Stephanie, said, "Stephanie burns me CDs of Dave Matthews and mails them to me. I would never have dreamed for a millisecond that my parents would be interested in the Grateful Dead or the Rolling Stones. Last week she left me the message, 'The new Springsteen album is great, Mom, you'll love it.' " Most of the personal stories that describe today's adult children's connection with their parents through television, movies, or music end with the parents saying, "I never would have thought to call my parents like my child calls me."

The Instant Electronic Age

Cell phones, e-mailing, and text messaging have become ubiquitous means for daughters to talk to their mothers, allowing a much more prevalent connection than ever before. Along with greater opportunity for connection, this easy access facilitates a higher level of dependence for longer periods. Megan, 25, recalls, "During my college years, my mother would call me every morning to make sure I woke up in time for class." While Megan didn't ask for this service, she never told her mother to stop. Megan never got the opportunity to know if she was competent to get herself up on time.

We have the capacity to connect with our daughters at any time, in any place, from an airplane on the tarmac to a summit in the Rockies, during happy hour at a bar, walking to the subway, and sitting in traffic. Jeri, who lives on the West Coast, refers to her daughter's cell phone as the "evolved Fisher-Price monitoring device," an adult walkie-talkie. In our focus groups, mothers shared so many rich, detailed stories about the ease with which their daughters use technology to communicate with them and its impact on their relationship.

Jo says: "My daughter calls me many days on her way home from work, when she is relaxed in the car, before she gets home and reads the mail and starts dinner. She is much more focused during her commute, and we enjoy this time."

Vicki says, "I think when you're used to being in touch so often, and you don't hear from them, your mind just goes off and you start worrying. Whereas, with my parents, I spoke to them every Sunday at ten-thirty A.M., whether there was something new or not. We didn't check in with each other on a daily basis."

Another mother said, "The cell phone for me feels very much like an appendage. It's both an independence thing, but then at the same time, I almost feel like I've given my kid a digital chip, just like a tracking chip. It's interesting to me, because in a way, it's kind of like that harness you used to see on kids in the mall. The kids may think they're independent, but the cell phone keeps them tethered to us; it's like an umbilical cord."

Numerous mothers tell similar stories describing the cell phone as an extension of them, something that draws their child physically closer and helps them to maintain a daily connection. Using cell phones to stay connected is a universal experience for this generation. In a *Washington Post* article, one young woman describes the cell phone as something she always wants near her: "You take your phone even when you don't take your purse or your keys. It's like a little person."

Social networking gives instant gratification new meaning. This means of communication has its pros and cons, according to some of the daughters in our focus groups. Lisa, 28, says, "Now that my mother is on Facebook, she has total access to me at anytime and anyplace. I love my mom and want to be close . . . just not this close." Many mothers maintain their daughters control the use of technology. Beth reports, "When I call my daughter, she often can't talk. I find myself waiting for her to call me back. However, if she can't reach me, she becomes agitated. It's okay for her to be out of touch, but not me."

Cell phones ring, buzz, sing, or vibrate anywhere at any time. With computers, the Internet, PDAs, BlackBerrys, networking, digital photography, and fax machines, we are always one beep away from checking in or being pursued. It is no wonder that this generation has little patience with delayed rewards. One mother shared her observation that her daughter's facility with the Internet was interfering with her ability to focus and find a job: "I worried that Leslie was missing her life day-to-day." As Peter Fraenkel says in *Psychotherapy Networker*, "Much of human life, especially with relationships, still proceeds at the rate of human emotion."

Technology has transformed relationships, including those between mothers and daughters. While technology keeps people in contact, it does not necessarily facilitate intimacy. Communication often becomes logistics; it allows ease of access, which can enable dependence, and it also creates the potential to confuse contact with friendship. Our daughters can notify 248 of their closest friends that they had a lousy day at work on Facebook in a millisecond or tell them via Twitter that they will be at a corner bar at 8:30 P.M. This is bulk mail, not intimacy.

3

Attachment vs. Individuation: Like Mother, Like Daughter

Thou art thy mother's glass, and she in thee
Calls back the lovely April of her prime.
—**William Shakespeare**

Mother Nature

What makes a thoroughly modern mother criticize her daughter in ways that echo her own mother, the one person she swore never to become? Why is a mother the yardstick against which a daughter measures herself? Can fear of becoming one's mother prevent the development of a mother-daughter friendship? These are some of the questions mothers in our focus groups asked as they observed their own style of mothering.

The mother-daughter relationship is affected by ongoing

developmental issues associated with life-cycle transitions, such as a daughter's transition to adulthood, career, marriage (at age 27 on average), and becoming a mother herself. At the same time, a mom is experiencing a transition to an empty nest, switching careers, changing primary relationships, and aging. Examining these life-cycle transitions and their interactions facilitates understanding of the mother and adult daughter relationship.

Much attention has been paid to adolescence, when daughters experience an avalanche of physical and emotional changes. Until now, few have examined how the relationships between adult daughters and mothers evolve. According to psychologist Dr. Rosalind Barnett, our most deeply ingrained sense of ourselves as women comes from our biological mothers or mother figures who serve as our most important role models. Our behaviors, attitudes, values, and interests are greatly influenced by our mothers. The change in the mother–adult daughter bond entails redefinition and renegotiation; the trick is negotiating this adult phase of the relationship collaboratively.

Mothers at Midlife

During this period, mothers and daughters go through different life experiences. Mothers go from *other* focus to *self*-focus, and daughters go from self-absorption to seeing themselves in the context of others: family, work, and community. It is important to understand the impact and complexity of these different life stages. This can enhance a mother's ability to understand that her daughter's life now includes new relationships that need to be nurtured, and can enable a daughter to accept the new boundaries her mother may need to nurture herself.

While mothers' circumstances may vary, they confront the challenge of reframing their lives when the needs of children are no longer front and center. At a certain age, mothers come face-to-face with the fact that life is finite. They find themselves grappling with the meaning of the second half of life in an ageist society that values youth and devalues age. One 50-year-old mother said, "I am at the peak of my game, but [I] find it sobering to know that I've already lived more life than I may have left to live." Many care for an elderly parent and are acutely aware of losing the buffer that keeps them from knowing they are next.

At the same time, some women discover a new confidence at midlife and become bolder, finding their voices and speaking out. Many women can count on years of good health and vitality and have a new appreciation of life. Some reassess their careers, others take trips to places they never dreamed of exploring, and still others leave husbands of more than twenty-five years or rebuild a marital bond. Kathy, mother of two adult daughters, said she envied the opportunities and lifestyle she had provided for her girls. After they both graduated from college and were on their own, Kathy went to Costa Rica to work for Habitat for Humanity, building homes. Her husband had absolutely no interest in going, but she knew life was too short to let that stop her. Kathy said, "I have no idea how long these legs will let me hike mountains and travel to places that don't have the comforts of home. I need to go while I still can."

The literature has shown that the mother-daughter relationship has the potential to be the most complex and emotionally loaded intrafamily relationship. For purposes of clarity and readability, we discuss attachment, shared biology, sex-role expectations, and achieving successful balance between attachment and individuation separately.

"The First Time Ever I Saw Your Face"

The concept of attachment is integral to exploring the mother–adult daughter relationship. Secure attachment and the ability of a young child to separate from her parents and to seek comfort when she is upset is very important because it provides the foundation for positive growth throughout life.

In infancy, closeness to a loving caretaker creates a foundation of security. During maturation, attachment may involve different people, but it still continues to promote a feeling of security. In an ideal world, all children have the opportunity to enjoy such warm and intimate relationships. The optimal attachment is a secure attachment, which permits a child to find a flexible balance between finding reassurance and connection to others and the capacity for exploration.

Healthy attachment lays the groundwork for connection because a securely attached adult is comfortable trusting others and is able to form lasting relationships. According to psychologist Janet Surrey, connection is based on the premise that infants are tuned to the feeling state or feelings of their mother or caretaker. Bonding is the positive emotional attachment that mothers form with their infants after birth. A mother's listening and empathetic responses create what Surrey calls an open relationship between mother and child. This interaction helps daughters to develop their capacity for mutual empathy and, in time, mothers and daughters can become sensitive to each other's feelings. For most children, attachment is a natural outgrowth of a mother's love and attention. For others, the process is more complicated. It is critical to understand that innate biological temperaments can affect a child's ability to form a secure attachment.

According to psychologist Jean Baker Miller, women develop in a context of attachment and connection with each other. Their sense of self is based on the formation and maintenance of relationships. Relationships are so important that many women feel the loss of a relationship as a loss of self. This fundamental need for attachment may explain why a mother will go to extraordinary measures to protect, stay connected with, and be involved in the life of her child.

This sometimes requires putting yourself second to your daughter's needs. Sandy, the mother of Vanessa, says, "After my divorce, I was available 24/7 for my daughter, Vanessa, and grandson, Jonathan, who were the source of great comfort. During the first year of Jonathan's life I was more than happy to babysit and help Vanessa in any way I could, because it was good to feel needed and was a diversion for my loneliness. Eventually I realized I needed to transition to a new life involving people my age. My friends and I planned a trip to New York City for the weekend to see shows, shop, and visit museums.

"After the plans were made, my daughter asked me to babysit for the same weekend because she and her husband were feeling the stress of two high-pressured jobs while raising a toddler. I could tell by the tone of her voice that she was barely holding it together and this trip was an important trip for her mental health. While I felt very disappointed at the thought of canceling my trip, my daughter, Vanessa, was suffering. My fear of her having a meltdown was more worrisome for me than the pleasure I anticipated from my own trip to New York. So, I bailed on my friends in order to give Vanessa the opportunity to spend a much-needed weekend alone with her husband."

Most often a mother's desire to maintain the attachment happens in the ordinary, everyday moments. Says Marcie, "I will do anything to spend time with my daughter. As winter turns to spring, while Morgan sits on the bed, I am stacking her hangers, collecting plastic bags, and sorting through her sweaters. Morgan offers opinions about what to discard and what to keep, while I am stacking, bagging, and tossing. When this kind of mundane activity brings me joy, I understand how much I want to be with her." This connection is precious.

Consistency in the caregiver's response during a child's developmental years builds the security that encourages the skills necessary for positive attachment and connection. However, multiple difficulties may arise in developing attachment. For example, separation due to illness, depression, or stress within the family may make it difficult for the primary caregiver to respond consistently to the child's emotional needs. *Attachment in Psychotherapy* author David Wallin explains that while a secure attachment creates the stability for infants to attach to caregivers and for young adults to handle relationships, many children who don't have this advantage can still be resilient and overcome insecure attachments.

Being in a Relationship

A secure mother may feel wistful about her daughter's need to be separate, but supports her individuation because it is a necessary part of the developmental process. In a mature and supportive relationship, both daughter and mother coexist mutually. It is critical that mothers respect their daughters' individual differences and do not view the process of individuation as a betrayal. For a daughter, it is also important that she not view her mother's respect for independence as abandonment.

Phyllis, mother of 25-year-old Christine, said, "I always told Christine that I hoped she would live near me when she settled down. I let her know how I moved five hundred miles away from my parents without realizing how nice it would be to have their support when I had a family of my own. So when Christine said she wasn't going to consider a job offer in Chicago, I worried that my propaganda [had] worked too well. I told her that, while of course I would miss her, I wanted her to use her wings to fly. I wanted her to know that this was my gift of freedom as her mother and not in any way a message that I didn't yearn to have her [be a] part of my everyday life."

Though established early in life, the foundation for relationships evolves substantially as a daughter and mother go through their life stages and/or passages. For example, during adolescence, the subtext of many arguments between mothers and daughters is redefining attachment—how close or how distant they are to one another. We believe mothers and daughters should strive for autonomy with connection, and as adults they should create what we call "respectful interdependence."

Just the Two of Us

The mother-daughter dyad is defined and complicated by shared biology, gender, expectations, rituals, and culture. Because mothers and daughters share the same gender, they have difficulty acknowledging both their differences and similarities. While their shared biology contributes to their potential for empathy and closeness, it also inhibits the process of differentiation and individuation. This powerful connection creates complex relationships in which mothers and daughters often impose their own projections onto each other.

A young daughter identifies with her mother as *the* person who takes care of her and tends to her needs. In its earliest stages, the mother-daughter relationship lays the foundation for all of the daughter's future relationships. This primary relationship determines a daughter's sense of self and continues to have immense power over her emotional life. Karen Fingerman, author of *Aging Mothers and Adult Daughters: A Case of Mixed Emotions*, writes, "Mothers continue to influence the way their daughters feel about themselves. Years after daughters are grown, daughters feel guilty and ashamed when their mothers criticize them and feel happy when their mothers are proud of them."

According to sociologist Nancy Chodorow, the solid mother-daughter bond serves as the most important context in which girls come to understand themselves as "relational" and "connected" people. Healthy mother-daughter attachments can foster the development of positive capabilities, such as motivations for action, self-esteem, and self-affirmation. However, this intense, close relationship also can be a breeding ground for conflict.

Erica, 32, says, "My mother and I are very close, even though we ride an emotional seesaw. I love her and sometimes I hate her. Sometimes she's the last person I want to see. But she's still the first person I call for advice." This is a typical example of the "push/pull" nature of the mother-daughter relationship. Mothers in our focus groups experience the same paradox. They rave about their daughters in one sentence and express hurt, frustration, and pain in the next. These extremes are common within the mother-daughter dyad. In describing her daughter Susan says, "Jenna is the joy of my life and the bane of my existence." The psychological connection between mothers and daughters creates an environment in which they are finely tuned to each other. This can result in both mothers and daughters vacillating between demonstrating appropriate empathy and behaving with insensitivity or callous indifference.

According to Terri Apter, author of *Altered Loves*, girls do not construct an identity, as boys are thought to do, by marking personal boundaries between themselves and their mothers. Instead girls construct their identity by emulation. Many mothers in our focus groups express feeling "tethered" to their daughters. Mary says, "Maggie can push my buttons more than anyone. It's as if we merge together as one person. It is different with my son, David, whose biology makes it clear that he isn't me."

This tenacious link makes it difficult for a mother to view her daughter objectively. Again, for reasons of gender, biology, and shared experiences, the mother-daughter relationship is considered to be the most complicated of human relationships. Rachel, a 32-year-old psychiatrist, says, "It is harder for daughters than [it is for] sons to separate and individuate from their mothers. When I think of many mothers who haven't adequately separated themselves from their mothers, they risk displacing some of their own fears and insecurities on their daughters. I think it's hard to articulate, but this lack of objectivity helps to explain why we have a visceral reaction when our mothers talk to us. The same exact words and tone could be used by someone else, but it just isn't loaded in the same way. We react this way because we believe that we and our mothers should feel the same way about things. Sometimes we're right and other times not so much. The relationship is filled with anxiety, contradictions, and collisions."

Brooke, 28, says, "My mother collects cats, and every time I see another cat figure in her house, it makes me cringe and I ask, 'Where did this one come from, Mom?' I may even say something cruel, like, 'Mom, you know you're becoming a weird cat lady.' Afterwards I bite my tongue and ask myself why I have to be so mean. But it makes me feel like my mother's odd, and I'm uncomfortable with her eccentricity. Other times I feel less annoyed and I may even buy her a cat statue, even though I feel ambivalent about it. Every time she gets a card from me with a cat on it, she loves it."

Another daughter, Melanie, says, "My mother collects orchids, and I feel my meanness rising inside me when I enter her home, and it makes me uncomfortable. I have to remind myself how sweet she is and try not to say something hateful. My mother frustrates me because she worries about her heat bill but makes sure the house is warm enough for the flowers. She buys a new orchid stand for each plant, and I want to scream, 'Can't you just get one big plant stand like a baker's rack?' I hate the plant stands. I want my mother's house to look more sophisticated and less cluttered. Yet, she has a magic touch and her orchids are filled with multiple blooms. Her orchids are gorgeous."

Brooke's and Melanie's stories are good examples of how a daughter doesn't want to be like her mother, and at the same time is uncomfortable she isn't like her. Each tells of wanting to criticize her mother's choices. Both Brooke and Melanie feel anxiety when they see how different their mothers are from themselves, and rather than feeling vulnerable, they become aggressive. As much as they regret acting mean, it's a less scary place to be than to acknowledge their mothers' differences.

Like Brooke and Melanie, our daughters separate and individuate, not just around big life decisions, but in the mundane everyday moments as well. Their nasty behavior comes out when they experience this "not alikeness." When we realize this is a normal process it is easier to see it as something different from insensitivity and callousness. Daughters are judgmental because their relationship with us is so important and it looms so large in their lives.

On the other hand, a mother struggles with her daughter's choices that she may not like, either because she disagrees with her daughter's decision-making, or because she is envious of her daughter's opportunities and freedom. This discomfort is not because her daughter's choice is necessarily wrong; it may happen just because it is different.

As Deborah Tannen, linguist at George Washington University, explains in her book *You're Wearing That? Understanding Mothers and Daughters in Conversation*, a mother's innocent comment can be misinterpreted too easily by her daughter. Mothers and daughters communicate on two levels; the words they speak exist in the context of a continuous underlying conversation. Carol laments, "My mother has been dead for thirty years, yet she is still criticizing my hair."

Denise, mother of 31-year-old Hilary, says, "My niece, Julie, just found out that she was having her third son and announced that she was done trying for a daughter. She lamented that she would never have a daughter and said, 'Oh, well, everyone tells me that boys love their mothers.' Seeing that she was wistful and thinking about my own twenty-seven-year-old son, I said, 'Julie, you're right, boys are wonderful. I agree they love their moms.' Not a moment later, my daughter, Hilary, butts in, 'There she [I] goes again. Can't you leave it alone, Mom? You only say that to get at me.' My daughter is hypersensitive to me. Whenever I make a positive comment about my son, Hilary interprets it as a negative remark against her. I had no ulterior motive in this instance, but I know that there have been numerous times in the past when I meant for Hilary to hear how well my son treats me." Our struggle is in knowing when a statement is loaded with meaning that comes from the past and when the comment is clean and in the moment.

Gail says, "It's like a mixture of oil and water. I'm always on the verge of an argument; something could explode at any moment. If I tell my daughter her hair looks good natural, she'll ask me why I didn't like her hair blown straight. I always feel that I'm dancing on wet glass and could slip." This mother is acutely aware that her words have the ability to evoke emotions in her daughter that may not make sense in the present. Even though we may think our comments are innocuous, our daughters often interpret our words differently from what we intend or we actually mean to say. With mothers and daughters, our conversations are often loaded because the present is infused with the past.

"Free to Be You and Me"

We have come a long way since society defined morality using a male standard. Carol Gilligan's 1982 study of adolescent females provided a wake-up call for other researchers and educators. She discovered that noted researcher on development Lawrence Kohlberg had based his theory of moral development exclusively on male responses to his questions of morality. This biased instrument was then used to make the false argument that women are less morally developed. After 25 years of progress, men and boys are no longer the norm for every standard, from symptoms of disease to psychological health.

While Gilligan criticized Kohlberg's male-based methodology, she was interested in the question he raised in his study: "Why do some individuals recognize a higher moral law while others simply are content to obey the rules without question?" She noted that males find hierarchy, being at the top, appealing, while females experience "the top" as isolating and detached.

Deborah Tannen artfully took up Gilligan's theme. Tannen and Gilligan reconceptualized the study of the differences and similarities between males and females. Women are now able to celebrate their different ways of operating and elevate the difference to be equal to, rather than less than, men. We no longer have to argue that for men and women to be equal their experiences in this culture must be one and the same. The original research and writings of Carol Gilligan, Deborah Tannen, and the work of the Stone Center at Wellesley College and others, normalize what women have known all along. Carol Gilligan concludes, "Women's sense of integrity appears to be entwined with an ethic of care, so that to see themselves as women is to see themselves in a relationship of connection."

Mothers and daughters are close because connection is both a powerful value and a psychological need. Women define themselves in the context of human relationships and judge themselves in terms of their ability to care for others. Judith Jordan, author of *Women's Growth in Connection: Writings from the Stone Center*, states, "Our self-esteem is rooted in feeling that we are part of relationships and value nurturing those relationships as we express empathy with others. Many women feel that preserving relationships with the primary people in their lives is still the most important thing."

On the whole, women favor connection with others over separation. They prefer collaboration over a hierarchy or a pecking order. We are reluctant to follow rigid rules. This is not moral relativism; women evaluate the intricacies of each situation. For example, for most women, while stealing is wrong, stealing to feed a hungry child is not. For women, there are fewer absolutes. Instead, the moral reasoning of women and girls is more likely to lead them to look for a solution that preserves life, relationships, and connection.

In the 1980s and 1990s, following this revolutionary research, books and studies about women proliferated. These works demonstrated their strengths and contributions, making women more visible in virtually all academic disciplines. However, as is the case with many human rights movements, the more we discover, the more sophisticated our analysis becomes. Currently, we find ourselves at another juncture. Researchers are now exploring how sex-role stereotyping affects men and boys and are studying both the negative and positive impact of socialization on the development of girls and women.

Our Mothers, Ourselves

A mother and her daughter share a unique and powerful intergenerational bond. In *Motherless Daughter*, Hope Edelman says that our own mothers are our most direct connection to our past. They set examples for us by their actions and inaction, by their strengths and weaknesses. Our relationships with our mothers inform us about our relationships with our daughters. We need to understand our relationships with our mothers to understand our own mothering and have the ability to resolve conflicts with our daughters.

Mothers shudder in the aftermath of an angry encounter or clench their jaws while forcing themselves to stay silent to avoid saying something that reminds them of their experience with their own mother. Every mother we interviewed has a story she'd like to buy back if only that were a real option. Suzanne, 47-year-old mother of Stacey, says, "I am the oldest child in my family and have put a lot of pressure on myself to keep my siblings from annoying my mother, who is often depressed. I am a classic 'good girl' who never breaks rules or lies. So when my daughter, Stacey, started to act out in high school, I came down on her hard. I had little tolerance for this girl who broke rules, talked back, and sometimes lied. In order to stop this conduct, I would sometimes threaten her with boarding school to let her know how 'good' she had it and how serious I was about her modifying her behavior.

"It was only when a good friend overheard my threats that I reflected on why I had such a low tolerance level for normal teenage behavior. I couldn't bear seeing my daughter do what I never permitted myself [to do]. My anger was much greater than was necessary. The ghost of my childhood 'good girl' behavior was present in my own home. I regret the anxiety I caused Stacey and wish I had [had] this insight earlier." Suzanne's story demonstrates that often there are three people in any mother-daughter relationship: the grandmother, the mother, and the daughter.

Karen and Laura share their stories of mothers who were not nurturing and the impact on their own parenting. Karen, mother of 33-year-old Erica, says, "My mother had me when she was twenty years old and was overwhelmed. In my little girl way, I taught my mother to be a good enough mother by telling her when she wasn't there for me." Laura reflects, "My mother wasn't at all nurturing. My father made it clear that I shouldn't upset her, and I learned to take care of my own emotional needs."

Karen and Laura had different reactions to similar childhood experiences. One nurtured her mother, the other turned inward, but they both parented their own daughters in a comparable way. By reacting to their own childhoods, each made a good effort, but still missed some important parenting responsibilities. Laura says, "Because of my own mother's lack of nurturing, I wanted my daughter to feel unconditional love. It felt good just to give." Karen agrees and adds, "I am so in sync with my daughter, I believe that I am the best mother for her. I have done the opposite of my own mother. Yet, if I knew then what I know now, I'd do it differently. I thought being empathetic and fixing things was good mothering, but I didn't know that giving her opportunities to be self-reliant was also important."

Laura adds, "Because I didn't have a mother who soothed me, my endless patience and reassurances inhibited my daughter's ability to self-soothe. I became codependent with my daughter. This was the impact of my mother. I became a nurturer, was able to repair what I had missed but didn't hold my daughter accountable for learning to tolerate her own feelings. Parenting should be more nuanced, and now I wonder how her dependence on me will impact her own mothering."

According to Judith Warner, author of *Perfect Madness: Motherhood in the Age of Anxiety*, "All around me, in recent years, I've seen women living motherhood as an exercise in correction, trying to heal the wounds of their childhoods and, prophylactically, to seal their children against future pain." Alternatively, if our wounds aren't healed, we as mothers can re-create those same patterns. We must be mindful not only of our mother's behavior, but of our responses and how these impact our mothering.

Women form their identities in a context of the mother-daughter relationship because, according to Nancy Chodorow, "Mothers tend to experience their daughters as more like, and continuous with, themselves." We are mirrored from head to toe, replicated by common genes, sexual makeup, and social experiences.

Mothers provide a genetic and emotional road map for their daughters. This bond is particularly strong during adolescence, a period that offers an opportunity for both mothers and daughters to rediscover their identities. Physician and author Nancy Snyderman reports in *Girl in the Mirror* that the "past, present, and future collide when we look into our daughters' faces. All of our dreams—those we've realized and those we consider beyond our grasp—are in the room with us."

For a mother, raising a daughter is like going back to the future, watching herself while watching her daughter. Observing our daughters reminds us of experiences we had as young girls. While this identification with our own past can provide us with greater empathy and understanding, it can also resurrect childhood pain and cause us to react in a negative way. For these reasons mothers often struggle to separate their own experience from their child's. This is easier said than done.

Patricia says, "I am grateful for the relationship that I have with my daughter. I didn't have it with my mom. She did the best she could as a single mom; she provided for us and had dinner on the table. My dad died when I was young, and I appreciate what she did for me. I did learn that when I had children I wanted to give them unconditional love. My mother was cold and didn't show her emotions and she was too concerned with what other people thought. We lived in the suburbs, where everyone else had two parents and weren't struggling financially like we were. She also was very successful as a young woman, but had to give up her career when she had children. When she had to work, she was limited as to what she could do without recent work experience. I think that was one of the reasons I was willing to help my daughter, Melanie, so she would be able to eventually take care of herself."

As the mother of a daughter, you inhabit two roles at the same time, the past role of daughter, which may not end until after your own mother's death or beyond, and the role as mother of your own daughter. In a sense, you are sandwiched between the expectations your own mother had for you and the expectations you have for your own daughter. These dual expectations resonate, creating a unique vulnerability and a sensitivity toward your daughter and her judgments about you. Many of us find ourselves wanting to please our own mother and daughter at the same time, often with differing expectations.

Many mothers in our focus groups discuss the desire to become different women from their mothers. They feel empathy and love for their mothers, but created a self in opposition to what they observed. Whether you want to be like your mother or develop in opposition, the relationship is powerful.

Barbara, a 56-year-old lawyer, recalls, "My father died when my mother was young and her life remained insular with very few outside activities. Even though she traveled a little bit, she never developed a life of her own. He was her everything, and I think watching what happened to my mother after my father died was the reason I knew that I was always going to have a career. Observing a mother who never developed her own identity motivated me to prepare for a meaningful career, like my dad. So I modeled myself after my father, not my mother. He had the life that I wanted to have. My father really enjoyed his work; he was successful and had an identity separate from our family.

"It wasn't surprising that my mother felt diminished by my

ambition and success. What I didn't know at the time were the real reasons behind this. My mother was embarrassed because she felt unintelligent. Only now can she talk about her difficulty in school. When my mom was in school, no one knew about learning disabilities and she was intimidated enough to drop out. My mother lived her life avoiding situations that would expose her illiteracy. She never went to parent-teacher interviews because my mother was too frightened to be in a room with a teacher. My success in school really threatened her. Now my mother can label her reading difficulty as a learning disability, which one of my daughters has inherited. She watched me help my daughter, and I think that's when she began to change her attitude toward me. And maybe I also began to understand how hard growing up must have been for her. My mom no longer treats me like I'm being spiteful to her when I succeed."

Most of the conflict Barbara and her mother have faced is based on misunderstanding each other's circumstances and feelings. As a child, Barbara couldn't fully comprehend how painful her mother's life had been. Barbara's experience as a mother eventually enabled her to make sense of both her mother's life and her own childhood. This understanding has the capacity to inform her own mothering and improve her relationship with her mother. Nancy Snyderman writes, and we think it bears repeating, "For every girl who makes the journey from child to woman, the first mirror in which she looks is the mirror of her mother's face . . . In the room with us are our past selves, the adolescent girls [young women] we once were. Our own mothers' words echo when we talk."

The most important homework we can do to prepare to mother our daughters is to recognize and manage our own baggage, which includes understanding our relationships with our own mothers—the good, the bad, and the ugly. Was your mother rigid or flexible? Was she restrictive or lenient? Was she empathetic or shaming? Happy, depressed, optimistic, or pessimistic? Our answers to these questions are influenced by our temperament and birth order as well as whether our other siblings are girls. What we experience as daughters is part of what we consciously or unconsciously bring to our role as mothers. Becoming more aware of our experience as daughters helps us to understand and maybe to cut ourselves a little slack when we hear ourselves saying, "I never thought I'd say that; I sound just like my mother."

"Every Breath I Take"

There is so much pressure on mothers. We are supposed to make everything comfortable for others, tending to their needs before we turn our attention to ourselves. According to psychologist Dana Jack, selflessness often drives a woman's thinking and behavior in her relationships. Jack explains that, for women, the "good me" and "good mother" roles are culturally dictated as primary goals of female development. These roles may involve stifling and/or delaying one's own wants *and* needs.

Because mothers often put the needs of their family before their own, many daughters assume their mother is available to listen to, sympathize with, or comfort them at any time. Beverly, mother of 29-year-old Margie, says, "My daughter feels comfortable calling me late if she needs me to comfort her. Last night she called at 12:45 A.M. on her way home from a movie that made her very sad. I go to bed late and had just shut my light when she called. I asked her whether she thought about the fact that I might have been sleeping, and she said, 'Mom, I thought about it and I knew I was playing the margins.' I wasn't surprised she would err on the side of waking me up versus allowing me to sleep. Regardless of her age, Margie expects I will drop everything to help her, day or night. And I don't expect it to be reciprocal; she shouldn't be the same safety net for me that I am for her. But I struggle with knowing when to set limits." The mother-daughter relationship is not a relationship of equals. However, years of putting our daughters before ourselves often creates unclear boundaries.

For mothers, it is almost counterintuitive to put our needs ahead of those of our children. At best, this is a tenuous balance, because mothers have competing needs. We need to nurture ourselves and we need to nurture our daughters. When those needs are in conflict, it is difficult to feel at ease with the balance between self and others. This is an ongoing challenge.

Traditional cultural models portray women as all-giving, having few wants and desires for themselves. Women who attempt to assert their individuality are often criticized. Mothers are expected to treat their daughters' needs as their own. Daughters have the same expectation. Many daughters in our focus groups, whether they are Latina, African American, or Asian American, all agree about their mothers' willingness to sacrifice anything for them. These adult daughters also discuss feeling guilty when they have taken advantage of their mothers because they know their mothers would do anything for them. They feel guilty because, even when their mothers are tired, they still say yes. Mothers in our focus groups also express feelings of guilt, but their guilt has to do with saying no, even when it's appropriate.

Stephanie, an executive with an insurance company, tells us, "I was in the middle of a meeting with a client talking about long-term care insurance when my daughter, Kim, called to ask for advice. Kim was job hunting and had just returned from an interview. I couldn't talk to her, even though I knew she was anxious and really needed to talk. I felt terrible, and she didn't make it easy when she sounded so disappointed. It feels that no matter what I'm doing when Kim needs me, I should stop everything and be there for her. I know intellectually that this isn't reasonable, but emotionally, my mothering instinct kicks in and I feel bad saying no." Mothers of adult daughters fight saying no because they instinctively feel the pull not to disappoint their daughters, while also meeting their own needs. The attachment pull is there for both; however, daughters love, but they don't feel the pull to the same degree. They usually don't understand this emotional bind until they became mothers themselves. This reality creates an inequity between the experience of being a mother and of being a daughter and limits the possibility that mothers and daughters can be best friends.

Andrea remembers her mother telling her to take advantage of her twenties because it is the only time in her life she can really think only about herself: "I couldn't know how wise my mother's advice was until my son, Carlos, was born. I can't take a shower without worrying that he might need me, and reading the newspaper seems like a luxury that I don't have time for anymore. I am either with the baby or I'm waiting for the baby to need me." Guilt is a universal experience for both mothers and adult daughters; it's an equal opportunity feeling of discomfort.

The expectation in all cultures that mothers should be selfless prevents them from being *best* friends with their daughters. Alice says, "My default mode is to help my daughter, regardless of how tired I am. I want her to know she can count on me, but often I think she feels entitled. I would never expect the same sacrifices from her." Many mothers struggle with knowing how much of themselves to give. Giving to our daughters should stop short of being self-exploitative. We've all maintained friendships out of guilt, but that doesn't make for a *best* friendship. A best friendship requires mutuality.

The Middle Way

Finding the balance between attachment and individuation is a high-wire act. It is the mother's job to support her daughter's independence without disconnecting, despite the inevitable confusion and tension. In doing so, a mother must struggle with redefining her historical caretaker role to allow, if not encourage, her daughter's developmental need for autonomy.

Our culture teaches us that being too close to our adult daughters produces a stifling symbiotic and enmeshed relationship. This negative assessment makes it difficult to view attachment and connection in a positive light. This is a problem for all people in our culture, not just for mothers and daughters.

In contrast to the United States and Europe, Latino, Asian, and African cultures discourage, if not hinder, a daughter's autonomy. Many are not expected to leave home until they get married, moving from one hierarchical family to another, where authority is primarily a function of age and gender. For them, the well-being of the family unit is of primary importance, and individuation is less important. There is some anecdotal evidence, however, that this value is changing among second-generation Americans and in urbanized Japan, China, and India, where capitalism and materialism are prominent and individuation is somewhat tolerated.

In most circumstances, the attachment between mothers and daughters shifts as the daughter matures. As a daughter goes through different life phases—graduation from college, work, marriage, and children—the everyday intimacy with her mother may be inconsistent. The strength of the mother-daughter connection is like a force field and the connection remains. But through all of these phases, by psychological osmosis, a daughter carries her mother inside her. Part of a mother is always implanted in her daughter's head. By midlife, the adult daughter hears her mother's voice integrated as a permanent and crucial part of her, some of which she, in turn, transmits to her own daughter.

Psychologist Rosalind Barnett believes the fact that adult daughters continue to need their mothers does not prevent them from becoming independent thinkers. Nor does it create a dependence that inhibits their ability to become independent. Dr. Barnett writes that the dependence is a byproduct of attachment and a mother and daughter's need to maintain a healthy connection. All people *grow* in connection, in relationship, even though they experience themselves as separate beings.

We believe the mother–adult daughter attachment can be

respectfully interdependent. The challenge for mothers and daughters is finding the balance between connection and separation. An adult daughter's interdependence and attachment to her mother may demonstrate psychological health rather than pathology. Many psychologists like Rosalind Barnett and colleagues also state that adult women are psychologically better off when they have good relations with their mothers. They posit the women have higher self-esteem, feel less anxious, and are less depressed than are women who are in conflict with their mothers.

A positive mother-daughter relationship protects our daughters by giving them a greater ability to cope with adversity. This relationship contributes to our daughters' resilience by providing the foundation for healthy emotional development. The relationship between mother and daughter is primordial because it sets the stage for all other relationships in a girl's life and provides her with a sense of well-being.

4

Differences Between Supporting and Enabling: She's a Young Thing and Cannot Leave Her Mother

Margaret Mead, noted anthropologist, wrote about her mother in a way that any "fix-it mom" could relate to. "I know that if I had written to her [mother] to say, 'Please go and wait for me on the corner of Thirteenth and Chestnut streets,' she would have stayed there until I came or she dropped from sheer fatigue."

Actions Speak Louder Than Words

For daughters, adulthood is a time to renegotiate their relationship with their parents. This transition is complex; our daughters are becoming more independent and self reliant, while at the same time still freeing themselves from emotional dependence.

While friendships also go through transitions, there is no analogous struggle for independence. In young adults' struggle for independence, a best friend is usually an ally. While a mother can be an ally, she can also be a deterrent and a focal point of the struggle. Best friends don't monitor your maturity; whereas as one mother says, "I always have my mommy light on."

While adult daughters are trying to wean themselves from economic dependence, many find themselves needing assistance. One of the more seminal experiences in the transition to adulthood is when a daughter moves back home temporarily. This presents a lifestyle transition for both parents and adult daughters. One mother says, "I find it disconcerting to have Laura move back after having been gone for five years. It's like a pothole on the road to her developmental maturity." In terms of lifestyle changes, moving back home is different from "crashing" with a friend in terms of expectations and levels of involvement.

A recent article from *Business Wire* stated that more than 60 percent of today's college graduates are moving back to live with their parents after college, between jobs, or after an emotional upheaval. Just when you thought the intense period of parenting is over, they're back! Some of our daughters also bring significant others, children, and pets with them; others come and go like a revolving door.

Bonnie tells us, "I love being an empty nester. I thought I would be lonely, but I love having my house to myself. I enjoy being free of thinking of what to make for dinner, being home at a certain time, and lounging around in sheer pajamas. I wasn't prepared for my daughter, Rebecca, to move back home. I certainly wasn't prepared for Rebecca, her new husband, and their golden retriever. First thing I had to do was transform her old room back into a bedroom. That meant getting rid of the treadmill and free weights.

"I love my kids, but I find it hard to stay out of their lives when they are in my face. I also find that my daughter expects me to do for her what I did for her as a teenager, like doing her laundry and running errands. It is too easy for me to fall back into old patterns. I understand that we are transitional housing while she saves for a down payment on an apartment, but it is interfering with my new hard-earned freedom. I am afraid that if I make it too comfortable, she either won't leave or they will come back again."

Many mothers in our focus groups enjoy the freedom of the empty nest; however, they agree a daughter's move back home has lost its social stigma. While it no longer means their daughters are not growing up, they are confused about their role as a parent when their daughters come back home not as children, but as emerging adults.

Whether daughters move back home or live apart from their parents, we believe they can be independent and productive and still remain close. During this transitional time between adolescence and adulthood, our daughters should develop what we call "respectful interdependence." Respectful interdependence requires mutuality, support, more collaboration, and less hierarchy. Parents are no longer the boss of their adult children. They can parent best now through discussion, coaching, compromise, and collaborative problem solving.

For every family, finding the balance between enabling and supporting adult daughters on their road to maturity and adulthood is complicated and difficult. While there are more opportunities to create a positive adult relationship, there is also the chance that daughters will remain less mature and more dependent for a longer period. Our daughters are often single until at least their late twenties and Mom may still be the "go-to person" until a daughter has a significant other or marries.

In the United States, parenthood is a private act. Like Americans of the nineteenth century who were told to "Go West," in the twenty-first century we still look for new frontiers rather than to our neighbors for help. Our society is characterized by the priority of individual goals over the common good. The value of individual liberty is more important than serving the majority. This cultural norm is the reason we don't yet have universal health care and a more comprehensive Family Leave Act. Unlike other Western countries, our society fails to provide an adequate social safety net to help support young adults and their families. For example, young adults are the least likely to have health benefits among eligible adults. For these reasons, parents with the financial means continue to take a more active role in helping their daughters with life's necessities, including health care, child care, and housing. Parents are frequently their children's only safety net.

The distinction between supporting and enabling can be blurred. Some of our daughters need more assistance, even while they are making a valiant effort to be self-reliant. Others require our help because we failed to teach them adult life skills. Most of them are somewhere in between. In this chapter, we discuss the divergent needs of adult daughters and how to determine what encourages growth and what is an inhibition. During this stage of our daughter's life, parents should be coaches and resources not personal assistants.

"Those Are Strings, Pinocchio"

Many mothers ask about the difference between supporting and enabling. There is a qualitative difference. Enabling occurs when mothers (and fathers) try to protect their children from the consequences of their actions and, thereby, fail to hold them accountable for their personal behavior. Enabling moms take on responsibilities their children should assume. Enabling behavior can be as overt as repeatedly bailing a child out when she can't pay her credit card bill or as subtle as sending e-mail reminders and text messages of tasks she needs to do, or being your daughter's human alarm clock. When we continue to be task completers we give our daughters the unintended message that we don't have faith in their ability to do things for themselves. By engaging in enabling behavior, we encourage our daughters to behave less maturely and to be more dependent. By doing things for them rather than coaching or letting them do for themselves, we deny them the opportunity to learn critical skills and face consequences.

Overdoing encourages our daughters to be irresponsible. Barbara, mother of 33-year-old Andrea, says, "Helping our kids so much also has limitations and consequences as they get older. Andrea wanted me to lend her money to pay taxes. I said I would if she would pay me back. Even now when she is financially independent and receives bonuses every year, she still hasn't offered to pay me back. This year I asked her to pay me back on a payment plan. She responded with, 'Good idea, Mom.' So far, I haven't received any money." In this case, it is important for Barbara to help Andrea to create a payment plan and hold her accountable.

If not, resentment can build and may interfere with sustaining a positive mother-daughter relationship. In contrast, rather than hinder their maturity we can offer our daughters the opportunities to develop and practice the skills of adulthood.

Emotional support is primarily providing adult daughters with encouragement and, when asked, counsel. It is based on active listening, rather than on giving advice. Physical support is doing something for your daughter that she is not able to do for herself. Supporting is bringing your daughter food when she is ill, driving her to work if her leg is in a cast, or picking up a grandchild from day care if your daughter can't leave work. Providing temporary help for your daughter is considerate and thoughtful. Most important, supporting is a temporary gift of assistance, money, or time until she can do for herself.

A supportive mom holds her daughter accountable for her behavior, sets boundaries, and fosters personal responsibility. At this stage of our daughter's life our goal is to help her become more able, not less able or unable, to do things for herself. This is also an appropriate time to give our daughter a chance to give back!

Deborah, mother of 26-year-old Kelly, says, "When my father was dying, I spent every evening after work at the hospital. I was so tired when I got home that I ate nothing that couldn't be microwaved or served from a can. Although Kelly would call to see how her grandfather was doing and went to see him, she never offered to grocery shop, cook, or even make sure that I ate. At first I was very disappointed waiting for her to offer help.

"I decided that this event was a good chance for me to tell her how I felt about her behavior rather than waiting until the opportunity passed. This was an important lesson for both of us.

Once I sat down and talked to Kelly, she immediately responded with warmth and empathy. I realized that I could still teach Kelly what mattered to me and that I shouldn't expect her to be a mind reader. The next day I came home from the hospital to a refrigerator filled with possibilities that were not frozen or in Mylar packets." Just as we need to tell our husbands and friends what we need, we should do the same with our adult daughters. The days of being only "The Giving Tree" are over!

It's easy to confuse enabling with support. An enabled childhood produces a young adult who may not be self-reliant. In one of our focus groups, a mother told us that her children refer to her as "GPS Mom." Her children know she is an excellent networker with a fabulous Rolodex, so they call her first, before they look for information on their own.

By the way, the extent to which we teach our children to expect us to solve their problems has nothing to do with proximity. Adele received the following phone call from her daughter, a financial development specialist for a private school in another state. She said, "Mom, I don't know whether to get into the shower. The water pipes are making these weird hissing sounds; I'm afraid they are going to explode. What should I do?" Adele replied, "Call your landlord. I'm not a plumber. What do you expect me to do?"

"Keep Me Hanging On . . ."

For our generation, the Holy Grail for mothers contains a contradiction. We encouraged our daughters' self-esteem but shielded them from the experience of failure. We wanted them to have high self-esteem without experiencing pain. Many of us remember end-of-the-year soccer parties when the team manager mom gave every player a trophy. We raised our children to believe they are special and can do anything. The unintended consequence has been imparting a sense of entitlement and, for many young women, a reluctance to stick with something when "the going gets tough."

When things didn't go well, we felt compelled either to eliminate the discomfort or fix the problem. We lobbied with coaches to get our daughter more playing time; we called her school to make sure she got the best teacher; and we persuaded other parents to make sure our daughter was invited to a party. Anna Quindlen describes our children as "the first generation to have homework-helping, soccer-coaching, essay-reading parents fluttering around them like moths with control issues." Many of us were devoted to making our daughter's life less difficult, if not easy, believing this would create a happy child.

Dawn, a psychologist, tells us, "My aunt had a hard childhood and she made sure that her kids weren't going to experience anything awful or unpleasant. By trying to smooth over all the jagged edges, my aunt rendered my cousin, Monica, pretty much unprepared for life. For example, Monica was a gifted pianist and she had an anxiety attack when her exams in music school got stressful. One time my aunt brought her home and told her, 'Honey, you do not have to write the exam.' Sadly, this caused Monica not to graduate. To this day she feels horrible that she never completed school. I really think my aunt had no understanding of the need to teach my cousin persistence. Monica is now thirty-four, and she continues this pattern by wrapping her own children in cotton batting. It's hard to watch Monica repeat the disabling patterns of her upbringing."

There comes a point when our job is not to park ourselves in front of our kids to shield them and get rid of all the bad stuff in their lives. Our job is actually to stand behind our kids as they face adversity or tough situations. "Watching their back" gives them the opportunity to learn for themselves that they can handle difficult challenges. This is where self-esteem comes from. Mothers must understand that crying and feeling a little pain sometimes is okay. Once a daughter deals with the pain and gets through it, she will be less afraid the next time.

In modern society, overbearing advocacy for our children has few limits. Parents filling out college applications say things like, "*We* have an application due on December fifteenth." They attend orientations in such numbers that colleges run separate programs for parents. And this doesn't end with the application process. Parents call the schools when their children's grades aren't what they expect and go on the Internet to read about course assignments. Mothers and fathers who have difficulty setting limits on their own involvement may produce adult daughters who have trouble doing things for themselves.

Sheryl says, "My daughter, Erin, called me last week on her way to her first anthropology class. At first, I was thrilled to hear from her. Then she asked, 'Mom, can you look up the course guide online and tell me where my anthro class is?' My mouth dropped and I thought, couldn't she have checked the information before she left her room? Then, as usual, I went online and told her where her class was being held. I did this as fast as I could, because, of course, I didn't want her to be late. Erin said, 'Thanks, Mom, I knew I could count on you. You are the best.' And I thought, what have I created?"

When you think about this story, and we all have stories like this, as mothers we have to take some responsibility for our daughter's continued dependence. It's very satisfying for a parent to feel needed, and for many of us the secondary gain of being praised and valued by our children is compelling. As children get older, parents often miss being needed by them. We interpret our daughters seeking us out for help as evidence that they still value us. We certainly want our daughters to come to us when they are in need, and we want to maintain our connection to them; it's how we define "need," distinguishing it from "want," that can be either enabling or supportive.

Before providing help, parents can support their adult daughters best by determining whether we wish to help them for their benefit or our own. Obviously, there are ways to identify a form of support that is mutually beneficial. This identification allows us to stay involved in our daughters' lives and help them in a manner that facilitates development of adult behavioral traits.

Often we don't know whether we are enabling immaturity or supporting maturity. Sometimes we both nurture success and allow temporary dependency, and this creates mixed feelings and results. Diana shares the following story: "My daughter, Nicole, went into a financially precarious career, opening up her own clothing store at twenty-three years old. She made her business out of whole cloth. Nicole had no previous business experience, but had a real knowledge of ready-to-wear. We were her financial safety net. It would have been a whole lot easier for us if she had become an accountant.

"I started to do extra consulting to provide her with income while she got on her feet. We provided her with seed money. A new business is a struggle. I was pleased to be able to help her, but also frustrated. For example, during this time period, she got a lot of parking tickets and it drove me crazy. Her cell phone and clothing costs were more than she could afford. She bought more expensive clothes than I did. I didn't like that I was judgmental about how she spent her money. I shouldn't have been in a position where I was so involved. However, she did achieve success. I am proud of the position of respect she has earned in her community, her level of expertise, and, finally, after a few years, her financial solvency. Because we could be her safety net, she was able to follow her passion."

When we make the decision whether to help our daughters or how much, we don't always know the results. Nicole's experience could have gone either way, and Diana might have regretted her decision to keep quiet over her concerns. Fortunately, Diana saw her daughter grow incrementally and become successful, and she felt comfortable with the outcome. Nicole was successful, and at the end of the day, this experience helped her to overcome her personal financial mismanagement. And her parents' support was a critical factor in her success and ultimate independence.

Many mothers feel that their daughters can't manage without a safety net. We disagree. They may not have as many choices as we could provide for them, but they do manage. In fact, having too much of a safety net often becomes a tool for enabling dependence and robs young adults of their hunger and drive. According to one adult daughter, "I know that I would be more successful if I knew that my parents wouldn't always bail me out. It would force me to be more ambitious and self-reliant. I wonder if it would help me be more satisfied with my achievements, instead of expecting to live like my parents do without all of the hard work."

Amy, a young woman, tells a similar story: "My friend Sarah's parents were paying for this luxury townhouse, even though she worked in banking and could have afforded a nice apartment herself. She wound up spending beyond her means and accumulating ten thousand dollars of credit card debt. Her mother wanted to bail her out, but her father didn't. He convinced her mother that unless they took a stand, this excess spending would continue. They would have to bail her out again. So her parents decided to draw the line. Sarah had to move out of her townhouse, rent an apartment she could afford, and get a second job as a financial advisor to augment her salary to pay off her debt." Sarah was furious with her parents and panicked for a while at the thought of working two jobs, but eventually she learned to live within her means.

Frank Furstenberg, a University of Pennsylvania sociologist, provides a cautionary word for parents who give their children excessive long-term support: "Young adults today may watch their parents providing support for so long—and be wary of becoming parents themselves. And that, of course, would be very bad news for boomer parents who aspire to become grandparents."

Many of our daughters have grown up with a sense of entitlement. According to journalist Dan Zak, "They expect a buffet of opportunities and are peeved when they don't materialize." Their expectations that we will pave the way emanates from our desire to protect and provide them with everything. This has created an "I generation," a term coined by Jean Twenge, a professor of psychology at San Diego State University. "*I* as in both iPod and me, me, me." Today baby girl T-shirts have sayings that support this attitude, such as "spoiled brat" and "Daddy's Little Princess." Stephanie Coontz, director of research for the Council on Contemporary Families, says in an article by Kimberly Palmer, "As a historian, I can tell you no older generation in history has ever spent so many resources on grown kids." Parents who don't have the financial means to subsidize their adult children offer to babysit for grandchildren or allow children to move back home. This trend highlights parents' decision to remain as their daughters' caretakers. Friendship is nearly impossible to maintain in such a disproportionate and dependent relationship.

Money Is the Root of Some Evil

To determine whether conduct is holding back an adult child, parents must assess the impact of their behavior on the child's ability to function independently. A mother must ask herself honestly whether she is contributing to, or hindering, her child's developing adult behavioral characteristics. As one mother asked us, "If, God forbid, anything happened to you, could those kids continue to function?" Another mother told us about her sister whose extended dependency on their parents made her unable to cope well into her forties.

When parents who have the financial means overindulge their adult daughter, they do her harm. When parents who do not have the financial means overindulge their daughter, they harm themselves and her. Generally speaking, friends, even best friends, do not undertake this burden. In fact, best friends don't ask each other for this level of financial support. Good parenting does not require putting oneself into financial jeopardy or threatening one's retirement.

Some adult children continue to take money from their parents just because they want to and feel entitled to it and the money seems to be available. Parents have a responsibility to be honest with their children about the sacrifices they are prepared to make to maintain them in a certain lifestyle. If they don't set these limits, parents rob their children of the opportunity to challenge themselves and solve their own problems. Parents certainly can still assist their children financially; however, they should always remember that excessive assistance can hinder their child's ability to learn the skills necessary to become independent.

Barbara says, "My daughter, Danielle, saved enough money to put down a deposit on her condominium. My husband and I decided to give her some money to remodel the apartment. I found myself looking at furniture, appliances, hardware, and tile that fit my taste and my budget. It took the contractor to remind me that Danielle did not have to start where I have ended. I realized that she could use her teapot to boil water and nixed paying for an instant hot." Parents must be very clear about, first, whether they have the money to give, and, second, even if they do have the money, whether giving it will benefit their adult child's maturation. By failing to set appropriate boundaries, parents facilitate their daughter's prolonged dependence and, possibly, her dysfunctional behavior.

Growing Up Is Hard to Do

Many mothers ask us, "When do I treat my daughter, and how much do I support her?" Kaitlin says, "I know my mother isn't my best friend because she always treats when we meet for lunch.

There's no way a friend would assume that role; it would feel unfair." Diane, mother of Allison, says, "We can't walk by a makeup counter without me worrying if Allison is going to fall in love with the newest wonder product. One day, she selected a lip liner and gloss and I said, 'Let me buy that for you.' I mean, lip liner and gloss could not set me back much and I thought it was a nice treat for her. I thought I could afford even the best lip gloss. I almost fell over when my Visa charge was sixty-eight dollars. This charge didn't even include the lipstick!

"I turned to Allison and said, 'I'm happy to buy you some makeup, but I can't spend sixty-eight dollars on lip gloss.' I did feel bad that what could have been a pleasurable moment became uncomfortable. Allison may have been disappointed, but I felt fine about setting limits." Many mothers in our focus groups talk about the difference they feel between supporting a lifestyle (wants) versus supporting their daughter's genuine needs. Appropriate support contributes to the self-esteem and maturity of adult children.

Determining the appropriate type and amount of support is tricky. One mother tells the story of her daughter who works for a large public relations firm. She says, "My daughter, Amanda, is so excited about her first real job. When she started to send me the drafts of her writing, I was happy that she wanted my opinion. My knee-jerk reaction was to edit her piece and send the finished product back to her because I knew she was nervous and wanted to make a good first impression. But after a while, I began to feel she was depending too much on me to get her work done, and it started to feel uncomfortable. After several nights of helping her meet her deadlines, I realized that I wasn't doing her any favors; I was enabling her dependence on my skills rather than building her own.

"My good intentions were eroding her self-confidence. I decided to tell Amanda that she was more than capable of managing her own work. Amanda responded, 'I know I can do it, Mom, but you always make me look a bit better.' The only way Amanda could appreciate her talent was for me to break the pattern. At first, Amanda was unhappy with me, but eventually she was proud of her ability to write copy because she learned that her work could stand on its own. That knowledge was worth everything to both of us."

Appropriate support is based on healthy connections with good boundaries. We can learn this from many sources: trial and error, our own experiences as daughters, parenting our adolescent daughters, conversations with friends, and self-help books. Many of us also learn from how our parents treated us when we were young adults; although, sometimes this knowledge teaches us how we don't want to parent. We then use these experiences to formulate our own ideas about parenting.

Stacey says, "My parents were physically there for me, but there was always a price to pay. Their assistance was conditional, judgmental, and punitive. I learned pretty early not to go to them, so I never wanted my daughters to feel about me the way I felt about my parents. I have definitely crossed the line a number of times with my daughters by being too intrusive. But as I've matured, I have really tried to be less intrusive. I think that it's so important to let my daughters know they can turn to me and ask that I give them support without that judgment, which diminishes them. I feel my support should be gladly given and free of conditions. When I am successful at this, my daughters are appreciative and respectful. As they have gotten older, our relationship has become more reciprocal."

Another consideration when determining appropriate support is that one size does not fit all. For those of us who have more than one daughter, each may require a different kind of parenting. Jean tells us, "It's easy to give to Lindsay because she never asks for anything unless she really needs it. I offer to give her money for groceries or to go out with her friends for a nice dinner or to buy a new down jacket. Lindsay usually tells me, 'Thanks, but I don't need it.' On the other hand, I have to hold myself back around Ellen. If I'm not careful, she will take all of my money!"

Similarly, Jocelyn says, "I have two daughters and the best way to describe the difference is if I give one daughter twenty dollars for an item that costs three dollars, she keeps the change. The other daughter will hand me back two dollars if the item is eighteen dollars. I want to be generous, but I have to be careful to clearly ask for the money back from one daughter, because if I don't, she takes advantage of me."

From just these two examples, it is easy to conclude that the appropriate amount of support can vary with the circumstances or the child. If help isn't suitable to the situation and/or the particular needs of a daughter, inappropriate support can result in excessive dependence. An adult daughter and her parents should be continually negotiating the conditions for support to preserve mutual respect.

A Room in My Heart

Most articles in the media sensationalize and criticize the phenomenon of adult children moving back home. The media popularize the notion that adult children move home because they are over-indulged and unable to function on their own. This assumption is based on an incomplete understanding of the facts. In most countries, and for culturally diverse families in this country, it is traditional for children to live at home and conserve resources. This is also true for families who have less wealth. As we learned from writing *Mom, Can I Move Back In with You? A Survival Guide for Parents of Twentysomethings*, adult daughters moving back home is frequently a sign of family strength. This transition often signifies the comfort level today's young adults have with their parents. Historically, children have always moved back home during difficult economic conditions. In 2003, 54.8 percent of 18- to 24-year-old males and 45.7 percent of females were living with their parents.

Today the data show that adult daughters are moving back home because they are transitioning between jobs and school or are still in school, find themselves in debt, are trying to save money, or are adjusting to the end of a relationship. Parents and their daughters intend for the move to be temporary. Unfortunately, many parents still see their daughters moving back home as their failure as parents to prepare them for adulthood. As more adult children move back home, this transition is becoming common and more accepted. Many parents welcome their children home, but are perplexed about which parenting skills still apply. The context has changed, because the person who is returning home is an adult and not the adolescent who left for the first time. During this stage, the rules for parenting adolescents have to be reframed for young adults. Parents need to negotiate different boundaries with adult daughters, such as privacy issues, curfews, calling home, and financial and home maintenance responsibilities.

Judith, mother of 29-year-old Zoe, says, "I've always been a great cook. It is one of the things of which I am most proud. So when Zoe moved back home last fall, I had to get used to her doing her own cooking. One night she was making guacamole and neglected to add cilantro. My mouth started talking before my brain could edit my words. I said, 'Zoe, guacamole needs cilantro,' and Zoe responded, 'Mom, *your* guacamole needs cilantro. Did you ever consider that mine is just fine without it?' At that moment, I realized that Zoe was right. Yet, she was in my space and I was unused to sharing. The kitchen has always been my domain, and this was a lesson for me that Zoe had her own way, and should have her own way, of doing things. She has a right to cook the way she wants. I am glad that we had this opportunity to live in such close proximity because it permitted us to work through some issues that otherwise may have taken a longer time to first identify and then resolve."

Respect, cooperation, and compromise are key in any relationship. An adult daughter returning home provides another opportunity to demonstrate these characteristics as well as the importance of empathy and thinking about others. Parents should be very intentional about making this time productive. A positive outcome is more likely if the parents maintain boundaries and expect their daughter to assume adult responsibilities. The parents' role is to uphold whatever agreement they reach with their daughter. This understanding is necessary in any kind of a long-term relationship.

As in any stage of parenting, having a sense of humor helps to keep harmony in the home. The unexpected is difficult enough for parents and children; having perspective about the situation can help to make their time together meaningful and fun. One mother has the following sign on her refrigerator: "If you take it out, put it back. If you open it, close it. If you throw it down, pick it up. If you take it off, hang it up." Setting the rules of the house makes them easier to accept, because they are meant for everyone, not just children who have moved back home.

Living at Home from Different Cultural Perspectives

Different cultures respond to adult children living at home from diverse perspectives. It is exceptional for parents outside the United States to subsidize their children's independence. In most countries, it is the norm for adult children to live at home. For example, in Belgium, families with children who move back home are called "hotel families." After all, Mom or Dad may continue to do the laundry, at least, for a while. In Italy, sons and daughters commonly live at home until they marry and can afford to live separately. In Germany, a 30-year-old son sued his parents to force them to pay his college tuition and won. In Britain, a poll showed that one in ten adult children move home on four different occasions before they finally settle in their own homes.

Even in the United States, it is common for culturally diverse adult children to live at home. Within these cultures, the family remains primary, and for economic reasons or tradition, adult children don't leave home until they get married. Often, more than two generations live together in one home.

It is expected that parents and other family members will provide support for one another in African-American, Asian-American, Latino, and Native American families. This support comes in many forms, such as financial, housing, and child care. Family interdependence is certainly seen as more important than individual independence.

Isabella, the mother of Sophia, 24, and Isela, 26, describes the traditions in her family: "My family is typical. My children lived at home through college. And after college, we all needed to pool our resources. They never even considered moving out of the house. Isela is just beginning to think about moving out. My mother and the kids help with our younger children. We have 'familialism,' a strong sense of family loyalty. I have raised my children to know that family comes before anything else. It is our strongest cultural value."

Another parent shares a similar story. Lola, mother of two adult daughters and two adult sons, says, "I am a single mother living with my children. Two are working, and two are still in school. They know they are always welcome. We depend on each other. I love having them in the house. I can't imagine why they would live on their own until they are married, and, frankly, neither can they."

In European-American families, children leave home early because they often go away to college, so when they return it's often a shock to the family. Even adult children with their own families return to their parents' home, or the home of other relatives, if they can't support themselves. As one adult child says,

"We don't look forward to that move, but there is no stigma attached to it either." The question for many families is what they can afford. Adult children want to move out when they can support themselves, without expecting any help from their parents.

The Yin and Yang of Support

Doing for ourselves builds and sustains our self-esteem and self-confidence. However, we often enable our daughters' dependent behavior because it is easier for us. Our fast-paced, 24/7 lives, where everyone is multitasking, frequently as single-parent families or families with two working parents, force us to cut corners. Diane Ehrensaft, author and sociologist, described trying to have a quality life with our children in her paper "Kindercult" as "squeezing a quality relationship with our children into only a 'thimble of time.' "

Annie, mother of Liza, says, "Liza ordered running shoes online. One of the shoes arrived with the security tag hanging on the tongue. I knew she would probably order a new pair before she would find a local store with the equipment to remove the tag. So I did the research and took the shoe to the store myself. Liza didn't ask for help; I just needed to get it done." We do more things for our children, rather than fewer, because it's quicker and easier than teaching them to do things for themselves. Teaching skills takes time, something we often have in short supply. We are often too impatient to let our children make mistakes and suffer the consequences. Our intentions are good, but our behavior actually disables our children, denying them the opportunities to learn adult skills. We instill the belief that we can take care of things better than they can.

Katherine says, "My daughter, Erica, lives in a lovely apartment in Chicago. She is going on a business trip, and my husband and I plan to use her apartment while she is out of town. When I asked Erica if this was okay, she said, 'Sure.' About five minutes later, she asked, 'Mom, my sofa is filthy. Can you wash my slipcovers when you stay over?' I answered, 'No,' which is not usually my default response. I thought I had answered her clearly. About ten minutes later, I received an e-mail from Erica and she wrote. 'Maaaaaa, PLEASE wash them after I leave town.'

"I think she thought that by behaving so babylike and cute I would change my mind. It's a job I hate doing. Putting damp slipcovers on a sofa and finding the right cover for each pillow is a pain. I wrote her back that I will help her after she returns from her trip. I was proud that I didn't fulfill her fantasy of washing her dirty sofa and arriving home to a spanking-clean loveseat. I was able to resist my need to make everything nice, mainly because I hate the job so much." Dependent and entitled daughters will try to hook us in, but Katherine is really doing her daughter a favor; now Erica will learn to clean her own slipcovers.

Our children will take advantage of our good intentions when we do too many things for them or bail them out of trouble too frequently. In doing so, we set up a pattern that is difficult to break. By giving young adults a false sense of reality, we deny them the knowledge of how to minimize the number of avoidable mistakes. The process of assisting our adult daughters to develop the behavioral traits necessary to minimize such mistakes begins with mutual expectations. These expectations include financial and emotional responsibilities that both parents and their adult daughters should meet.

The Markers of Adulthood

Our generation had a road map. We went to college, we found a boyfriend, and we went from our parents' home to the home we shared with our husbands. Our daughters follow a more circuitous route to adulthood. Today, many young women experience their early twenties as culture shock. Until this time, their goals seem obvious and the rules to follow to reach those goals easy to master. But after college graduation, when they enter the world of work, the path from point A to point B is often unclear. Life does not progress linearly, and it lacks definite objectives. The endless options and choices can make them feel anxious and confused.

These days, the old markers of adulthood no longer apply. The markers that were once self-evident—getting married, having children, finding a job that might last a lifetime, becoming economically independent, and owning your own home—are more elusive and harder for many young adults to achieve. Many young adults marry later and delay having their own children until they're in their mid-thirties. Satisfying, career-track jobs are also more difficult to find, and changing jobs is more common.

Mental health professionals are counseling parents who ask them advice about their 28-year-olds, who they thought would have already been launched and independent. In the absence of clear guidelines for parents, we have identified characteristics of adulthood that provide mothers with alternatives to the disappearing traditional markers.

The new characteristics of adulthood give sociologists, educators, parents, and mental health professionals guidelines to help today's youth negotiate "adultescence" (the process of growing up). This period is one of the great challenges of twenty-first-century parenting; the following behavioral characteristics can help to fill this void.

What Are the New Characteristics of Adulthood?

Today's mothers can use the following behavioral characteristics as guideposts instead of the traditional markers of adulthood. As a result of our observations over the last eight years (consisting of holding multiple focus groups, one-on-one conversations, clinical practice, interviewing psychologists and sociologists, and presenting at conferences and workshops throughout the country), we have successfully identified, synthesized, and codified new markers of adulthood. We have learned from experts such as Daniel Goleman, author of *Emotional Intelligence*, that emotional intelligence consists of qualities that include, "self awareness, impulse control, persistence, self motivation, empathy, and social deftness." These are the traits that enable people to live successful adult lives.

This sociological shift is not bad; it is just different. We believe it has a silver lining, which is reflected in many stories from mothers who tell us that they are much more connected to their daughters than they were to their own mothers. We believe connection is what sustains all people and helps to build resilient adults and a better society. Employers describe young adults requesting time to be at their children's parent conferences, and pediatric nurses describe both parents wanting to learn how to diaper and feed their infants. These are positive examples of some of the changes. The two generations know more and share more of each other's daily lives, and this shift affects all facets of life.

We believe the characteristics of the New Adulthood include the following:

Personal responsibility: Accepting responsibility for their actions builds resilience. Parents can help by letting their daughters know they have the competence to be responsible for their own lives. Have reasonable expectations of it being a process. Avoid being rescuers.

Financial responsibility: Accepting more responsibility engenders self-confidence and self-reliance. Teach your daughter money management skills as early as possible, and as she gets older, provide financial help on a selective basis. Negotiate for planned independence. Avoid being lifestyle subsidizers.

Respectful interdependence: Being independent while staying connected helps to create mutual respect. Independence doesn't mean having less of a relationship.

Empathy: Develop an understanding of how their behavior impacts others. Learn to anticipate the impact of their behavior.

Model behavior that demonstrates how to act for the greater good. This includes placing the needs of others before their own.

Appropriate boundaries: Set and maintain appropriate boundaries so they are able to begin to chart their own course. Respect each other's privacy. Healthy boundaries are not only important to creating privacy, they also help to build personal integrity, develop limits to protect themselves, and engage in appropriate behavior toward others.

Engage in mature relationships: These relationships may include marriage, forming committed partnerships, and, perhaps, having children. This transition provides parents with a wonderful opportunity to treat their daughters as adults. Expectations shift because the boundaries created by committed relationships influence new behavior by both parents and their adult daughters. Children learn about relationships by watching their parents.

Cultural competence: Our daughters are growing up in the most diverse society in our history. Successful adults will require skills to participate in the global economy. The ability to get along with people and understand different perspectives is essential in the twenty-first century.

Understanding environmental context: Our daughters appear to be sophisticated, but they often seem unaware of what is appropriate in different contexts. Successful adults need to be aware of what expectations are in a given context, such as the workplace.

They need to understand what behaviors are suitable and what the consequences are if they don't present themselves appropriately.

The earlier parents and others start to cultivate maturity, the more likely daughters are to become healthy, resilient adults. We need to ground our daughters in reality and give them the opportunities to master their own domains. A mother of a high school senior observes, "Having just completed college tours, I was struck by parents who asked all the questions and gave us the feeling that they wanted to pick their kid's courses, roommates, and majors. Colleges not wishing to alienate prospective parents/students play along with this when they should simply tell parents: 'Please, have your children ask the questions.' I, like so many parents, have raised two college-aged kids who have traveled around the world yet can't function effectively on a day-to-day basis. So in one sense they are 'worldly,' but [they] often don't demonstrate much common sense."

Mothers and/or fathers who micromanage their daughters' lives find that their daughters are often unable to cope with disappointments and rejections. Daughters need to have opportunities to learn and practice life skills. Because so many of them have not had opportunities to develop these skills, parents are often surprised at their daughters' extended dependence throughout their twenties and thirties.

This generation has experienced many changes that have transformed them, such as women working in greater numbers, divorce and the increasing number of single parents, technological change, the contraction of the economy, and the extraordinarily high cost of housing and healthcare. All of these have changed the landscape for our daughters. As a result, the process of becoming an adult is different and takes longer. New definitions are needed, and maturity comes incrementally and at no particular age. As mothers, we must respect our daughter's pace while looking for and taking advantage of those teachable moments.

We believe that the behavioral characteristics of adulthood described in this chapter provide you with new and useful guideposts as you continue to parent your adult daughter and develop a more mature relationship with her. Ignoring this new developmental stage of adulthood prevents you from assisting your daughter to become independent, while preserving a strong connection. This is a delicate balance for both you and your daughter. Whether our daughters come to us for skill development geared toward employability, for intellectual exploration, or for emotional comfort, we can mentor and give them new perspectives on their lives that will enable them to perform capably and comfortably with their multiple adult roles. This is the fundamental challenge and the ultimate benefit of a transformed relationship between mothers and their adult daughters.

5

Characteristics of Friendship: "You've Got a Friend"

Long after a child is grown and has left the nest, if she makes a single misstep, painful signals are triggered in a maternal body far away, as if from a phantom limb.

—Sarah Blaffer Hardy, *Mother Nature: A History of Mothers, Infants and Natural Selection*

Healthy Friendships but Not Best Friends

I (Susan) remember as a young girl watching my mother get dressed to go out with my dad on Saturday evenings. She looked so beautiful and confident in her peach organza dress with a wide patent leather belt that cinched her waist. After getting dressed she would go to her fabric-covered jewelry box to find the perfect earrings to go with her coral choker. I wanted nothing more than to look like her. An image like this may be pushed to the back of our adolescent girl's mind, but it remains indelible. It is one of the first mirrors in which we see our adult selves. The relationship between a mother and her adult daughter provides another opportunity to re-create this shared intimacy.

If close, the mother-daughter relationship can simulate friendship through the common characteristics of empathy, listening, loyalty, and caring. However, the mother-daughter relationship has other characteristics that distinguish it from a best friendship. These characteristics include a hierarchy of responsibility, the mother's role as primary emotional caretaker, inconsistent reciprocity, and the past intruding into the present. The mothers and daughters we spoke with in our focus groups agree with these distinctions. For these reasons, in her book, *Among Friends*, Letty Pogrebin doesn't include mothers and daughters in her pool of friend categories. She agrees that equality is essential for friendship, and there is always an imbalance when one person in the twosome is the parent of the other. Karen Fingerman, researcher and author about mother-daughter relationships, also concludes that a best friendship is not possible because mothers and daughters are never at the same life-stage at the same time.

Nancy, mother of 32-year-old Natalie, says, "I never wanted to be my daughter's best friend. We are close and go to each other for important life decisions. She is thirty years younger than I am. I appreciate the importance of age-related friendships. I was never my mother's friend, let alone best friend. We weren't that close. I want my daughter to have her own contemporaries as friends."

Marina, 27, says, "I love spending time with my mom, but I wouldn't consider her my best friend. She's MY MOM. Best friends don't pay for the dress you covet in a trendy clothing store that you wouldn't buy for yourself. Best friends don't pay for your wedding. Best friends don't remind you how they carried you in their body and gave you life, while in return, you gave them stretchmarks and, sometimes, gas! Best friends don't assume they are wiser based on their age and experience. I love my mom, and I want her to remain a mom."

The fact that mothers and daughters by our definition aren't best friends doesn't mean they can't be very close and share a satisfying relationship. While some mother–adult daughter relationships are troubled, many women find them to be extremely rewarding. Many moms spoke to us about how happy they are to be finished with the "eye rolling" and dismissive looks from their adolescent daughters, looks that say, "You must come from a different evolutionary chain than I do." Daughters also adopt the famous Mark Twain quote about aging when discussing feelings about their mothers: "When I was a boy of fourteen, my father was so ignorant I could hardly stand to have the old man around. But when I got to be twenty-one, I was astonished at what he had learned in seven years." This analysis also applies to mothers and daughters.

This generation of mothers and adult daughters has a lot in common, which increases the likelihood of shared companionship. Until recently many mothers and daughters shared the experience of being homemakers and shouldering the responsibility for maintaining and passing on family values, traditions, and rituals. In addition, contemporary mothers and daughters also share experience in the workforce, which may bring them even closer together.

Best friends may or may not continue to be best friends, but for better or worse, the mother-daughter relationship is permanent, even if for some unfortunate reason they aren't speaking. The mother-child relationship is, therefore, more intimate and more intense than any other. One of our favorite *Gilmore Girls* episodes demonstrates this intensity. Rory is starting her first day of college at Yale University. Her mother, Lorelai, like thousands of moms, helps Rory set up her new dorm room. When it is time for Lorelai to leave, Rory is not quite ready. She text messages her mom and asks her to come back to Yale. Rory says, "You ruined me. I am still a mama's girl." Lorelai winds up spending the night. This gesture is exactly what Rory needs to be ready to let go and begin her life as a college girl. This is not something you would ask of a best friend. Lorelai knew more than anyone else that just one night together would permit her daughter to move on.

In this chapter, we explore why mothers and daughters are not best friends, what a mother-daughter friendship looks like, the shared experiences as women that contribute to their companionship, some of the difficulties in staying connected, the necessary boundaries to maintain a healthy relationship, and the joys of having an adult daughter. We focus on the period when, in most families, both the mother and the daughter are in good health and before a daughter may need to care for her mother. The umbilical cord, now invisible, remains, but provides enough flexibility for a mother and daughter to enjoy each other and develop a sustaining relationship.

PERMALINKS

While in our view mothers and daughters aren't best friends, their relationship can have characteristics of a friendship. In our focus groups, mothers and daughters told us about the experiences and similarities they share, including spending time together, common interests, the experience of being women, life in the workforce, family, shared biology, history, religion, and culture. Dr. Lucy Rose Fischer, who has studied mother-daughter friendships, identifies additional qualities that create good friendships between mothers and daughters in her book *Linked Lives: Adult Daughters and Their Mothers*. They include: realistic and objective expectations with respect to one another, significant involvement in each other's lives, maintaining appropriate boundaries, and valuing and respecting each other's independence.

Mothers and daughters can approximate friendship; however, they do have some different and interesting expectations. The following examples may seem very familiar to you. Daughters screen your phone calls and call you back every third call. They never say no if you offer them money. They still expect you to be "On Demand" or their personal "OnStar." They prefer your washer and dryer to the one in their building. Miraculously, when the two of you go shopping or out for a meal, it is your credit card that gets used. When they go on a trip, you slip them a few dollars; when you go on a trip, they slip you a request for a gift! Mothers and daughters have very different expectations of one another from what they expect of best friends.

For many mothers and daughters, there is generally a desire to maintain a connection and to modify the mother-daughter hierarchy of previous years. This is easier in contemporary society where, according to psychologist Dan Kindlon, "Our kids are probably more precious to us than any previous generation of parents." We live in a more emotionally open society and have less of a generation gap. Our daughters are often single for longer, so we have more time to form an adult relationship with them before their affections are transferred to their significant other, spouse, and family. Between cell phones, the Internet, text messaging, and

IMing, the connection to our daughters is more immediate than ever before. This accessibility is unprecedented.

And, thankfully, the adolescent angst has passed. Nancy, mother of two adult daughters says, "Having adult daughters makes all of the earlier maintenance worthwhile . . . soccer, braces, homework, etc. You finally reap the benefits without all of the antagonism." Teenagers often pull away from their mothers, and young adults usually move toward their mothers.

Joanne tells us this story: "I am a single mother of a twenty-five-year-old graduate student in economics. Our relationship is very close. Even though she lives out of town, we talk all the time and text or e-mail one another many times during the week. I don't give her advice unless she asks for it. We have normal arguments, but we also discuss her hopes and dreams. She usually welcomes my opinions. I am ready to help her whenever she needs me, but she is very independent and self-reliant. I love when she comes home and we can spend time together, but I don't expect her to be as supportive of me as I am of her. That is the responsibility of my best friend, not a daughter. Her ability to be okay without me doesn't take away from the companionship and trust we feel for each other."

Our generation and our parents' generation had a pronounced ideological and social gap between them. Our parents were much more authoritarian, in contrast to the democracy that has existed in many of our households. We are the first generation of mothers with a wide range of lifestyle and occupational choices. Mothers and daughters have always shared the more traditional roles of homemaker—managing families and raising children. Today, many share the challenge of balancing family and careers.

Since the 1970s, women have joined the workforce in numbers greater than ever before. For some women, work outside the home was always the norm. For example, culturally and ethnically diverse and low-income women have always worked, and have had to balance work and family. Unlike middle-class European-American women, this is not a new phenomenon for them. Many daughters working outside the home say they feel comfortable talking about workplace stressors, career decisions, and handling work and home responsibilities with their mothers. Liza, says, "My mom is the first person I go to when I have a question about my job. She's run her own business for almost thirty years and has sage advice. Her experience helps me to sort out my feelings about work, when to start my family, and how to manage the two." Sharing our experiences, while at the same time giving our daughters the freedom to make their own choices, makes for a good friendship.

Good-bye, "Matraphobia"

At many points in a girl's development it is normal for her not to want to grow up and be like her mother. Someone saying, "You're just like your mother" or "You sound just like your mother" could cause a daughter to become apoplectic. This relationship does evolve, however, and as adults most contemporary mothers and daughters enjoy each other's company, admire each other, and get along well. Common experiences frequently offer them the opportunity to create more of a peer relationship in which they can seek each other's counsel.

Lily, 24, tells us about her relationship with her mom, Margaret.

"I talk to my mom at least every other day about what's going on in my life. I do omit topics that I think would make her uncomfortable (like my sex life). I don't consider myself dependent on my mom, but we do go to each other for guidance. My mom is divorced, and now that I am an adult, she sometimes asks me for dating advice. My mom has always given me lots of freedom, and I love having a close relationship with her. I know she feels the same way."

When a daughter asks her mother for advice, she relies on the fact that her mother has the daughter's best interest at heart. This exchange of ideas may be both good and sometimes confusing for our daughters, because embedded in a mother's opinion are her fears and values. A mother may feel comfortable discussing only certain issues with her daughter, but this new intimacy and more positive communication is an important step in modifying the mother-daughter hierarchy. With their common experiences, "matraphobia" (fear of becoming like your mother) is less of a concern.

Mama Goodies

Spending time together is an important characteristic of friendship. Many mothers and daughters talk about the activities they enjoy with each other, from sports to shopping, and shared interests, from religion to discussing the latest episode of *American Idol*. But, again, this is just one part of friendship and doesn't make for best friends.

Cathy, mother of 30-year-old Anna, says, "A best friend isn't just about doing things together, enjoying each other's company, or sharing the same love of music and movies. A best friend is somebody that you can always count on, whose life experience is not necessarily the same, but comparable enough so that you feel a kinship. I love being with my daughter. We have great talks and enjoy running together, but my best friend knows me in all of my multiple roles. Anna only knows me as her mother." A mother still has to balance independence with caring, and individual growth with family ties. It is important for a daughter to be able to both separate from and stay connected to her mother. This consciousness allows for companionship, but not a best friendship.

Arranged Relationships

Mothers can't and should not be their daughter's best friend. The mothers we interviewed overwhelmingly agreed with this conclusion. Kate, mother of 30-year-old Jenny, articulates this when she says, "My relationship with Jenny is always filtered through my *mommy eyes*. I mean there is a little white noise always present that sifts everything through my *mother brain*. Jenny and I do friend things together. We have friendlike conversations and girlfriendlike experiences, but I always feel the overarching mother thing, especially when we're talking about a sensitive subject. I always want to be her mother more than her friend. However, I love having friend experiences with her. I love it. It's so much fun, and the older she gets and the more she matures, I enjoy our time together more and more. I know Jenny has her best friends and I'm happy she has them. She needs to talk to them about the things that she won't bring to me."

Recent articles, such as "Mommy Is Truly Dearest," which

appeared in the *New York Times*, and "Best Friends: Mothers and Daughters with the Deepest Connection," which appeared in the *Pittsburgh Post-Gazette*, focus on daughters who say their mothers are their best friends. While this gets your attention, the real story behind the new headlines is that "social, demographic and technological changes have made it more common for adult daughters to keep their mothers' apron strings tied tighter—and for longer." What may appear to look like friendship to these young women is an extension of the recent trend in hyperparenting.

We believe that daughters are not describing a best friendship. The title "best friend" is being used without any consideration of the complicated nature of the mother-daughter relationship. We have identified some of the unique aspects of the mother-daughter relationship that preclude it from being a best friendship. First, the mother-daughter relationship is not equal. Although this distinction decreases as a daughter matures, there is an inherent hierarchy that prevents them from forging a friendship on a level playing field. For example, Judy states, "I mean, in a friendship, sometimes a friend takes care of me, and other times I take care of my friend. Over the long haul, the friendship, if it endures, ends up equal. This never happens with your child because in many ways a mom is always the caretaker."

A mother remains the primary emotional caretaker in her family because she is biologically hardwired to protect her offspring. Lynn, mother of 31-year-old Stacey, says, "Mothers are still the ones who are responsible for holding the family together. We are expected to put our problems second if one of our kids has a problem. As long as the women in the family are the emotional caretakers, we usually feel responsible for our children's happiness." Mothers in virtually every culture are responsible for maintaining the emotional well-being of the family. We see young fathers taking on more of this responsibility. But even if they do, most mothers remain heavily invested in and available for their children. This role of emotional caretaker creates a deep connection, not a best friendship.

The sense of protection a mother feels for her child can't be expressed in words. Marion shares this sentiment: "I will not automatically, unequivocally lay down my life for my girlfriend, but I would lay down my life for my child. For a friend, you don't expect them to give up their life; you expect to be cared for. Likewise, your friend doesn't expect you to make such a sacrifice. It's a very powerful force that compels most parents to protect their child before they protect themselves. Perhaps it's an existential connection to immortality, I don't know. I just think, how could a mother-child relationship ever be equal?"

A daughter should not feel responsible for her mother's emotional well-being. Not that a daughter shouldn't care deeply about her mother, it's just that she shouldn't be burdened with her mother's psychological health. It is out of order for a daughter to have this responsibility. As one mother said to her daughter, "I would gladly dive under a bus for you, and there is no way that I'm diving under a bus for my friends." Her daughter responded, "And I'd gladly let you dive under the bus to save me!"

Tina tells us, "My sister was in an extremely serious car accident and she was in the emergency room about to get two hundred stitches on her face. Her first reaction was she didn't want to show our mother her open gash; she wanted to protect her from seeing her wound. While listening to my sister, I remember thinking, 'Oh, my God, I could never protect my mother, she'd have to be there to make it better for me.' My older sister, Jackie, was like another mother to me. In this instance, Jackie also mothered our mother. What is interesting to me is that we each needed a different kind of caretaking from our mother, which influenced our mother-daughter relationship." This story demonstrates how two daughters in the same family develop a different relationship with the same mother. The patterns in a mother-daughter relationship are created early and are always affected by temperament, birth order, and family dynamics. In adulthood each daughter goes on to have a very different friendship with her mother. This is a familiar experience for mothers who have more than one daughter.

A Game of Telephone

The patterns we develop early also apply to communication between mothers and daughters. This early blueprint sets the stage for so much misunderstanding, which is often at the heart of mother-daughter conflict. With a best girlfriend, we have the freedom to say what we want without feeling like we have to bite our tongue or self-edit. Not so with a daughter. Daughters want our blessing more than they want our advice, so much of what mothers say has a double meaning; the words live both in the present and in the past.

In her book, *That's Not What I Meant*, author Deborah Tannen explains that the miscommunication between a mother and a daughter stems from their inability to distinguish between messages—the literal meaning of the words we speak and the "meta-messages" that are the meanings our words imply. Simply stated, what we intend and what the other person perceives are not always the same, particularly for mothers and daughters. Dawn says, "Often, I make a conscious effort to ask my daughter a benign question or I might even give a compliment. Just yesterday, I suggested that she consider cutting her bangs while we were reading a fashion magazine together. This comment evoked a response from her that would only make sense if I had yelled, 'Your hair looks like crap!' Her response to me makes me feel frustrated, and we invariably end up in an uncomfortable and familiar place. It's the same place, with the same feelings that we've butt heads against in the past."

Mary, the mother of an adult daughter in her twenties, says, "The communication in our relationship is always on her timetable, not mine. My daughter needs to know where I am at all times. She goes crazy if she can't find me. Yet, I'm not entitled to the same information. I am expected to be on call 24/7, but generally speaking, when I ask her about her whereabouts, she is frequently annoyed and/or doesn't have time to talk." Mary's story illustrates that our daughters are often in contact with us, but it's usually on their terms. This double standard is normal.

Many of the mothers who spoke with us believe that to maintain a healthy relationship with their daughters, with less conflict, they have to self-edit. Mothers often worry their daughters will avoid their phone calls and generally be unavailable if they perceive their mother to be intrusive. Some mothers would rather duct tape their mouths shut than chance disconnection from their daughters. Says Hope, the mother of two daughters, "I understand that the things I say have the power to sting deeply. The tricky part is that this sometimes happens even when I say something that I do not realize is loaded." With friends, there aren't as many loaded conversations, so we have much more freedom to say what is on our minds and to move past misunderstandings.

Brenda, mother of 24-year-old Tonya, says, "My daughter wants me to be a friend to her. I can't do that because, more than anything, I want to keep her respect. Her friends' mothers are younger and getting tattoos and belly button piercings with their daughters. Tonya is looking for that kind of relationship with me. She tells me, 'You're a mean mother; you're not cool like my friends' mothers!' I tell her that even though Hallie's and Lisa's mothers go to clubs with them, I'm not about to do that." Brenda decided that her role as a mother, and the respect she wants, would be jeopardized if she twisted herself into becoming her daughter's playmate and peer.

Brenda is right; there should be a distinction between a mother's role and a friend's role. A best friend is somebody who listens to everything you need to say. She appreciates you for your good points, tolerates your bad points, shares your high moments, and supports you during stressful times. Unlike friends, mothers often try to protect their children from many of their low points. As Chris asks, "Would I unload some of my frustrations regarding my husband onto my daughter? No, I would never do that. I respect how much she loves her father and imagine my frustrations with him would hurt her. There will always be some issues that I won't discuss with my daughter because they can be painful for her to hear. It's my responsibility to find safe people who are peers."

Another example of this tendency to be protective is Julie's story about a conversation with her daughter, Leila. Julie recalls,

"Leila called me yesterday when I was in the middle of a meltdown about my job. When I started to tell her what was happening at work, I could tell she was listening to me and was appropriately concerned. But I also noticed that she cut me short and didn't want me to talk about the details. I think Leila didn't want to hear that I was really having a hard time. The next day she called to see if everything was better. I could tell by her voice that Leila needed to know I felt better. Even though things were not resolved at work, I decided to spare her the grim details, because she had heard enough. I could tell by her voice that she was relieved."

Another reason why mothers don't burden their adult daughters is because many admit that they protect themselves from the disappointment of their daughter's lack of engagement in their emotional suffering. It isn't that daughters don't care; it's more that they find it scary to know their mothers are failing to take care of themselves. Moms have to be problem-free, competent, and in charge! This reality further defines the daughter's aversion to knowing her mother's struggles.

Tangled Vines

Even though mothers and daughters can't be best friends, they can be close and enjoy each other's company. Every relationship in our life has a different purpose and function and brings both satisfaction and frustration. Mothers and daughters are no different, but they do provide an opportunity for a unique connection. For many of us, as our daughters mature, parenting doesn't stop, but the relationship does become more balanced. The hierarchy diminishes and there is more opportunity for daughters to give back. For mothers, this opportunity for reciprocity provides both gratifying and disappointing experiences.

This bond is one of the significant relationships in our lives, and we are motivated to make it work. For the relationship to develop positively, we must be mindful of certain "friendship breakers." Because the relationship is so sensitive, dissatisfactions with daughters and/or mothers are felt intensely. Mothers and daughters share strong biological and social ties, which engender the expectation that they truly know each other. Therefore, they are both deeply upset and wounded when they are surprised by unrecognized characteristics or insensitive behaviors.

During this transition from childhood to adulthood, many mothers search for ways to be part of their newly adult daughters' lives. Janice, the mother of a 24-year-old, said, "My daughter's life is so stressful and busy. She is juggling work and her social life and I see her mostly when she asks for my help. I find myself looking forward to tasks like helping her hang shelves in her apartment and shopping for food to stock her kitchen. I'm hungry for time with her."

Both adult daughters and their mothers are experiencing major life transitions while they are creating these adult relationships. Daughters are taking on adult roles, such as starting careers, marrying, and becoming mothers themselves, and mothers are adjusting to empty nests, redefining or reassessing careers, and caring for elderly parents. Mothers should expect that their needs and those of their daughters are often at cross-purposes because they are always at different life stages.

Good Enough Mother

The notion of a "good enough mother" was coined in 1953 by pediatrician Dr. Donald Winnicott. This notion gave women permission to be human, rather than perfect mothers. He maintained that the "good enough mother" provides for her children's needs, but not necessarily the minute they want a need to be met. The importance of this idea is to allow for a relationship that can tolerate both good and bad—Mom is not all good, nor all bad and is a separate and imperfect human being. And this kind of mother is certainly "good enough."

Still, some mothers feel burdened by expectations to meet their children's needs perfectly. Barbara, mother of 28-year-old Heather, says, "Sometimes, I don't answer the phone if the caller ID says it's my daughter because I don't want to feel guilty saying no to some favor she may ask. Last week she forgot to get a birthday present for a three-year-old's party. She e-mailed me to buy the present. She works all week, and I work all week, but I usually feel that she thinks I have endless energy regardless of what's on my plate. So rather than risk disappointing her, I sometimes avoid her."

Another mother, Trisha, says, "My daughter, Lisa, still wants me to take care of her. She forgets that I can also feel tired after a twelve-hour day of work. If she thinks I'm wiped out and unavailable, then she worries I won't be available to take care of her in the way she needs. For example, Lisa called me last week to ask me to review her resumé when I was in the midst of writing two different briefs. I was so overwhelmed with work that I hadn't gone grocery shopping for two weeks and ate peanut butter on Triscuits for two days straight.

"When I couldn't review her resumé, and told her that it would have to wait for the weekend, she proceeded to provide me with a laundry list of all of the things that were on her plate. I reiterated how exhausted I was and she said, 'Mom, I am, too; are you trying to compete with me?' I knew I had set up the expectation that I would drop everything in order to meet her needs. I just expected that once she became an adult, it would be more reciprocal. From her point of view there is nothing I could be doing that is more important than being the kind of mother I had always been." These are the times when you realize that your daughter's self-centered requests are part of a learned behavior. To have a healthy adult relationship, this is the time to set boundaries. Setting appropriate boundaries is essential, but it doesn't always eliminate your guilt.

Other daughters present the challenge of blaming their mothers when life is not treating them well. Debbie tells the story about her daughter, Alexa, who is expecting her third child. "Alexa has two daughters, and she and her husband really wanted the third baby to be a boy. I told her before her sonogram that it was okay if she felt disappointed with another girl. It goes without saying that the most important thing is the baby's health. An initial disappointment is totally normal. Alexa called me from the car after the sonogram and I could tell from her voice that the baby was, in fact, another girl. I tried to be as upbeat as possible because I knew she was disappointed. Alexa accused me of not being supportive and blamed me for her frustration. I was the one to blame as she transferred all her negative feelings onto one of the safest people in her life." For many of us, feeling frustrated that you can't do it right or feel guilty that you aren't a "good enough mother" is just part of the territory.

Cheryl, mother of 27-year-old Emma, says, "Mothers and daughters share an emotional history. Daughters fall back into old patterns of behavior from their childhood, and mothers never stop parenting. I think mothers and daughters struggle, especially if one or the other is not mature." A mother's relationship with her own mother makes this relationship more complicated and impacts the mother-daughter relationship in good and bad ways. Mothers and daughters have to be prepared for conflict even in the best relationships. The past is always with us and outdated expectations last forever.

Creatures of Habit

Many of the mothers we spoke with discussed their relationship with their daughters in the context of their relationship with their own mothers. Beth says, "I am grateful for the relationship that I have with my daughter, Michelle. I didn't have it with my mom. She did the best she could as a single mom. While she provided for us and had dinner on the table, she was cold and didn't show her emotions. My dad died when I was young. I appreciate what she did for me. I learned from what I didn't have. When I had children I wanted to be a warm mommy who gave them unconditional love.

"My mother was also too concerned with what other people thought. We lived in the suburbs where everyone else had two parents who weren't struggling financially like we were. After my father died, my mother was limited in what she could do without current work experience. Because my mother suddenly found herself the breadwinner of our family, I wanted to make sure that my daughter was always prepared to take care of herself. Additionally, I wanted Michelle to feel the warmth of an affectionate and nurturing mother." According to Amy Richards, author of *Opting In: Having a Child Without Losing Yourself*, the relationship between mothers and their own mothers is always a subtext in any conversation about mothers and daughters. The topic is unavoidable, and there is as much fascination with our mothers as with the mothers we have become.

Not Without My Daughter

We believe even though mothers and daughters aren't best friends, the friendship they offer each other is one of companionship, trust, and pleasure. A mother really enjoys sharing her experience and wisdom with her daughter. It's her way of passing on her legacy and a touch of immortality. For a daughter, a close relationship with her mother can enhance her identity and emotional health.

Many mothers agree with Marnie's sentiment: "One of my greatest rewards is my daughter and I think of her as my living legacy and my greatest accomplishment. The biggest challenge is to keep the roles defined and to try to reinforce that I am the mother. My daughter and I have always considered each other close friends. This is both a blessing and a curse. My mother was not my friend, and there was very little I could discuss with her. My daughter tells me everything, much too much, things I really don't want to know."

Vicky, mother of 27-year-old Lauren, says, "My daughter and

I talk every day and e-mail as well. I have to make myself call my own mother out of duty. I'm hoping my daughter calls because she really wants to hear my voice. I try very hard to withhold the negatives, even when I want to give her constructive advice or tell her she is acting like an idiot. My daughter is a gift, and I hope she can learn from our relationship and do better with my granddaughter. My only wish for her is that when she messes up we can laugh at the situation together and that I can keep my mouth shut." Any successful relationship includes humor.

Lois says, "I always censor myself because, as I'm getting older, I'm sounding just like my mother and don't want to press those buttons that made me crazy. At these times I tell my daughter it was my evil twin speaking, not me." With appropriate boundaries, humor, and realistic expectations, the mother-daughter relationship can be extremely enjoyable.

Colleen says, "I don't expect to get back as much. I'm lucky to have a daughter who is really caring. Olivia is so caught up in her own life, trying to survive and be healthy, I don't think she has a lot of extra energy to be that giving and I don't expect it. When Olivia is more comfortable and secure, older (now twenty-seven), she will be more thoughtful. She has a ways to go. Olivia is trying to cope, and my job is to help her to do that."

Many mothers conclude that they welcome friendship with their adult daughters, especially after the ascent out of adolescent hell. Robin says, "Listening to and watching my daughter be successfully independent, with her own ideas about many things that I didn't have a clue about at that same age, is very fulfilling. I love to listen to her ideas about politics, music, literature, relationships, and religion (even though they are very different from mine). I think I nurture our relationship by listening, only giving advice when it's asked for, and always with a willingness to hear her ideas. She says I nurture her by being her biggest cheerleader and by thinking she can do everything wonderfully."

While many relationships are very positive, others are a struggle. Just know that for those of you who fall into the latter category, you are not alone. Not every parent and child will become friends, but even if both sides have behaved badly in the past, there is still the opportunity for change if they want a better relationship. In talking to mothers and daughters, we know that relationships are dynamic and changing.

How your relationship functions today is not the way it must be forever. Don't worry if you and your daughter aren't friends now. This situation can change at any time. Therapist Dr. Susan Gordon works mostly with women trying to negotiate relationships with important people in their lives. She says, "Any relationship can be negotiated if you have the skills." These include friendships with other women, a spouse, your mother, or your daughter.

Phoebe shares her honest assessment about her behavior toward her mother, whom she loves and adores. "I react differently to my dad than to my mom. I overreact to my mother like no one else. When my mom makes an empathic error, it's so big for me, and when she's on, it's so good. I make little comments and stinging barbs. I now see them as part of the process of growing up and this is helpful to me. My mom's generosity drives me up the wall and I react in a way that is uncalled for. She is so different from me and it's scary to be alone on my own. So I turn on the source of my anxiety—my mom. It's a given that my mom will be over the top with her generosity and I'm not always grateful. I allow myself to exploit her generosity of time and attention, and yet I'd be very defensive if she called me on it."

Phoebe's observations suggest to us that many adult daughters do not want to hear their mothers say no. They want to be treated as independent adults, but at the same time they want to continue to be nurtured. These contradictory emotional needs and behaviors are specific to the parent-child relationship. Best friend relationships are much more transparent.

A daughter knows she can turn to her mother to seek comfort, and she understands intuitively that the investment her mother has in her happiness is different from that of even a best friend. According to journalist Jan Hoffman, "Parents are now exponentially more entwined with their offspring, including to place their children's well-being above their own." Only moms are willing (and able) to give so much time and energy to support their adult daughters. One young mother's nanny was out of the country and she asked her mother to fly in to babysit for seven days. Another grandmother goes to her daughter's house every morning before work to help her daughter get the children ready for day care. These are not favors you would either ask of or expect from a friend as easily. They do, however, bond mothers and daughters together, enable them to spend quality time, and develop their own type of friendship.

Mothers are often distressed to discover a stranger at the end of what one woman calls the "invisible umbilical" connecting them to their female offspring. In *Friends for Life: Enriching the Bond Between Mothers and Their Adult Daughters*, Susan Jonas and Marilyn Nissenson illuminate a paradox: "By giving up the outmoded wish to control our daughters . . . we're not losing a connection but actually gaining a stronger one." For example, Shari says, "I want my daughter to be independent. As she has gotten older I enjoy the fact that she doesn't only rely on me. I love our time together. I don't have to do the heavy lifting. By giving up control, I have gained a friend."

We have also given our daughters more life choices than ever before, which both overwhelms them and provides them with unparalleled freedom. We can be proud of these accomplishments. Our similar lives give us the opportunity to get to know each other in new and different ways and can engender gratifying adult relationships. Claudia expresses what many other mothers feel: "When I come back, I want to come back as my daughter."

Survey: Mother and Daughter Friendships

Take the following survey to explore your friendship with your daughter. This may help you to think about and maybe talk to your daughter about what you both find satisfying and what you may want to change.

1. Do you set boundaries with your daughter? If so, what are they?

2. How do you handle it when your daughter makes choices with which you disagree?

3. Do you enjoy each other's company? What do you like to do together?

4. Do you feel appreciated?

5. Can you be yourself without fear of criticism?

6. Is there such a thing as being too close with a daughter?

7. Is your relationship with your daughter different from your relationship with your mother? If so, how?

8. Can you make a decision for yourself that favors your interests over the interests of your daughter?

9. How is your relationship with your daughter similar to that of your relationship with a friend? How is it different?

6

Archetypes: Mother Superior . . . My Mom Is Running My Life from Across State Lines

. . . the precursor of the mirror is the mother's face.

—**Donald Winnicott, *Playing and Reality***

"Our Love Is Here to Stay"

The model of a mother as her daughter's best friend is *a* model, not *the* model. Relationships exist on a continuum, ranging from real intimacy with weekly or daily communication, to more careful conversations and obligatory visits, to miscommunication, mistrust, and estrangement. For the most part, separation, individuation, and connection remain the salient themes for mothers and daughters.

This chapter explores the range of mother–adult daughter relationships that reflect more challenge. From our focus groups we have developed seven archetypes that form a continuum of behaviors that describe these more challenging relationships. The flashpoints we see occurring between mothers and daughters include:

- miscommunication
- entitlement
- self-absorption
- not really knowing each other
- lack of appreciation
- lack of emotional support
- distance and unavailability
- control
- judgment
- lack of boundaries
- shaming
- idealization of childhood

These behaviors are the genesis of issues that can't be swept under the rug. Conflict is inevitable and can be harmful to the development of an adult relationship if it isn't resolved in a mutually respectful and appropriate way. With few exceptions (mental illness, narcissism, and other personality disorders), certain qualities can help mothers and daughters to overcome barriers.

Nobody is perfect. Children are very resilient and can accept imperfections when their mothers exhibit the above flashpoints. Parents can also accept flaws if children demonstrate empathy. We define empathy as an awareness of the impact of one's behavior on others and a sense of responsibility for this. Empathy is the foundation for mature relationships; it promotes connection by inviting intimacy.

For comparison purposes, it is important to observe the characteristics of a close mother-daughter relationship versus a best friend relationship or one that creates barriers to friendship. As we create new models, we must understand the problem of trying to be both mom and friend to our daughters. We begin the discussion about challenging relationships with the model we believe is the most centered and reasonably balanced. We refer to this preferred archetype as the Perfectly Imperfect Mother.

The Perfectly Imperfect Mother meets almost all of her daughter's needs when she is a baby, and as she grows, slowly frustrates some of her daughter's needs to give her the ability to deal with failure. The Perfectly Imperfect Mother gives her daughter the message that she wants her daughter to be moral and responsible, to have the strength to make her own choices and appreciate her own abilities and talents. The Perfectly Imperfect Mother doesn't see her daughter's struggles or frustrations as proof that she isn't a good mother. Instead, she sees these behaviors as appropriate individuation. She understands that her daughter may make very different choices in life from the ones she made and doesn't interpret this as a rejection or as a failure of her mothering.

The Perfectly Imperfect Mother acknowledges that, by being

imperfect, she is helping her daughter learn to face the complexities of life. Her role is to help her daughter adjust, cope, and persevere. Mothers shouldn't try for perfection because perfection creates an impossible ideal, one that no daughter can either emulate or live up to.

Lily, mother of a 3-year-old daughter, says, "Sometimes my mother was not the person that I would have wanted her to be, but I think on the whole she was exactly what I needed. I used to feel frustrated when she seemed preoccupied with her own life and didn't make as big a fuss about birthdays and holidays as my friends' mothers [did]. She would say, 'Lily, those are Donna Reed mothers and I will never fit that mold.' Now that I'm a mother, I can appreciate the pressure on mothers to make childhood into a child-focused treadmill of activities. When my girlfriends ask if I've signed my daughter up for dance, guitar, and/or ceramics, I feel like my daughter and I are on a hamster wheel. Most mothers I know try to provide their kids [with] an ideal childhood, and many of them try to become the perfect mother. I'm lucky to have my mother as a role model; her example makes me sane when my stress level goes haywire. She doesn't preach to me; she lets me vent and she really listens."

Perfectly Imperfect Mothers respect boundaries and demonstrate empathy toward their daughters, enabling a close relationship, but not necessarily a best friendship. A close friendship between mothers and daughters is a modern phenomenon brought about by a smaller generation gap and a more informal and open culture. The transition from mom to friend is clumsy and may create conflict because the boundaries are less well defined.

Fault Lines and Archetypes

Even during conflict, the mother-daughter bond is so powerful and enduring that the majority of mothers feel positive about their relationships with their daughters. On the other hand, many of these same women wish that their relationships were better. Marianne Walters, founder of The Family Therapy Practice Center, goes so far as to say: “If mother is the cornerstone of family life, the mother/daughter relationship is the brick and the mortar that holds them together.”

The bedrock of women’s relationships is talk. According to William Doherty, Professor of Family Social Science at the University of Minnesota, “Men bond around common interests and occasionally turn to a buddy for help. Women bond through confidences.” Sharing personal information is central to women’s friendships. If a daughter can’t communicate with and feels misunderstood by her mother, or vice versa, their friendship will be built on an unstable foundation. Any cracks that are present in the relationship before adulthood may fracture the most sincere effort to form a friendship.

Unsatisfactory relationships with disconnection and/or emotional turmoil vary in their intensity. We have identified seven types of mother-daughter dyads that provide a framework for some of the more challenging relationships. These dyads may be causally related. This chapter comes primarily from the stories of adult daughters in our focus groups. You will hear the voices of daughters more than the reflections of their mothers.

It is important to remember that the sources of division are not absolute; some of the challenges can be worked through. For example, a daughter who has a Guardian Angel Mother may be prepared to be taken care of and/or rescued by her mother. Despite this kind of relationship, acceptance and understanding may promote growth, serve both the mother's and daughter's psychological needs, and allow a successful relationship to develop. As we learned writing our book *Mom, Can I Move Back In with You? A Survival Guide for Parents of Twentysomethings*, this period of parenting emerging adults offers an opportunity to renegotiate the mother-daughter relationship.

The archetypes create a *risk* of failure, not a *certainty* of failure, to nurture rewarding adult relationships between mothers and daughters. It is definitely possible to negotiate a satisfying relationship between an adult daughter and any one of the following archetypal mothers. Each situation requires its own kind of special care. Mothers described in each archetype have an attachment style that provides a framework for understanding their adult daughters' sense of security and capacity for love, connection, and disconnection. According to developmental psychologist Mary Ainsworth and her colleagues, who contributed to the creation of attachment theory, *secure* adults find it relatively easy to form close relationships and are comfortable depending on others and having others depend on them. They don't spend their time worrying about abandonment or getting too close to others. *Avoidant* adults are somewhat uncomfortable being close to others; they find it difficult to trust and difficult to allow themselves to depend on others. These definitions of attachment are fundamental and help to clarify a mother's behavior and her influence on her daughter. Whether a daughter feels secure or insecure depends on the nature or quality of the communication between mother and daughter. This understanding gives us insight into how these archetypes influence adult daughters and their relationships with their mothers.

The following archetypal stories help to flush out the complexities and contradictions of the mother-daughter relationship. They don't tell the whole story, but they do begin the conversation. Like any classifications, the archetypes may overlap. Mothers and daughters may find parts of themselves in more than one archetype and need to add their own nuances to complete the picture.

GUARDIAN ANGEL

The Guardian Angel Mother tries to protect her daughter from any failure or disappointment. She defines her child's happiness in terms of her own needs and perceptions. She believes that by fixing everything for her daughter, her daughter will be happy and have all the best opportunities open to her. This mother may be experienced as smothering or always hovering, which has earned mothers like her the name "helicopter" moms. The daughter of a Guardian Angel Mother has a sense of entitlement, and she may have difficulty with compromise and disappointment. This daughter may also lack empathy for her mother because her mother neglected to make her own needs known. Often this hypermothering results in a daughter who does not feel competent to do for herself. A daughter of a Guardian Angel Mother is confident that her mother will always respond to her needs because this type of mother has an extreme need for and values attachment; she is consistently reliable.

It is hard to be best friends with someone who is hyperfocused on your life. This type of relationship is likely to remain unbalanced. Some mothers stay overly invested long past the time when, at the same age as their daughters, they were emotionally and economically independent from their own mothers. The extended parental relationship into adulthood also develops in part from the pervasive attitude of parents who say, "We are invested and we're staying invested!" These parents are protective of their "investments." A mother who is overly committed to her daughter's success and happiness does not allow her to experience any failure or disappointment, if she can help or fix it. The Guardian Angel Mother believes she can intervene to prevent challenging and/or adverse experiences.

Dawn tells the story of her daughter, Clara, who panicked when she realized her passport just expired. Dawn says, "When Clara asked me to fix it, I went into hypergear and researched the quickest way to expedite her passport. I called our congressman's office for help. Through my efforts and resources, I was able to get Clara a passport in time to travel outside the country. I thought by [my] being a competent mother, she would learn how to do things for herself. But in reality, Clara learned to depend on me to fix everything for her." A mother who always fixes things or eliminates disappointments and/or consequences may cause her daughter to feel a lack of competence and a sense of entitlement.

A Guardian Angel Mother's behavior begins early, and many experts are now writing about this phenomenon. Parenting expert and author of *The Blessings of a Skinned Knee: Using Jewish Teachings to Raise Self-Reliant Children*, Wendy Mogel, observes the extended adolescence of today's twentysomethings results in college deans referring to overprotected kids without the ability to handle their problems with roommates or laundry as *teacups*, and burned out, dazed survivors of bewildering boot camp as *krispies*. Hovering does not always produce the intended result.

Susan, mother of 29-year-old Alison, tells us, "My daughter wants flowers that are out of season for her wedding, making them twice as expensive as flowers in season. She has no regard for how this impacts me. Everything she chooses is 'just a little bit more.' This wedding is beginning to feel like an arterial bleed. I know that daughters want a perfect wedding, but mine has a touch of Bridezilla and doesn't know how to prioritize or compromise. I have always made everything too easy and now her expectations are not in line with reality. Who told her she was Princess Di? Maybe the problem is I was the one who made her feel like a princess. I know I have to feel more comfortable with saying, no. It's hard for me to refuse her anything."

While daughters take advantage of their mothers' overprotection, many are mindful of the fact that this may inhibit the development of their adult competencies. Renee, 30, says, "I respect my mother's character, her strength, her willpower, and her willingness to sacrifice anything for me and my brother. Yet, I'd love to model this, but know that there is a limit to my capacity to serve. I also wonder if it hinders my ability to grow up. I don't want to be in my forties and expect my mother to help me pay my car insurance!"

Christina says, "My mother has the patience of a saint. You can push and push and push, and she'll still speak to you without expressing any anger. I wish I could be so patient. I go to her for direction when I can't figure out my life and rely on her telling me what to do. I have a lot of anxiety when I have to figure out what's best for me by myself. As I get older, I wish that she had given me the opportunity to develop the skills necessary to be my own decision maker." Christina is experiencing insecurity because she has relied so greatly on her mother. She doesn't trust her own voice or internal compass to find her way. The Guardian Angel Mother's conduct is seductive, and resistance to this behavior jeopardizes the relationship as defined by the mother. To separate, a daughter may attack her mother, when she can't otherwise individuate.

Barbara says, "Sometimes I am aware of my daughter's disapproval when I begin to speak. I think I'm being articulate and funny and I can see in her face that she thinks I'm just *too much*. I see myself as a complete pain in the ass and it makes me uncomfortable. Just because she is different doesn't mean she should make me feel embarrassed and ashamed of my style. Sometimes I wish she wasn't there with me so I could just feel comfortable with myself. I don't want to worry that her disapproval is the whole truth. I struggle with how to change what needs to be fixed, ignore her distortions, and keep my self-respect." Barbara's daughter has not come to terms with how different she is from her mother. When she sees her mother act in a way she disapproves of, it makes her uncomfortable and she has a bigger emotional reaction than necessary. While this story may be true for other archetypes, the lack of individuation for the daughter of a Guardian Angel Mother makes healthy and normal autonomy more painful for her mother as well.

Caroline, mother of 32-year-old Jennie, agrees with Barbara

when she says, "When I'm with Jennie, she's often self-absorbed. I am so careful when I speak because I know there is a ninety percent chance she will misinterpret what I say. Her criticism makes me feel bad about myself. I am first and foremost a mother; it's where I live. So when she criticizes me it feels bad. I experience this as Caroline being intentionally disrespectful." For most of us, we are our best selves when we are with those who support and validate us. When we are with those who judge us, we naturally become self-conscious.

Individuation is particularly difficult between mothers and daughters because we are much more sensitive to one another's judgments and feelings. As a result, both mothers and daughters lack objectivity during this process. A Guardian Angel Mother has a harder time letting go, and her daughter has a harder time believing she should or can let go.

ALPHA MOTHER

An Alpha Mother is faultfinding. She can be disapproving, controlling, and/or hypercritical. She is also judgmental. One of the pitfalls of this type of mother is that she may find plenty of opportunities to be disappointed in her daughter. For example, as a critical mother, she may censor and condemn people, associations, and professions that are not to her liking. An Alpha Mother may wield her power through fear and shame. Shame is often a byproduct for a daughter. Physical affection and communication may be conditional. Things run smoothly as long as it's "Mom's way."

A daughter of an Alpha Mother is seldom able to express her true feelings and hides parts of herself for fear her mother will find fault with her. This daughter loves her mother, but experiences her as controlling, invasive, and inconsiderate. A daughter who doesn't live up to her mother's expectations feels like a failure. No matter what her daughter does, an Alpha Mother is never satisfied. A daughter who tries to be friends with her mother runs the risk of never being good enough. In turn, this produces a broken connection and a lack of communication. A daughter feels this as an incalculable loss, because she can't talk to the person whose DNA is closest to her own and must discover who she is by herself. Alpha Mothers are usually organized and run their families like well-oiled machines. Think of an Alpha Mother as a CEO of an efficiently run corporation, a person who has high executive functioning skills. Imagine what it is like for a daughter to have a mother who appears to do everything perfectly.

A mother who insists on controlling her emerging adult daughter's life in the same way she did when she was younger is not sought out as a friend. Many of these mothers want to be close to their daughters, but their behaviors distance them. Lisa tells the story of refusing to go out of town to a second cousin's wedding, a cousin she hasn't seen since she was 12 years old. Her mother offers to pay for her transportation and hotel room, but Lisa has other plans and has absolutely no interest in spending a weekend with family members she hardly knows. Lisa says, "My mother is more concerned with the appearance of family unity at the wedding and won't listen to what works for me. She was so unglued about my refusal to go that she brought up past disappointments with me and didn't talk to me for days. She is constantly trying to control my social calendar without regard for my feelings.

This fits in with her telling me to get a haircut, wear bootleg or wide-bottom pants, and date only professionals."

An Alpha Mother has trouble giving up control and allowing her adult daughter the freedom to mature. Daughters report feeling that their Alpha Mother's love is conditional. Andi, 23, says, "My mother and I have been in a constant battle for control over my body. For part of my teen years she watched everything I put into my mouth, complaining I didn't need four cookies after dinner, the ice cream I had after lunch, or the M&Ms at the movies. When I started to watch my weight, my mother complained that I wasn't getting enough calories. Now that I care about my weight, I either eat too much or too little. She gets furious when I tell her to back off and she tells me I need her hypervigilance." Andi's mother confuses this experience of individuation with betrayal. An Alpha Mother uses anger, blame, and guilt to try to control her adult daughter, who should no longer be under her control.

It's impossible to be best friends, or even friends, with your sergeant major! Jen says, "Sometimes my mother gives me her opinion when it is not appropriate, and that is never appreciated. Right now we aren't talking because she said I'm high maintenance because I get manicures once a week. It's my one self-indulgence. It's unacceptable for her to comment on my choices. I work fifty hours a week and shouldn't have to defend giving myself a treat." While it is appropriate for a mother to be concerned about an adult child's well-being, it is disrespectful and invasive to battle over the details of her life. The consequence of having a mother who wants to control a daughter's social calendar, what she wears, whom she marries, and her career choices is that the daughter can't really share her life; this discourages communication, let alone friendship. To stay sane, the daughter of an Alpha Mother has to separate herself from her mother, sometimes with great distance. This controlling and critical behavior denies both the mother and daughter time with each other and their families. Similar to the daughter of a Guardian Angel Mother, the daughter of an Alpha Mother sometimes feels that, to protect her own ego, she must remain secretive about her life. The difference between them is the intensity of the conflict, between telling someone firmly to stop (Alpha Mother) and a metaphorical slap. The Alpha Mother behavior creates the possibility for greater conflict.

To make a course correction if you see yourself as an Alpha Mother is to act on the fact that your daughter is a grown-up and has to learn to make mistakes on her own. One reformed Alpha Mom says, "I find myself saying to myself: 'There is a fine line I don't want to cross when Monique is going in a direction that I don't think will benefit her.' I tell myself, 'Butt out, let her fail, and she will learn from it.'" An Alpha Mother has a difficult time accepting that closeness doesn't have to mean knowing everything, making judgments, and controlling a daughter's every move. It can mean accepting that, if she needs you, she will willingly ask for your assistance and opinion. Only with this acceptance is there potential for developing an adult friendship.

LONG-DISTANCE MOTHER

The Long-Distance Mother may attend to all of her daughter's custodial needs, including food, school, extracurricular activities, and shelter, but not her emotional needs. This mother may be disconnected from her own feelings and/or lack emotional intelligence. The Long-Distance Mother may be reserved and have a hard time showing physical affection and warmth. She appears to be detached, which a daughter may experience as indifference and a lack of love. A daughter may disconnect from her mother as an adult, even though she can appreciate that her mother does provide basic necessities. Both mothers and daughters lose because they miss out on forming an intimate relationship. A daughter with an unresponsive mother looks into a mirror without a reflection and sees an abyss.

This style of mothering is dismissive of attachment, and a daughter learns to avoid seeking contact with her mother. She may learn to hide her anger or distress, which may appear to others as being unemotional about the lack of connection with her mother. This daughter learns not to go to her mother for comfort because she most likely will be unable to provide it. A daughter of a Long-Distance Mother often adapts by inhibiting her need for connection because she anticipates her mother's rejection. A resilient daughter of a Long-Distant Mother learns to find comfort and support elsewhere.

Katie, a 29-year old mother of 1-year-old Sophie, says, "When I think about my experience with my parents, the harm done was not in their being 'too close,' but in their inability to be emotionally safe, empathic, and connected. From the outside, my family looked fabulous—just like Ozzie and Harriet. On the inside, it was certainly not a safe harbor and a far cry from 'best friends.' I doubt that anyone would have asked whether my mother and I were close enough—no one would have worried about that dynamic. It took many years of therapy for me to understand what was lacking and to find my self-worth."

A daughter who doesn't feel unconditional love from her mother often experiences a lack of connection and an inability to trust relationships. This detachment has a powerful impact. The daughter has to figure out who she is on her own, and trailblaze rather than learn from example.

Holly says, "My mother's role was traditional, but she was neglectful. She was herself neglected and, therefore, neglectful of me. I think she was probably depressed her whole life, so we really had to take care of ourselves. My brother and I fixed our own dinner and washed our own clothes. We were not nurtured; we were not taken care of. When I was growing up, I had to reach out to others. I had a lot of friends. I sought nurturing from my friends because I knew I couldn't get it from my mother. My ability to find substitute relationships was my saving grace. My mother and I now have conversations about my childhood and she understands how I must have felt. I knew my mother couldn't take care of me, because she couldn't take care of herself."

Erica, 33 and a daughter, says, "I'm embarrassed to admit that when my mother got sick and was in the hospital, my sister and I barely went to visit her. In stark contrast, when my father was sick, we made it a priority to run to the hospital. I guess because my mother didn't nurture us I don't feel connected to her and that makes me feel sad. I'm sure it is hard for her to see how attentive we are toward my dad. It's depressing not to want to care for your own mother. While it's gotten better since her illness, I am personally not proud of my relationship with my mom." With a Long-Distance Mother a lot of resentments may build up over time. While the Long-Distance Mother may feel that she cared for her daughter and did enough, she may have missed what her daughter really needed. Therefore, her daughter might express her frustration, sadness, and disappointment with a lack of connection and anger.

In a *New York Times* article, Erin Brown writes, "Make no mistake: My own parents loved me. It's just that their love was manifested in ways that I began to see as indicative of an East-West divide. When I left home, it was as if my parents had sent me off in a covered wagon to claim my own plot of land in the valley. Everything I needed, they assumed, was already in the wagon." A Long-Distance Mother may build a resilient child, but that child may feel as if she is flying on a trapeze without a safety net. Building skills without fostering a close connection may create an adult relationship that is functional and pleasant, but less interdependent and connected.

Many mothers create a relationship with their own daughters in reaction to an unsatisfactory relationship with their own mothers. Terry, mother of three adult daughters, says, "My mother was extremely unavailable, and it was a tremendous lesson for me as a mother. I decided to do the opposite with my three daughters because I didn't want them to suffer as I had. My grandparents were immigrants, and my mother had a lot of responsibility. She was raised in a family that tried to survive without an expectation of intimacy. I experienced her lack of emotional warmth as neglectful. As a reaction to my own upbringing, I never hang up the phone with one of my daughters without telling her I love her. I may have made a lot of mistakes, but I know I demonstrate to my daughters how much I care."

Daughters of Long-Distance Mothers must learn to self-soothe because they can't expect nurturing from their mothers.

Unfortunately, they may repeat this pattern as mothers, but they also can become Guardian Angels to their own children. Long-Distance Mothers may not get the opportunity to form adult friendships with their daughters because, over the years, they haven't shared intimacies.

SHADOW MOTHER

A Shadow Mother is self-denying and feels powerless to stand up for herself and unworthy of expressing her needs. She denies her own validity. These women are what Dr. Murray Bowen, one of the pioneers of family therapy, in his book *Family Therapy in Clinical Practice*, describes as "deselfed," unable to defend themselves. They obliterate their own needs and punish themselves. A daughter of a Shadow Mother views her mother as dependent, depressed, and childlike. This daughter is often angry and does not want to be like her mother. She also may feel guilty when she surpasses her mother's achievements. A Shadow Mother is weak and dependent, and a daughter may become her mother's mother. Daughters resent this role. A disempowered mother cannot teach her daughter how to claim her own voice and be her own person. According to Rosjke Hasseldine, author of *Lifting the Veil on Mothers and Daughters*, a daughter often ends up being angry at her mother's fragility and for exhibiting a disempowered picture of femininity.

This daughter is encouraged to be assertive and becomes impatient with her mother's silence, tears, and timidity. Some daughters find their mother's behavior intolerable; others experience it as manipulative. The mother's expressions of neediness, dependency, and weakness may be another way of controlling.

When a mother feels disempowered and can't find her voice, she also can't teach her daughter how to be powerful and find her own voice. Her daughter is likely to end up being angry and distant. Julia remembers being angry with her mother during adolescence: "My mother always seemed bored and frustrated. I didn't like the picture she portrayed of everyday life. I saw an educated, yet unfulfilled woman who did not know how to either identify her needs or fulfill them. I felt angry and let down. I needed her to teach me how to listen to my own voice to be able to make myself happy and satisfied." Julia's story demonstrates that a mother who doesn't take care of her own needs can create a daughter who distances herself from her mother's choices and feels residual anger. A mother who feels powerless to take charge of her own life can also create a daughter who assumes the burden of caretaking and/or feels guilty about her own successes and joy.

Another characteristic of a Shadow Mother archetype is the frequency with which her daughter takes on the parenting role. This child is often called a "parentified child," one who has to behave in ways that are emotionally older than her years because her mother is not able to protect or take care of her. The consequence is that this child doesn't feel safe or nurtured by her mother. For example, the daughter of a Shadow Mother assumes adult responsibilities because her mom is overwhelmed and/or depressed.

Beth says, "My mother was slightly depressed my whole childhood. Sometimes when I would come home after school, I would find her still in bed. My mother would tell me that she was just getting up from her nap, but I knew better. I had to make sure there was food in the house, otherwise my sister and I would not have meals. I would start my homework, and my mother would say that she would start dinner, but by the time I finished my homework, dinner was never on the table." Another young woman says, "My mother calls all the time. It drives me crazy because I feel like I'm the only one she's talked to all day long."

A daughter of a Shadow Mother learns to be self-reliant, but at a price, the loss of her childhood. As an adult she struggles with managing her mother's well-being versus taking care of herself. Sofia says, "The months following my parents' divorce were the most difficult. My father walked out without any warning, and my mother was in total shock. I had to pick up the slack and keep the house together. I missed out on my own childhood because I had to do the caretaking. I was focused on making sure my mother was okay. When I had the chance, I moved as far away as I could to get the separation I needed. I grew up in New York City, and California looked pretty good to me. The move was very hard because I considered my relationship with my mother close, but we also fought a lot because she didn't have good boundaries. Taking care of her shouldn't be my job." In a functional relationship, the mother is the caretaker, not the other way around. It is difficult to be friends with a Shadow Mother, who lacks an accurate self-image. This problem is the opposite of an Alpha Mother, who demands control and accepts responsibility. A Shadow Mother abdicates responsibility. Both archetypes create unbalanced relationships.

Opposition often results between the Shadow Mother who is trapped in "old" ways, whose life has not been fulfilled, and the "new" and "modern" daughter who is liberated, or at least sees the possibility of liberation and growth. Louisa says, "My mother had me when she was so young, and I don't think she's done what she really wants to do in life. And that kills me. I want what's best for her and don't know how to help her, and I worry that she won't help herself."

Amanda says, "I wanted to go out with friends and I wanted to hang out with boys, but knew that my mother wanted me to stay home with her. On Saturday evenings she would order Chinese food and we would watch *Love Boat* and *Fantasy Island* together. We would lie in her bed eating Chinese food and I was her date." Many daughters express sadness and feel wistful about their mothers' unrealized dreams. Others may resent their mothers' failures to take charge of their own lives. A daughter of a Shadow Mother often feels guilty when she is taking care of her own needs and having fun, especially when she knows her mother is unable to make a satisfying life for herself.

Some Shadow Mothers are emotionally absent, not because they are depressed, but because they are working hard to keep their families afloat. This kind of Shadow Mother is able to take charge of her life, but is necessarily absent from the lives of her children. Children have an easier time recovering from this absence because it is usually temporary and serves the interests (usually financial) of the family. If the situation is explained properly, a child can rebound and form a positive adult relationship with her mother.

Emily says, "My mom went to law school when I was seven years old. I literally tucked her in for three years. I remember saying, 'Good night, Mommy,' and she couldn't move from her bed. She woke up every morning at five to study, made my lunch, and then woke me up for school. She was the queen of multitasking and I was proud of her, but she was not around in those years." There are mothers who are Shadow Mothers for valid reasons such as being the sole support of their families. This kind of Shadow Mother has more success forming a positive adult relationship with her daughter because her absent behavior is understandable. Children are very forgiving when they see their parents making an effort for their well-being and understand that the behavior is in the interest of the family.

MINI-ME MOTHER

While somewhat similar to the Alpha Mother, the Mini-Me Mother is controlling, but uses this control to replicate herself. The Mini-Me Mother uses her influence to mold a daughter into her own image and/or the type of daughter she thinks her daughter should be. This mother wants to create a replica of herself without consideration of her daughter's separate identity and needs. The daughter of the Mini-Me Mother may have a difficult time knowing where her mother ends and where she begins. She may be sad when her mother is sad and anxious when she's anxious. Wanting her mother's love and approval, a daughter may sacrifice her individuality to morph herself into a version of her mother.

The Mini-Me Mother *needs to be the center of attention.* She allows neither real separation nor mutual respect to develop. This mother decides what her daughter wants and needs. This daughter's happiness is defined in terms of her mother's own needs and perceptions. She may say she is hungry and tells her daughter to eat; she may feel cold and tell her daughter to put on a jacket.

According to Arlene Harder, author of *Letting Go of Our Adult Children*, Velcro Mother or Mini-Me Mother is enmeshed with her adult daughter and concentrates on her daughter rather than on herself. Outwardly this can look like a close relationship, but it comes with conditions. Often a Mini-Me Mother can't distinguish between her daughter's problems and her own.

Livvy says, "My daughter, Samantha, wants to be a performance artist, and they even have majors in school for this profession! I think she will not be able to support herself because it is a dead-end job. Whenever I try to talk some sense into Samantha, she gets crazy with me. She will say, 'Mom, remember you went to college with a visual arts scholarship and you decided not to follow your dreams. That was your decision. I am not you. I want the freedom to make my own mistakes and life choices.' Her choice makes me anxious, because I think she won't have a steady paycheck." Samantha needs to find her own way, which may not mirror what her mother wants for her. To be close, her mother has to relinquish control.

A Mini-Me Mother has a vision of who she wants her daughter to be and what she wants her daughter to look like. Carolyn, mother of 28-year-old Vanessa, acts like a mind reader and projects her own need to be thin and fit onto her daughter. Carolyn says to Vanessa, "I know you don't like yourself when you're heavy." Vanessa never has a chance to decide what body weight feels comfortable for her; her mother makes this decision. Carolyn believes that Vanessa has twenty pounds to lose. Vanessa doesn't agree with her mother's assessment. Vanessa says, "Mom, I am not fat, I am just a little chubby. Just because you are a fitness freak doesn't mean I have to be a gym rat."

A Mini-Me Mother tells her daughter what her ideal is and tries to convince her daughter that she knows better. Carolyn tries to influence her daughter, and as much as Vanessa believes she is not fat, she is vulnerable to her mother's opinions. It is very damaging when a mother projects her own image onto her daughter. A daughter may forfeit her own needs and values to get her mother's approval. The danger of "helpful" suggestions from a Mini-Me Mother, such as offering hints on how to fold fitted sheets or poach salmon, can quickly morph into a lecture that sounds as if she is saying her daughter can't do anything right. A daughter interprets this as disproval and worries that her mother thinks she's incompetent.

Some mothers have such a strong attachment to their daughters that they merge their identities without consideration of the daughter's need to individuate. Talia, 29, says, "I have four older brothers and I'm the youngest and the only girl. My brothers thought it was funny to call me Mini after my mom, Mickie, when we both wore jeans skirts on the same day. Until I was twenty-four, I was Mini and, if I had kept that nickname, we would be Mickie and Mini. I finally got rid of that nickname after college. Somehow having this as a nickname made the identification with my mother much stronger. I never questioned that I should not do things the same way that she does."

Talia adds, "My mom is very traditional, stayed home, cut coupons, baked cookies, and made her own applesauce. I struggle with buying cookies, which makes me feel guilty. This fusing with my mother has made it more difficult to find my own path." Forging an attachment that forces a daughter to lose her own identity, or makes it hard for her to establish one, does not create a foundation for an adult friendship. A daughter needs an environment that allows her to build on her own strengths rather than bend to the ideals of her mother.

CHAMELEON MOTHER

Inconsistency is the most consistent quality of a Chameleon Mother, who is sometimes attentive and other times negligent. She is sometimes overprotective and sometimes absent. In other words, she is unreliable. A daughter can't count on this type of mother. Sometimes she is available, and other times she is a vanishing act. This mother sets up a pattern of unpredictability, so her daughter doesn't know what to expect or how to behave. As a consequence, the daughter's needs sometimes go unanswered, and she may grow up being afraid or unsure of attachment. Chameleon behavior leaves a daughter feeling disappointed and may render her distrustful of relationships. In addition, because the Chameleon Mother is undependable, her daughter may also cut herself off as a way of protection.

Many of the qualities of a Chameleon Mother may overlap with the criteria of a diagnosable problem such as substance abuse, borderline personality disorder, bipolar disorder, or some other underlying mental illness. However, as we explained earlier, for purposes of this book, we are not focusing on these causes. Yet, many Chameleon Mothers do have some limitations (such as attention deficit disorder) that overlap with symptoms of some of the above, which are not pathological, yet create real difficulties for their daughters and interfere with consistent mothering.

According to daughters in our focus groups, a Chameleon Mother is unpredictable. The following stories all describe this inconsistency. Ava recalls, "In order for my mother to really pay attention to what I am going through, all the environmental variables have to be lined up for her to be present. The phone, an article that catches her eye in the newspaper sitting on the table, the crawl on the TV screen can distract her. I can't keep her attention. When she can be present once or twice in a row, I start to expect her to be there and be reliable. When she disappoints me after I begin to trust her, it makes me feel worse because my expectation was that she can change and be counted on."

Mixed messages and intermittent reinforcement are more powerful than regularity. If the behavior is uniformly bad, a daughter knows what to expect and develops coping skills. With a Chameleon Mother, a daughter feels disappointment when her mother doesn't come through and learns to protect herself by not counting on her mother. This inconsistency makes the relationship volatile, much like being on a roller coaster.

Thirty-one-year-old Janie says, "My mother is incredibly anxious and vacillates between smothering me and being unavailable. I think that her anxiety sometimes draws her toward me, like when I was a young girl, she would lie down with me until I fell asleep or expected me to call her every time I arrived back to college. She does these things to make herself feel better. Yet, when I need to unload my fears and talk about the things I can't handle, she's invariably busy and needs to call me back. My mother is not there for me when I need to vent. My fears overwhelm her, and just when I need some hovering and protecting, she goes AWOL."

Heather, 32, says, "My mother was so inconsistent. Whenever my mother would pick up me from school, she would promise me that she would be on time and about six out of ten times she'd be late. I'd complain and she'd shape up. I'd begin to trust her and then I would have to wait forty-five minutes because she got stuck at work and didn't call me. I still never know what to expect and it's very unsettling."

Erin, 28, says, "I missed out on having a more solid and reliable relationship with my mother because I was stuck in the caretaking position. I had to take care of her emotionally all the time. My mom was relatively young, beautiful, and single in Philadelphia and she loved being thought of as my sister when we'd go out. Sometimes we would go to dinner and someone would approach us as if we were peers, not mother and daughter. My mother was lonely, which made it my responsibility to make sure she had companionship. On the other hand, when my mother did have friends, she could get preoccupied, even forgetting to call me when she wasn't going to meet me for dinner. I never knew whether the disengaged mother or the needy mother would show up. This pattern of unreliability also exists today."

Ava's, Janie's, Heather's, and Erin's experiences are consistent with other daughters of Chameleon Mothers. These mothers are overwhelmed by their own needs and can't suspend them long enough to take care of their daughters. Many daughters of Chameleon Mothers are both frustrated and disappointed by this behavior. Some protect themselves by pulling away to avoid being upset, others may pursue these mothers, hoping to make it right, believing mom will finally be reliable. Danielle, 26, sums up this dilemma when she says, "My mother is either lovely or ready for battle." Many other adult daughters describe their Chameleon Mothers as sometimes protective, relaxed, or playful and at other times intense, distant, hurtful, or disinterested.

The Chameleon Mother is unpredictable, so her daughter must develop a strategy for dealing with her mother's inconsistent responses. A daughter may adapt by distancing herself from her mother or by getting angry after being disappointed once again. Because this mother's style is so unreliable, the daughter of a Chameleon Mother is caught in an anxiety-producing paradox. When she turns to her mother for safety or comfort, she doesn't know whether her mother will reassure her or ignore her. A mother who needs comforting herself is incapable of soothing her daughter. This mother's lack of consistent and sensitive responses to her daughter may result in an anxious, ambivalent, or insecure relationship.

MOTHER WHO STRADDLES TWO CULTURES (TRANSCULTURAL MOTHER)

Women from different cultures sometimes have different needs and expectations. Research involving more than 150 women, ages 25 to 35, conducted by Dr. Mudita Rastogi, Associate Professor of Psychology at Argosy University/Chicago and a licensed marriage and family therapist, shows significant variation between mother and daughter relationships in different ethnic groups. Dr. Rastogi found in general that, from the daughters' perspective, European-American women want to do fun activities with their mothers, but also want to maintain certain boundaries. Asian-Indian and African-American women generally turn to their mothers for support, wisdom, and advice. Latinas want to be dutiful daughters and help their mothers.

"Even though these ethnic groups varied somewhat in terms of relationships, all of the women in the study wished for the same level of connectedness with their mothers," says Dr. Rastogi. "Almost all of the women reported that they wanted respect and trust in their relationships with their mothers." Even though these mothers and daughters want to be close, the conflict between the culture of origin and contemporary American culture can be troublesome.

The values and beliefs of mothers who are immigrants or first-generation Americans may conflict with mainstream American culture. This creates the potential for conflict with their daughters. Simi says, "My mother is very stubborn and strict. Whenever I would ask her for something, I could predict that her answer would be no. Even when my dad said yes it didn't count. We had to ask her permission for everything, like sleeping over [at] a friend's house or dating, which we were never allowed to do. So my sister and I would lie and tell my mother that we were going to libraries with girlfriends or sleeping at a friend's dorm when we were out partying.

"Her behavior distanced me, and I feel much closer to my dad. Her need to control has continued and I am now a married woman. My husband and I have moved two thousand miles away to escape her strong hand. Respect for your elders is such an important value in my culture that my anger and need for independence makes me feel guilty." Like Simi, other daughters in our focus groups explain how they may sidestep, or even defy, their mothers' wishes. Daughters also express how the conflict between their mothers' hopes and their own ambitions for themselves create constant anxiety.

Transcultural Mothers in our focus groups feel foreign in both language and culture. These mothers share with us their feelings of isolation and alienation from American culture and, as a result, they take refuge in their culture of origin. A Transcultural Mother is often defined not by herself but by her services as a daughter, wife, and mother. Daughters tell us that their mothers put tremendous pressure on them to conform, serve the family, and not individuate. Daughters who resist conformity and seek a more contemporary American identity, for example, in career choices, social life, or marital partners, face conflict, resistance, or rejection from their families. Unlike their mothers, these daughters struggle with cultural identity.

A daughter may worry that, while attractive, assimilation may be perceived as giving up her native culture, distancing herself from her family. She often feels as if she has to choose. A daughter is caught between having to accommodate her mother and fitting into a less traditional society. She may feel guilty about her desire to separate from her mother because, as a daughter, her devotion to her mother is expected.

Maria says, "I want to feel like I am a good daughter, but I feel so much guilt when my mother calls and I don't want to answer the phone. I know she is proud of me, but she just doesn't understand my life. I can't always talk to her when she needs to talk, and because she doesn't speak English very well, she turns to me to explain everything. I just can't do it all the time; I have to work and I have to have a life, a life she will never accept. It isn't my mom's fault; she doesn't know what it takes for me to be successful here. It seems like no matter what I do, it is never enough. But I want to do the right thing for my mom; just sometimes it is in conflict with what is right for me."

Mainstream American culture places great value on the individual and independence and generally devalues attachment and dependence. In other cultures, staying close to family and interdependence are primary values, so there is a disconnect between foreign-born or first-generation mothers and daughters who desire to be independent. While daughters are expected to assume greater personal responsibility, as they become adults, allegiance to family remains the priority. In these relationships, some of the conflicts between mothers and daughters are based on misunderstandings about each other's feelings and beliefs.

Ying says, "In our culture you are also expected to show a lot of respect for elders. We are not permitted to reason with them, even if we are right. It is assumed we are always wrong. When I moved away from home, it seems that with every conversation my mother would find something to scold me for and our discussion would end in an argument. I know she thinks that I have completely lost my cultural background, which makes me feel sad."

In most of the issues we address here, the mother has the primary responsibility for making the relationship work. However, the daughter of a Transcultural Mother legitimately has this responsibility. She has the motivation and the opportunity to change her perceptions. Unlike her mother, she needs to be comfortable in both cultures.

Silvia says, "I know I'm going to have to look after my kids, my husband, and my parents. I know I'm not going to have anybody else to turn to and rely on emotionally or financially. It will be my responsibility to make it all work. Even if this seems unfair, I want to be a great daughter."

Many of the daughters with whom we spoke told us that their mothers don't understand why they feel torn between both communities. Mothers can't relate to their daughters' feelings about the resulting sense of confusion. Juli, 26, says, "Sometimes, I feel more connected to one heritage than the other. My mother is well intended, but overly simplified. You are Chinese and American and I am their daughter . . . therefore, the world must see me as a reflection of them, that is, Chinese or American. It's true that not all of us have cultural identity issues, because every experience is unique."

Teresa, six months pregnant, says, "My mom and I have a role reversal. In some ways she can be very strong-willed, and in other ways she is very dependent. Language is a barrier. We just got a notice in the mail, and she asks me, 'What does this mean?' I am always translating for her. I feel the need to call my mother to keep her company because she doesn't have many friends that she can speak to in Spanish. I take on the role of friend, and she tells me more than I need to know. I love talking to her and we share almost everything, but there are certain things that I can't share with her, like me going out with friends at night. She is overly protective, and in her culture, a married, pregnant woman does not drive alone at night to meet friends. I find myself hiding things from her so I don't upset her."

Living in two cultures doesn't always mean the mother adheres to the expectations of her own culture. Sometimes a mother can behave in a way that is contrary to her culture of origin. Susie's mother worked, unlike other mothers in her culture, who stayed home. Susie says, "My mother had a tough time growing up and believed that you can't count on anyone else; you need to do it on your own. She taught us the importance of education and having your own career. She stressed our education a lot and burned the midnight oil with us until one or two A.M. the night before an exam. My mother put so much pressure on me that when I received a ninety-two percent on my history exam, she wanted to know where the other eights points went."

Susie adds, "I want my mom to say that she is proud of me and the woman that I have become. I don't know if I will ever hear this because she believes that by picking on me and being critical I will become a better person and more successful." While this has the desired effect on academic success, for Susie to reduce her stress level she has had to distance herself physically from her parents. The distance helps, but it doesn't eliminate the conflict and guilt of having to choose between being a good daughter and creating her own life. Susie's experience is confirmed by the author of *The Joy Luck Club*, Amy Tan. When asked by interviewer Deborah Solomon how her mother responded to her book's success, her response was, "When I was on the *New York Times* best-seller list, at number four, I told my mother and she said: 'Wha' happened? Who's number three and two and one?' "

A daughter of immigrant parents straddles two worlds. She is caught between a society that still forces her to define herself by some kind of hyphenated American label and a world whose face is being changed forever by technology and the globalization of trade and travel. One hopes that accepting author Thomas Friedman's assumption that "the world is flat" will enable the daughter of a Transcultural Mother to maintain her culture and define her own life.

Christina says, "I am now strong enough to pay attention to what my grandmother told me before she died. She said, 'Listen. Listen to what your parents say.' When I was younger, those words made me feel unworthy, but now I finally understand what she was saying. I know that I inhabit two different worlds and

I am the possessor of two cultures. I am my mother's daughter, and she has passed her culture and heritage down to me. I must define myself by what I know and not by what others think of me."

Now and Forever

It is often difficult to figure out why a mother takes on the behaviors of one of these archetypes. A mother's personal history is key, including her history as a daughter.

Some mothers have positive childhoods, others have more negative ones. Some mothers are more resilient and emerge from a difficult childhood with fewer scars and maladaptive attachments, although they carry the legacy with them. Even a mother who has a positive childhood may not possess the social skills or empathy necessary to create a satisfying friendship with her adult daughter.

Mothers and daughters who struggle with their relationships as adults often repeat unhelpful behavioral patterns developed when the daughters were young. When this behavior occurs, the adult daughter hears her mother's words with the ears of a child. In addition, the temperament of the mother and daughter may also prevent closeness.

Many mothers in our focus groups question whether it is possible or even desirable for mothers and adult daughters to be best friends. The archetypes we present here demonstrate that mother-daughter friendships can be difficult to obtain, let alone best friendship. We have introduced the Perfectly Imperfect Mother archetype to demonstrate that to develop a gratifying relationship a mother must integrate her past without contaminating her relationship with her daughter. She also must evolve emotionally to allow the relationship to mature. For a friendship to develop, a daughter must accept the knowledge that, like all other human beings, her mother is flawed. She must also accept her own responsibility and contribute to making the relationship work. Many adult daughters begin to have more empathy for their mothers when they become mothers. They realize it's not an easy job.

It is generally in a daughter's best interest to create a positive relationship with her mother. A mother is ultimately the standard against which a daughter measures herself, in education, career, relationships, or motherhood. Whether their relationship is tense or calm, antagonistic or friendly, a daughter needs her mother, if only to validate her and to help guide her along the way. This need is universal.

It is also important for a mother to understand that even a lifetime of devotion and care doesn't guarantee that she will have a mutually satisfying relationship with her daughter. Few parents escape feeling guilty, believing that they do too much or too little. How we behave and what we say always affects the relationship. We have to take responsibility for this. Wanda, mother of 25-year-old Kendra and a tenth-grade teacher, tells us, "I love being a tenth-grade teacher and take my responsibility very seriously. I bring the same guidelines for assessing the needs of each student to my responsibility as a mother. If a child fails in my class, and it's on my watch, it is my responsibility to figure out what the child's learning style is and to teach her in the way that she can learn. I feel the same way as a mother. Often being a better mother requires me to have self-awareness and then make adjustments." The effort to forge a positive relationship with an adult daughter is worthwhile for many reasons. Similar to the benefits for daughters, mothers find that a good relationship with their child is linked to their own well-being.

To determine whether you can overcome some of the more difficult archetypes, you need to ask yourself the basic question: Do I accept my daughter as an adult? Some ways to demonstrate acceptance are withholding judgments about her friends, allowing her to prepare a family dinner in your kitchen with a guacamole recipe different from yours, and accepting how she spends her money. You respond affirmatively to these situations because you trust her to make her own decisions. Our adult daughters have to carve out their own lives, which may look very different from ours. Our daughters have the right to make their own choices, and we will not always agree with them. Recognizing this is fundamental to a friendship.

Provocative Questions for Mothers to Ask Themselves

1. When your daughter discuses her feelings with you, do you interject your own feelings?

____

____

____

____

2. Do you feel jealous of your daughter?

3. Do you think you are empathetic?

4. Is your support conditional?

5. Do you think your daughter feels close to you?

____

____

____

____

6. Do you demonstrate that you love your daughter? If so, how?

____

____

____

____

7. How do you cope with crises in your daughter's life?

____

____

____

____

8. How focused are you on how others might judge you?

9. How do you react when you are hurt and/or feel as if you've been criticized?

10. Are you able to speak your mind and express your feelings?

11. Have you blamed your daughter for dissatisfactions with your life?

12. Does your daughter feel your acceptance?

13. How critical are you of your daughter?

14. Is it difficult for you to separate your needs from your daughter's?

____

____

____

____

15. Are you reliable?

____

____

____

____

16. Did you rely on your daughter when she was younger?

____

____

____

____

17. How controlling are you?

18. Do you compete with your daughter?

19. How important is it for you to have things just right or your way?

7

Marriage, Motherhood, and Divorce: From Here to Maternity

Perfect love sometimes does not come
until the first grandchild.
—Welsh Proverb

All in the Family

Many mothers find the transition from having a single daughter to a daughter who is living with a significant other or is married to be an awkward time. Phyllis, mother of two adult daughters, says, "I live in dread of my daughters getting married. I love my relationship with my girls and I don't want it to change." Mothers feel this way because, unlike our parents, we are much more involved in their daily lives. The transition from single to a committed relationship presents a new and sometimes difficult change for our generation of mothers. Mothers in our focus groups voice apprehension about their daughters' adult relationships and how they will affect the friendship that many of them developed after college. Our daughters are getting married and having children later. It was different for us because we married in our early twenties and left our parents' house to form our own home. We spent most of our twenties solidifying our marriages, not our relationships with our mothers.

Many of the focus mothers found that once their daughters marry, intimate contact is sporadic. Leigh says, "My daughter calls from the taxi on the way home, and the conversation ends either when her battery runs out or when she has to pay the fare." Another mother adds, "I talked to my daughter for an hour while she was walking home from work and I was stuck in traffic. It was like a perfect storm, I caught her when she was available and had juice in her phone."

Susan says, "My daughter's job is so demanding. She has dinner meetings most evenings, and she calls from her car on her way home because it's her only free time. That's the only time we have alone, and I feel a tremendous loss. I love her husband, but I want more of her. Talking to her after work feels like I'm just keeping her company. Our phone calls are not intimate or substantive. Since she's married, her substantial conversations are with her husband and not with me. I'm glad they have a good relationship, but it's hard to be pushed aside; more than that I feel I'm less on her radar screen." Even though this is as it should be, the mothers in our focus group find the change difficult.

Parenting has transitional phases such as graduation, work, marriage, and grandchildren, which produce complex emotional feelings. Some are easier to accept than others. Like any other transition, this new stage requires adjustment. For example, when your child first goes off to school, the experience is bittersweet.

You may feel both a sense of satisfaction and of loss. One of the difficult consequences of a daughter's entering into a committed relationship or marriage is intermittent communication and no longer being the "first responder."

It is unrealistic to think that marriage doesn't change a mother-daughter relationship. Says Charlotte, "I couldn't go over to my daughter Rebecca's house when my son-in-law, Brad, was there. One day I was at Rebecca's house working in the garden and Brad came home earlier than I expected. Rebecca warned me and I grabbed my gardening tools and left the house without him seeing me. I don't feel comfortable being at the house fixing things because I don't want him to feel that I'm taking over his home."

Lorna says, "I self-edit when I'm with my son-in-law. I want him to like me and don't want him to see me at my worst." A relationship takes time before all involved are comfortable being themselves, but more caution is still exercised, even in the best of relationships. There are a number of adjustments to be made that also impact the mother's relationship with her daughter. In all likelihood the two family styles have differences. Your son-in-law sees your family's style through the lens of his own experience. Sometimes what you intend as helpful, he perceives as overprotective and intrusive. Visiting and planning require negotiating three schedules, rather than two. When your daughter marries someone, it changes your access, and you are no longer the "go-to" person; her husband is and should be. Your daughter may set boundaries that you either support or don't, but at this juncture in her life, your job is to respect her wishes and follow her lead. Sometimes this can be a relief.

The relationship changes once again when your daughter has

a child. According to AARP (2003), "Family life taps our deepest emotions. It's not surprising, then, that conflicts can arise as tiny but very demanding infants join the family circle. After all, we all have egos, opinions, values, and goals of our own. We all want a sense of belonging, to be treated well, to get our share of attention. Parents, grandparents, aunts, uncles, in-laws, and older siblings must adjust to new roles when a child joins the family."

This new stage provides lots of opportunity for establishing new connections between mothers and their adult daughters, and at the same time offers some new and familiar responsibilities. Women are returning to work more rapidly after having their first child. In the early 1960s, 14 percent of all mothers with newborns were working six months later, increasing to 17 percent within a year. Today, 83 percent of moms return to work by their baby's first birthday. Because of the scarcity of affordable and high-quality child care, many grandmothers often help their daughters care for their children.

We don't know exactly how many grandparents provide child care for their grandchildren. The U.S. Census Bureau says that grandparents provide child care for almost a quarter (23 percent) of children under age five. According to AARP (2003), that number is even higher for children who live only with their dads. Grandparents watch more than one-third (34 percent) of these children. An even higher proportion (38 percent) of Latino preschoolers are cared for by their grandparents. Almost one-quarter (24 percent) of these grandparents watch grandkids between ten and twenty-nine hours a week, and about 7 percent stay with grandchildren more than thirty hours a week. That's a lot of caretaking.

We live in a rapidly changing world, which now includes genetic testing, ultrasound pictures in 3-D, parking spaces for expectant mothers, midwives and doulas, spas for pregnant women, and family and friends in the delivery room. Lots of things change, but one thing remains the same: our children still need us. This need can take many forms. Maybe it's being a good listener; helping paint the baby's room, or providing reassurance that the changes our daughters are going through are normal. In this chapter, we focus on these experiences, transformative for us and for our daughters—marriage and/or a committed relationship, motherhood, and divorce. This is a time when we need to work on the relationship to preserve closeness with our daughters. It is also the time to lay a foundation for our relationship with our daughter's significant other and, if we're lucky, our grandchildren.

"Sadie, Sadie Married Lady"

Many mothers in our focus groups agree that once their daughter is seriously involved in a relationship, they feel anxious and unsure about their role in her new life. For the first time, mothers may be hesitant to contact their daughters or to make plans. Lydia says, "I almost always call my daughter on her cell phone. I only call on her landline when I know her husband is not at home." Bonnie says, "Once Meredith became engaged, it was the first time in our relationship in all these years that I was confused about what my place was in her life. When I do ask her about making plans, Meredith answers with, 'Let me check it out with Phil. Let me see what he thinks.' My reaction, although I keep it to myself, is 'What do you mean, let me check it out with Phil?' I know intellectually it is what she should be doing, but it still feels strange."

Joanne, a 61-year-old single mother, says, "My daughter, Stacey, called to let me know that she might be getting engaged soon. The timing isn't good because I am about to move. I said, 'Stacey, if you're thinking about a wedding, you know I just bought an apartment in New York City.' Her immediate response was, 'Mom, sell it!' Some things never change!"

Looking in the Rearview Mirror

Most parents know from their own experience as young married couples that there are lines parents shouldn't cross. Marian, a 53-year-old mother of an adult married daughter, says, "My parents crossed boundaries when they thought that after I had two children my husband and I were not going to have any more. So, while I was at work one day, my parents gave away all of the baby furniture and baby clothes. I was furious and pitched a huge fit. I will never be so intrusive with my children." Parents certainly should not make assumptions about their daughter's plans or decisions and act without discussing the situation first, especially because parents' assumptions are rarely free of their own biases and expectations.

Negotiating transitions is often challenging for all concerned. Some young couples must blend different family models, for example, the super-autonomy in one family with close family interdependence in another. As Alison, newly married, tells us, laughing, "I don't understand why my husband doesn't love my parents as much as I do, and want to be around them as much as I want to. I could live with my parents and be really happy. My husband is less involved with his parents. It's especially hard because we live close by. We have a 'no dropping by' rule, but my parents would never do that anyway."

This is a time to step back and take our cues from our daughter. Once again, this doesn't mean we can't maintain connection and provide support, but we must value the process of the creation of their own family unit. Our own experience should help to prepare us for this process. Gail, a 52-year-old mother of an adult daughter, says, "I was twenty-two years old when I got married. I felt like a hamburger stuck between my parents and my husband. I didn't establish myself as Mark's wife at the beginning of our marriage. Instead, I straddled two identities: Gail, the daughter of Joyce and Bill, and Gail, the wife of Mark. My mother is a faultfinder and my father is a peacemaker who never told my mom to stop intruding. My biggest regret is not standing up to my mother in Mark's defense.

"I should have told my mother to stop criticizing. Most of my fights with Mark during our first years of marriage revolved around my intrusive mother and my more passive father. At fifty-two, I finally feel comfortable in establishing my own priorities and can tell my mother she can't come over when she's on the warpath. I wish I had done this earlier in my marriage. I told this story to my daughter, Terri, when she recently got married. I want her to know that Justin should be her 'go-to' person and they should be each other's first priority."

Once your daughter is married, your role should be one of

support rather than providing direction or giving advice if you want your relationship with her to continue to be positive. Eileen, mother of Alexandra, says, "Alexandra and my son-in-law are a couple, and I want to be a positive support for their relationship. They have to establish their own relationship and values." Your daughter has to shape her household with her spouse, and if they have children, raise them according to their own values and lifestyle. These beginning years are crucial to your daughter's creation of a solid foundation for a long-term marriage. A mom's (and a dad's) understanding of this is critical. Sometimes a mother has to reinforce boundaries even when her daughter is not ready to accept this change.

Carolyn says, "The biggest fights I have had with Brett have been about boundary issues. He is very clear about wanting me-and-you time. There can be me-and-you-and-my-parents time, but Brett wants much more of me-and-him time. It's very hard for me. This is the biggest challenge. My family was my brother, my parents, and me; that was my family. Now there is Brett and me, and I thought I would just bring him in, so it would be Mom, Dad, my brother, and Brett and me.

"I thought this plan would work, but Brett isn't so into the plan. He loves my parents, but there are times when he says, 'I can't [be with your parents] tonight,' and I have to be like, 'Okay, I understand that.' And then I get mad at him. My mom is the one who tells me to 'back off.' She will say, 'He's right; you can't force him to want to be with us all of the time.' And I'm still, 'You know what? Yes, I can!' "

Carolyn's mother understands the importance of setting and keeping boundaries. Carolyn continues, "My mom will say, 'I'm thinking about coming over tonight; what are Brett's plans? I don't want him coming home from work and finding me just hanging out.' It's hard for me to remember that Brett isn't as comfortable as I am around my family." The transition from one family to the next is difficult for adult daughters as well as their mothers. What is significant here is that Carolyn's mom understands how Brett feels and is able to set and respect new boundaries, even though her daughter would just as soon not have them.

Another daughter in our focus group tells a similar story about the benefits of boundary setting. Melanie, a 25-year-old newly married daughter, says, "I didn't have to set up any boundaries. My mother, Carol, did that. Neither of our families live[s] in the area, but I don't really think that matters. My mother is determined to be the best mother and mother-in-law; she makes her own boundaries. While we were engaged, she called me and said, 'I spoke to Teddy [my husband] about dinner plans for Friday night, is that okay?' I said, 'Of course. If Teddy says it's fine, then it's okay with me.' She's always mindful of how I feel. She says to me, 'Tell me if this bothers you.' I don't think I am ever going to have to say to her, 'Listen, back off.' My mother is so respectful of my feelings. Her respect for both Teddy and me makes me want to spend more time with her. My mom has made it easy for me to talk to her, and Teddy and I have made [it] a rule to always talk about issues as well." This is a wonderful opportunity for parents to be positive role models for their newly married daughters and to stay close.

Advice or Vice

How do you know when to give advice and when not to? This is an easy question when everything is going well, but what do you do when you see a problem? The simplest rule is to offer your married daughter advice only when she specifically asks you for it. Even then, try to frame your advice as suggestions for discussion or consideration that she and her husband can think about and then either accept or reject. We all see our daughters making choices we wouldn't make. Throughout our daughters' lives, one of the most difficult challenges for us is to allow them to learn by failing, even when we know the potential consequences. One mother explained this challenge in the following way: "Sometimes we can see them about to veer off course, and we have to hold ourselves back from grabbing the wheel, because the wise part of us knows that they need to experience the consequences for themselves." Of course, this is easier said than done.

Joanne, a 57-year-old mother of two adult daughters, remembers when she was newly married, some thirty-two years ago. She tells us, "When I was first married, I got into the biggest fight of my life with my mom about how to make cranberry sauce for Christmas dinner at my home. And through some divine intervention, I realized fairly quickly that this was not a fight over a recipe, but over 'I'm a grown-up. This is my house, and my mother is trying to take charge.' But I came to the conclusion that, you know what, I don't really care. Maybe if I lived in the same town it would drive me crazy, but if she comes three or four times a year and she wants to organize my closets, I don't really care." Joanne has the maturity to understand what she can live with and what issues are worth battling over. A different set of rules and understandings based on firm boundaries may be necessary when mothers and daughters live near one another.

Another mother, Barbara, agrees about the importance of picking one's battles when it comes to interacting with her newly married daughter. Her advice is, "Don't say anything. My daughter has found her soul mate. Both of them don't care if the clothes get washed. They'll pick something off of the floor and say, 'I'll wear it one more time.' They are both wonderful, brilliant kids, but they have no sense. They don't complain, and they are very happy with each other. If they come to our house and we have food or don't have food, they really don't care. She doesn't like to cook, so he really does all the cooking. And she does her thing, but they keep meshing and there's no lack of compatibility. Other people might look at the way they live and say, 'Ohhh!' But we don't say anything. People ask, 'How do we do it?' We don't say anything, because my daughter is just like my son-in-law, and we can't believe they found each other." Barbara knows this is a wise choice, because her daughter and son-in-law are both eating and have a roof over their head. Her children have developed their own lifestyle, and she realizes that it has to be right for them, not her. This mother doesn't expect her daughter and son-in-law's lifestyle to mimic her own standards and values, and she avoids this potentially harmful battle.

Barbara avoids being the Mini-Me Mother or Alpha Mother to maintain a close relationship with her daughter and son-in-law.

She realizes she can't will them into being who she wants them to be and still maintain a close relationship.

Face-Off: Making Different Choices

Amanda, 31, says, "For me, career-wise, right now I'm at the top of my game. So I don't want to risk not achieving my career goals to have a baby at this time. Yet, for my husband, Danny, he doesn't have to give up anything. Gender still matters. No one at his firm will worry that he won't be available to give one hundred percent after he has a baby. But for me it's different. My mom always taught me that a career is important for a woman." Amanda's mother, Nancy, says, "Be careful what you wish for. I feel like it's my fault that Amanda is making a decision to postpone having a child. I valued being a mother who could be a role model for her to be independent and find a career that she could be passionate about. I feel like I should have been more careful and/or clearer about modeling a balance between work and family. Now I wonder if she took in one part of the picture and not the other."

Even when mothers try to create balance between work and home, daughters still have their own perspective and have the right to make their own choices. For example, we may not want our daughters to lose sight or dismiss the importance of family and children. At the same time, we don't want them to give up their career dreams. We believe if women choose to have a career and family, they, like men, should be able to have both. Regardless, mothers often feel that, when their daughters make contrary choices, it is always their fault. This is normal and serves as an example that no matter how prescriptive you are, you can't control the outcome, nor should you.

A mother has to learn that not everything is her fault. As our relationship with our daughter becomes more equal as she matures, she has to assume more responsibility for her decisions as we assume less. This doesn't mean that we love, worry, or care about our daughter less; nothing could be further from the truth. Certainly when your daughter marries, it is time to establish less of a hierarchal relationship and more of a friendship. Again, this is easier when you and your daughter are on the same page. What happens when you are not?

An adult daughter may choose an alternative lifestyle and form a relationship with someone who is of the same sex or is racially, culturally, or religiously different. A mom can choose to be supportive, or she can attempt to stop her daughter from making her own life choice. When a mother attempts to control her daughter's choices, she should expect a battle where either one or both parties may lose. The following story illustrates this point.

Rachel, a 25-year-old graduate student, knew in high school (and probably earlier) that she was gay, but by high school she stopped fighting the feelings so much. Rachel was the victim of countless incidents of harassment. She tried to make herself more and more invisible until she could get to college, hoping to find herself in a more diverse and accepting environment. Rachel believes her parents always knew, but chose to ignore her sexual orientation. At the same time, she regrets not having shared her lifestyle with her parents earlier. Rachel says: "I finally decided to talk to my parents when I started a relationship with Jill. I wanted to be as respectful of their feelings as possible. I wrote them a letter to give them time to absorb the information. I didn't hear from them for days. I finally couldn't wait any longer, and I called them from school. My mom couldn't talk without crying, and my father refused to talk to me at all. I love my parents, but I have to live my own life. I haven't seen my parents in over a year, but I am still optimistic they will come around.

"Jill's parents have totally accepted us. I go to their house for holidays now, but I miss my own family. I think if my parents understood how much happier I am, they would be more willing to accept me. But, right now, they can't let it in. I know they love me, and I also know they are as hurt as I am over the rift between us. I am still hopeful that, over time, we'll be a family again." The decision of Rachel's parents to try to hinder her relationship with Jill has hurt everyone. In spite of large differences, there are circumstances where parents and children can compromise.

Lara, mother of 28-year-old Haleh, says, "My daughter, Haleh, has been dating Adam for a few years. They both come from different religious backgrounds, one Muslim and the other Jewish. When my daughter began to date Adam, I tried to tell her that the likelihood of a successful relationship was doubtful. I spoke with her about the difficulties she would face from both their families and society if they remain together. We had many discussions about these issues, but Haleh and Adam decided to stay together anyway. I decided I could live with their decision, but, at the same time, I knew I couldn't protect Haleh from society or family members who wouldn't approve of her relationship. I wanted her to understand what she would face as an interfaith and intercultural couple in a post-9/11 world."

Haleh's mother insisted that her family members be respectful. However, she couldn't insist on her family embracing a relationship they disapproved of or that caused them discomfort. Although she and her husband accepted the relationship, they respectfully warned Haleh to be prepared for their relationship to become a source of family conflict.

Mothers (and fathers) have a responsibility to support their daughters by providing them with a realistic understanding of the world they will face. Relatives may disown them, they may not be included in family events, some people may shun them, and their own children may encounter prejudice. Parents and siblings may sustain them, but discussion needs to take place about how they may react when extended family members and, possibly, some siblings treat them rudely, when invitations don't come, or when their own children are excluded from family events. Parents can best support their daughters by helping them to prepare for the challenges they will face. With this openness, you can be a Perfectly Imperfect Mother and offer support.

Nonetheless, all mothers agree that it is still an adjustment when their daughters are married. Says Diana, "It's shocking that they don't call you to help them make decisions, to ask, 'What do you think about this or that?' I am happy that their relationship is working, but I still can't help but feel left out." Mothers must figure out where they fit in this new configuration. Daughters are partners in this renegotiation. What we know about children, even adult children, is that they eventually come to another phase, which offers both opportunities and challenges. Usually, the next stage after marriage is pregnancy and having a child. They come back for advice, layettes, comfort, and the closeness of sharing a common experience.

The intermittent connection that often comes with a married daughter can change with maturity and the desire of our daughters to become mothers. Barri says, "I adjusted to our new relationship about three to four years into my daughter Ellen's marriage. Then one day she called and wanted to talk about her future plans. I was cautious at first, then our conversation felt like our old conversations. It was intimate, and we discussed pregnancy and about her choices of where to relocate with her husband. She really wanted my opinion. Ellen talked in a way that was inclusive. By stepping back, and allowing Ellen and Frank to solidify their relationship, the intimacy we always shared returned as if it never left." Many mothers observe that daughters come back when they have a baby.

Welcome to Grandparenting

You're going to be a grandmother! You may find out in person, over the phone, or by voice mail or e-mail. Once you know, nothing in your life will ever be the same. According to Sheila Kitzinger, author of *Becoming a Grandmother: A Life Transition*, "When a grandchild is born, all relationships in the family shift and change. A woman often discovers that she becomes closer to her daughter, and many mother/daughter conflicts begin to be healed once the younger woman is herself a mother."

Some mothers in our focus groups say that their daughters' pregnancies created opportunities for many new connections.

According to Jacqueline, "My moments of closeness with my daughter, Lucy, lessened after she got married. But now my pregnant daughter is obsessing about zipper sheets, bumper pads, and strollers. She knows nothing about babies and baby products. Until Lucy got pregnant, it was never on her radar and now that she is, she's overwhelmed. I said, 'Sweetheart, this is not important, do you remember what color your bumper pads were?' And she said, 'I don't even know what bumper pads are.' I told her all that matters is that you love this baby. Lucy was getting caught up in the minutiae of having a baby, and she wanted me to be in my old mothering role of telling her not to worry. I reminded her that she has the right values, knows what's important, and the rest of these things don't matter. Lucy said, 'Mom, thank you for that.' It was one of those lovely moments."

Many mothers in our focus groups agree with Jacqueline. They were also used to having more moments of connection with their daughters before they were married. When these new moments of connection happen, as one did with Jacqueline and Lucy, they hold the promise of a new kind of closeness. Similar to parenting your married daughter, it is important to find ways to connect without offering unsolicited advice or taking over. In this instance, Jacqueline helped her daughter become grounded by telling her that she already had the most important components needed to be a good mother to her baby. Our approval still provides our daughters with great comfort, especially when they are beginning a new stage of their lives.

A grandchild provides a bond that brings the family together. During this new stage, forming a relationship with our grandchildren and being with their parents gives us another shot at getting things right. It's fascinating and somewhat intimidating to observe your daughter doing things differently from the way you did. A daughter who grew up in a family with a lot of arguing and screaming may not permit this behavior in her own household. A young mother who grew up with an alcoholic parent may not allow drinking in her house. On the other hand, sometimes we watch them repeating the same rituals from their own childhoods, and this feels satisfying. You may hear your daughter singing the same songs to her child that you sang to her when she was a baby. You may see your daughter using the same expressions of endearment that you said to her as a child. The arrival of a grandchild gives us a unique perspective. We watch the new family grow, while keeping an eye on the old one.

Just as you renegotiated your relationship with your daughter after she married or chose a partner, you will need to renegotiate your relationship with her when she has a child. Here we caution you again, much in the same way we did in our discussion of a daughter's marriage. Her expanded family needs to establish a strong foundation, which may also include you as an important source of support. However, your daughter and her husband must establish the rules of their family. You must take your cues from them. Once your daughter becomes a mother, she shifts her role and becomes the expert. She has the last word on how she mothers her own child. While most mothers give lip service to this advice and say they agree, it is, once again, easier said than done. Marilyn says, "When I told my girlfriend that my daughter was pregnant, she said, 'Marilyn, I have one piece of advice: You need to buy packing tape and cover your mouth,' and how right she was."

Mum's the Word

It's impossible not to compare how our children raise our grandchildren with how we raised them. We may not say it aloud, but many of us feel that what worked for us should be good enough for them. When you feel this urge to instruct your daughter, resist—stop yourself. Instead, give your daughter advice only when you are asked for it and withhold judgment. This doesn't mean you can't ask your daughter questions respectfully, particularly if you think your grandchild's safety is at stake. You can have a different opinion, but understand that your daughter has the last word regarding her child.

Watching our children parent differently may feel like an indictment of our style of parenting. This can be painful. Try to remember, child-rearing is a moving target. When we were pregnant we could drink wine, eat tuna, drink Coke, and have a cup of coffee. These are all taboo today. We fed our children on demand and put them to sleep when they were tired. Our social lives revolved around taking our children to one another's homes and letting them fall asleep on a sofa, in a guitar case, or in the car going home late at night. Rather than argue about the right way to do things, we need to realize there is not a single right way. We need to keep our eye on the prize, which is connection with our daughter and our grandchildren. This may require our making an accommodation with a different child-rearing philosophy.

Sally wanted to be the perfect grandmother when her grandson was born. It didn't take long for her to see that her idea of perfection was very different from that of her daughter, Becca. When her 2-month-old grandson, Jacob, began to wake up several times during the night, Sally begged Becca to give Jacob some oatmeal to reduce his hunger. Sally says, "Becca got furious. She refused and told me, 'No one gives their baby food that young.' And I barked back, 'Oh yeah, I gave you cereal at one month old and you've lived to become a mother yourself.' It killed me to watch Becca be so sleep-deprived when I had a solution. I even went on the Internet to show her that my solution worked for other mothers, but she still wouldn't listen." While Sally thinks she is being helpful, her daughter, Becca, finds her infuriating. You can talk to your daughter and give her your opinion, but you have to be ready to accept that she may disagree with you.

Many people don't have the courage to bring up problems with their grown kids. They may be afraid of honest conversations and hurt feelings. Others feel discounted. Rather than engage in a difficult conversation, they may silence and distance themselves. When a mother is fearful of conflict and doesn't know how to have healthy disagreements with her daughter, she tends to avoid conflict at any cost. The problem is that dishonesty and/or silence, which is dishonesty by omission, prevents intimacy. Acknowledging your daughter's right to make her own decisions and engaging in conversations while keeping an open mind is essential to maintaining a positive relationship.

"And Baby Makes Three"

Becoming a grandmother is transformative. Janet says, "When my daughter, Michelle, told me that she was pregnant, I was ecstatic. She told me over the phone and I started to cry. I was filled with happiness and joy. Yet I knew that things were going to change. Our family was about to become child-centered again. If I wanted to take my daughter and son-in-law out for dinner, we would have to go early with the baby or they would have to find a babysitter. The carefree days of just us adults were going to end." Janet is so right, especially for the first grandchild. It's amazing how several adults can stare at one baby in rapture. Your first grandchild represents the beginning of a new generation in your family, which comes with mixed emotions, ranging from sheer delight to anxiety. In addition to the happiness you feel with your new grandchild, becoming a grandmother signifies that you are aging.

Laura says, "My world changed when my granddaughter, Sophie, was born. It was an existential milestone. I feel invigorated because I am seeing the world anew through her eyes. Watching her face the first time I pushed her in a swing made me feel young. But when I calculate how old I'll be at her high school graduation or wedding, I feel frightened that I might not make it."

However, our idea of old age has changed as well. According to Sheila Kitzinger, "Women in their sixties and seventies do not get old. Instead we enter an active and satisfying 'third age,' and after that, at eighty a happy and contented 'fourth age.' " Today's grandmothers are very different from their mothers, the grandmothers of yesterday. Most of us are healthier, more active, and better educated. Our lifestyles are more casual, and we are less formal. Kathryn and Allan Zullo, authors of *The Nanas and the Papas*, say, "Most boomer grandparents work hard and lead vigorous, often stressful lives, where time is a valuable commodity." Many of us are also caring for elderly parents at the same time that we are expected to help with our grandchildren. We have to find ways to balance caretaking for our parents, work, and supporting our daughter's new family. Our daughters are also leading more stressful lives, and we are all stretched pretty thin.

Many grandparents help take care of their grandchildren. Retired, full-time working, and part-time employed grandparents all have different resources to offer. A mother needs to be clear about how much time she has to support her daughter when the baby comes. A daughter must understand that her mother has other responsibilities that may limit her ability to contribute. While the mothers in our focus groups choose to handle the time requirement differently, each one agrees that the most important thing is to be clear about how much support she can offer. Some mothers, who live in the same city as their daughters, choose to cut down on their work and give a day to their grandchild; others choose to give time on a "spot basis." Other grandmothers give in other ways. Beverly, mother of Julie, says, "When Julie's nanny was on vacation, I took off from work and flew to North Carolina to fill in for her. During that week, my twelve-month-old grandson, Zach, and I totally bonded. Because I live in Detroit, I worried that he wouldn't know who I was, and nothing substitutes for bathing and rocking him to sleep. After spending that time with him, he blows me kisses on the phone and recognizes me in photos."

Young moms can feel isolated, and one way to compensate for this loneliness is to call their own mothers. Due to the tremendous increase in the percentage of working mothers, today when a daughter has a child, it is more difficult for her to turn to friends for support. Many are on different schedules. This phenomenon gives a mother an opportunity to contribute and spend intimate time with her daughter and grandchild.

Beware the Cookie Monster

While many of us took our job of mothering very seriously, buying educational toys and reading books on child development, we are surprised by the intensity our daughters bring to mothering their children. For instance, *Sesame Street*'s 1960s DVDs have been reissued with an adult material warning label. Cookie Monster is considered a bad role model for overeating and eating unhealthy food. Oscar is too grouchy and lives in a germ-infested garbage pail. Young children play on a city street without supervision. Parenting today seems more rigid and fearful. Everything is scheduled, measured, and sanitized, even *Sesame Street*!

Lois says, "It's amazing that my children survived. I used to drive them in the 'way back' of my station wagon. Now I'd be pulled over, given a ticket, and maybe turned into the authorities. My daughter Erin's crib had a thick quilt with plastic bumpers. I put her to sleep on her stomach or in a hammock surrounded by her stuffed animals to keep her from moving. I brought her to germ-infested public places at three weeks old and never asked anyone to wash their hands before they touched her. She rode in shopping carts without the special fabric seat to shield her from the other toddlers' infections. I gave her Dimetapp for her colds and Dramamine for carsickness. In restaurants I cut up her food and put it directly on the filthy table without the plastic placemat that sticks to the table. How did she survive?

"When my grandson was born . . . Erin began her war against germs. I carried Purell in my purse, in my car, and washed my hands so often they were chapped. I told my daughter she was raising her boy in a bubble. But after I spoke to my friends, I realized that many new mothers and fathers were working hard to manage all of the dangers they perceive to surround them. What happened to the idea that children get stronger when they play in dirt and are exposed to germs?" Anne agrees: "Last week I was babysitting for my granddaughter and panicked when I realized that I put her down on her stomach for a nap. I wasn't worried about whether she would be okay, but I couldn't decide whether to keep my mouth shut and let my granddaughter sleep or confess to my daughter, who I knew would wake her up and turn her over. I let her sleep and didn't tell my daughter."

"Help, I Need Somebody, Not Just Anybody"

Many mothers in our focus groups expressed concern that giving their daughters too many instructions could prevent them from developing their own parental judgment. Carol says, "When my daughter was a toddler, a Doberman jumped into my brand-new car before I could get her out of her car seat. When I bent over to unstrap her, the dog jumped between my daughter and me, growled, and bared his teeth. He then began to mark his territory by peeing and pooping all over the front and backseats. I was terrified until the dog finally jumped out of the car. After my daughter went to sleep, I spent the rest of the afternoon scrubbing the filth and smell out of the car.

"If this happened to my daughter, she would have called me from her cell phone expecting me to access every bit of adrenaline in my body to either will that dog out of the car or call the animal rescue squad to get that Doberman away from my grandson. Her expectation is that I can and should fix everything. I never expected to have my mother jump in and save me. Sometimes I feel like I should go into a phone booth (although they are hard to find these days) and change into some caped Supermom costume."

We give our daughters the idea that we can do anything and are available at any time. Marilyn goes to her daughter's house at 6:00 A.M. every day to help her get the children ready for day care, and then she goes to work. Her daughter has a husband, but she relies on her mom, instead. This expectation comes from years of service and bailing out our daughters. For them to assume the role of mother fully, our daughters have to make sacrifices, understand that they will miss things, and learn to make compromises. The problem with repeatedly saving our daughters is that they will miss the opportunity to establish realistic expectations in their new roles as mothers and to become competent.

At some point a daughter has to accept the responsibility of being a mother. It is impossible for her to do this if we interject ourselves too much and take on the mother role rather than the grandmother role. Many mothers in our focus groups agree with the sentiment expressed by Jean: "It is our time, also. If you can't manage with three kids, you shouldn't have them. When we go on vacation, it is our vacation, too. Some mothers are expected to deal endlessly with their grandchildren. My friend Karen said she is relieving her daughter Laura of the burden of taking care of her own kids. Karen complained that she never had a moment to herself."

Abby says, "My daughter's baby is due in three weeks, and she is one of those planners. Her schedule is mapped out months before. She says to me, 'Mom, I have two weddings, one in Richmond and one in South Carolina. Why don't we drive to your house with the baby, pick you up, and then you'll come to the weddings with us and care for the baby.' I started to hyperventilate. First of all, what about my life? My work? My plans? She has mapped out my life without my participation, let alone my permission."

When our children were young, there were many times when we frequently stayed home or missed an important event because our child was ill. Grandmothers share lots of stories where they do step in. This is fine when it is your choice. A problem may arise between you and your daughter when she has to change her plans because you're not available. Megan was on her way to a baseball game, and her mother, Cheryl, was taking care of her grandson. Cheryl and her husband had tickets to a concert that evening and had hired a babysitter. Her grandson got sick and Cheryl didn't feel comfortable leaving him with a new babysitter. She called Megan on her cell and asked her to come home so she and her husband could attend the concert. Megan was very upset with her mom and expected her to cancel her plans and stay with the baby so she could stay at the game. Cheryl didn't agree, and Megan and her husband had to come home.

When our daughters were younger, we protected them from stress and frequently made motherhood look easy because we wanted both to take care of kids and work outside our homes. We micromanaged every millisecond. The term *Supermom* was coined for our generation. No wonder our daughters expect parenting to be easier, and when it isn't, they expect us to pitch in. Trudie tells us, "My daughter, Gretchen, and her husband, Nathan, are having a hard time. They are very scheduled, and the baby is not behaving consistent with their very ordered life." No matter how we appeared as parents to our daughters, parenting does not come without frustration and sacrifice.

Helen says, "When my two children were young, my husband was in his medical residency and never home. It was totally normal for us to have dinner without him. The kids would hardly notice. No one would ask, 'Where is Dad?' I did much of the custodial child care without him. I did the laundry, the shopping, and the housecleaning. I remember putting Marni in the grocery cart late at night. I had her out in the dark of night when she should have been home in her crib because it was the only free time I had to grocery shop. I contrast this with my daughter, Marni, who has extensive child care and still asks to be relieved on Wednesdays when she's alone with her boys. She would never disturb the boys' nighttime schedule by taking them shopping. It's unimaginable. I'm thrilled that my son-in-law and daughter moved back to Connecticut, but when they first came to town, I told them, 'Remember my name is spelled, HELEN, not HELP.'"

Some daughters do understand that their mothers are not

available 24/7. Trish says, "My daughter, Carly, has a tough life because she is in a big corporate law firm, has a baby, and is married to a husband who has an equally demanding job. Carly took only two weeks off in the summer for maternity leave. Her schedule is so different from mine when I was a young mother. I worked part-time when my children were young and didn't go back to work full-time until they were in school. Carly works in a law firm where she has to have a minimum number of billable hours. Her firm thinks nothing of contacting her on her BlackBerry ten o'clock on a Saturday night. I would like to give her support because she needs it, but I'm busier now than when my children were young. I have worked for years building my career; I love what I do and I'm not ready to cut back yet."

Trish has already raised children and doesn't want to be the backup mom. She feels, like many mothers, that Carly and her husband need to find a solution that works for them without being overly dependent on her. She made compromises with her career as a young mother with the expectation that she could devote herself full-time to it later. She hopes her daughter will understand her inability to fill in on a day-to-day basis and this will not prevent them from remaining close.

Another mother, Wendy, says, "I worked and worked and raised my kids. Now I'm at the point where I want to have a little more free time, more downtime, and more balance. I'm loving the fact that I have a granddaughter and I want to see her. But I'm done with the minute-to-minute child care." Janice agrees, "I've been working for thirty years, and I really look forward to my hard-earned flexibility. If my daughter, Caitlin, lived near me with the baby, I'd constantly be thinking about whether or not I need to be somewhere else rather than where I'm at. I don't want a weekly commitment to provide child care for my daughter. It's an expectation I don't want to fulfill. I've raised children. I juggled home and work without an involved husband. I want to be a good grandmother; I just don't want to be [the] mother." Having previously limited their career advancement when they had young children, these mothers want to have a grandmother relationship that is satisfying and helpful, but one that also works for them.

A mother may not want to accede to her daughter's sense of entitlement, but she still wants to stay involved. While a mother often must preempt her needs with those of her children, absent special circumstances, a grandmother doesn't have the same responsibility. At the same time, most grandmothers love to spend time with their grandchildren and daughters. Gloria says, "I love my grandchildren, but I don't want them to be my life. I want to have a life."

At this time of our lives, we are being pulled in many directions, balancing work, leisure, taking care of elderly parents, and still parenting children and grandchildren. It's harder to maintain the community we developed as younger mothers. Grandparenting, in addition to all of its joys, may separate us from our women friends.

When we were young, our children often brought us together with our friends. But now that our children are having children, the new family unit pulls us away from our friends. Marcia says, "I called my best friend to see about getting together; we spent much of our younger years with each other's families, including celebrations, birthday parties, Thanksgiving, and vacations. We also talked daily on the phone. We filled in for each other with carpooling, picking up meals, surrogate parenting; we were family. Now she spends all her free time with her daughter and grandchildren, leaving little opportunity to be together. This is a big loss and makes me sad. We spent our twenties, thirties, and forties creating a community, and I assumed the relationship would sustain me after my children left town. We have reverted from an extended family to two nuclear families. Where once we were each other's family, we are now just friends." This loss is particularly acute when one friend has grandchildren and the other does not. You don't rely on your friends to help you with grandparenting, but you do rely on them to help you with your parenting.

To sum up, we can support our daughters by recognizing that being a new mother is an exhausting and scary experience. Try to remember what it was like for you when you were raising small children. You can provide comfort by acknowledging your daughter's experience and offering her your support and empathy while taking care of your own needs. The reward is an enriched connection with both your daughter and your grandchildren.

Divorce: Till Death Do Us Part

Our daughters have lived with unprecedented rates of divorce, first as children and then again as wives and mothers. As late as the 1950s, the norm was that fathers were absent from the home because of military service or death. According to sociologist Stephanie Coontz, today, "The U.S. divorce rate hovers at about forty-five percent. That's down from the seventies and eighties . . . Somewhat surprisingly, a majority of divorces are initiated by women." In our focus groups, divorced mothers of divorced daughters express feelings of guilt, and worry they may be to blame for their daughters' failed relationships. Both the divorce and the way we respond to it can have an adverse impact on our daughters. While it is not our fault, what is important is how parents handle this difficult transition.

Thankfully, today divorce doesn't have to be ugly. Many couples cooperate with one another, especially if children are involved. Our grandchildren may even experience a sense of relief, because the conflict in their homes has ended.

In the past there were fewer positive single-parent role models. Currently, there is a body of burgeoning helpful research and increased numbers of professionals who work with parents to help them be more collaborative after divorce. Every child remembers the moment when his or her parents announced plans to divorce. However, the legacy of divorce is not an insurmountable challenge. Like so many other experiences in our daughters' lives, mothers can change the landscape by providing a safety net and support for their daughters and grandchildren and, if appropriate, encouragement for the children's relationship with their father.

Divorce Legacy

In our focus groups, many adult daughters talk about their parents' divorce. Beth says, "My mother's veins start to pop when I mention my father. He had an affair with our neighbor, so it was hard for my mother to get past the betrayal and humiliation. Now that I'm thirty-two, I can intellectually understand that, while he was a good father, he was a lousy husband. But my mother confused the two. She couldn't separate what he did to her from how he treated me. I was always stuck in a loyalty bind. By loving my dad, I felt disloyal to my mother. It's not fair. I've paid my dues by protecting my mother. I never shared that part of my life with her, because it would hurt her. But that meant I had to compartmentalize, life with Mom and life with Dad. I wish my mother could have moved on, but she stayed stuck in the role of victim. I've fashioned my ideas about my life in opposition to hers. I don't want to get divorced; I don't want to be alone. But if I am, I hope I know how to take care of myself."

Another daughter, Coleen, says, "After the divorce, my mother and I became really close; she would confide in me. My mom told me she trusted me more than anyone else because I wouldn't let her down. While it was a compliment, it was also a burden. I wished my mother had close friends she could have confided in." Divorce can leave a child feeling a sense of obligation, if not a burden. For Coleen, this manifests itself in her attempt to ensure that she is not emotionally and financially vulnerable in the event of her own divorce.

The impact of divorce can be felt beyond the nuclear family and can include friends, aunts, uncles, cousins, and grandparents. The model for what well-known lecturer and counseling psychologist Constance Ahrons calls the "good divorce" revolves around cooperative parenting and recognizes that anyone important in a child's life before the divorce remains important to a child after the divorce. In the past, use of the term "broken family" may have suggested that significant relationships were severed by the divorce. We believe descriptors like "broken family" should be shelved with such other archaic terms as "illegitimate child."

Some adult daughters express relief that the years of conflict between their parents ended. Sarah says, "For years, I kept my relationship with my mom and dad separate, never mentioning one's name in the presence of the other. But after I married, I started to make Thanksgiving at my house and asked my mother, father, stepfather, stepmother, and half-brother to come. It's cool; we are like a big, neurotic family laughing and teasing each other. It's been over twenty years, and the emotional rawness is finally gone." Mothers can help with the healing by cooperating with their daughters' wishes to maintain a family life and minimizing the conflict for her. A daughter shouldn't have to choose between her mother and father.

Stopping the Trickle-Down Pain

Grandparents become touchstones for their grandchildren, who are understandably confused when parents separate. After the divorce, grandmothers who stay out of the conflict and remain close to their grandchildren can soothe them by providing comfort and reliability. In the best interest of grandchildren, grandmothers should stay out of battles between their daughters and ex-husbands. We need to remember that her "ex" is still the father of our grandchildren. Linda, the mother of 33-year-old Heather, says, "Heather got divorced two years ago, and I made sure to stay in contact with her ex-husband, Michael. We had a good relationship when I was his mother-in-law, and I didn't want him to feel like a stranger after the divorce. He is the father of my granddaughter, Lily, and I care about maintaining family ties.

Sometimes it's tricky because I don't want to offend Heather, so I'm careful about the boundaries. Helping Lily maintain her relationship with her daddy is important, and Heather understands.

Linda says, "After the divorce, Lily found it difficult to express with words how she felt to her mommy. Instead, she would cry and tell Heather that her tummy hurt her. At that time, we would sit in my kitchen and she would tell me her worries. I believe Lily felt safe expressing herself to me because she understood my neutrality and knew that I loved both her mommy and daddy." An emotionally intelligent grandmother will make sure never to criticize her grandchildren's father in front of them. This restraint gives our grandchildren permission to talk to us about their relationship with their dad. When we offer equanimity, we give our grandchildren the message that they have the right to love each of their parents. We can help them experience less of a loss.

Debbie agrees: "My granddaughter, Olivia, has a good relationship with her other grandma. I want her to be comfortable talking about her with me. Olivia asks me questions that she is uncomfortable asking her mother. I believe she doesn't want to hurt her mom's feelings if she says something nice about her dad's mother." Debbie's approach is both sensitive and wise; she knows her granddaughter is coping with enough without having to feel torn by a sense of divided loyalty. It may be easy for a grandmother to compartmentalize because, in many cases, her contact with her daughter's ex-husband will be limited. However, one hopes that the ex-son-in-law will stay involved in his child's life. We believe that feeling loved by both parents after the divorce sustains a child's sense of well-being.

Often a grandmother becomes an active and necessary safety

net for her daughter by being much more involved in the daily care of her grandchildren. In times of crises, grandmothers can become welcome sources of stability. Holly says, "My daughter was in shock and needed my support in order for her to be able to parent and comfort her confused children. Regardless of how overwhelmed I felt, I knew that I wanted her to know she could rely on me." Holly understood that her own need to mourn her daughter's failed marriage would have to wait. Divorce is difficult, and while most people heal, this process requires a significant period of readjustment.

Walking a Tightrope

Mothers must avoid interfering in and assigning fault for their daughter's divorce. This can be a challenge, especially if you blame your daughter for either initiating or causing the divorce. Rosie says, "My daughter was unhappy in her marriage for the past five years but never told her husband how miserable she felt. Instead she had an affair with a guy she met at work. She said it started as an innocent friendship and became romantic after she confided in him. She thinks she has found her true love, and I'm scared and disappointed. I think she's been irresponsible and reckless and I'm struggling with finding a drop of empathy." According to journalist Mireya Navarro in her *New York Times* article "My Child's Divorce Is My Pain," "To minimize exposure to the acrimony of the warring spouses, parents of divorced children are advised to avoid taking sides or criticizing, even in cases when the parents may disagree with their own child's behavior, such as infidelity." If we aren't careful, judgments can jeopardize our relationship with our daughter and her family.

Ruth says, "When my daughter, Lizzie, told me she was separating from her husband, John, my first thoughts were for her children and I worried how they would react to the absence of their father. I looked at her in shock and said, 'Lizzie, how could you divorce John, he's one in a million!' I was heartbroken. It was the beginning of my attempts to mediate reconciliation and involve myself in a very private matter between my daughter and my then son-in-law. Their divorce became a big part of my life." According to Jill Curtis, psychotherapist and mother of a divorced daughter, "On the whole, grandparents, parents of the divorced couple, find little support. People do not consider what a wrench it can be to lose a much loved son- or daughter-in-law so most grief at this loss is unacknowledged. It can hurt, too, for friends to say they could 'see it coming' or that they 'had never liked him/her in the first place.' " Many grandparents say that it's difficult to find guidelines for their behavior and/or sympathy for their situation. While this is understandable, the feelings of the divorced family and children come first.

Pack Up Your Sorrows

It is difficult to be a source of support for your daughter if *your* feelings become front and center. Our job during this challenging period is to hold our daughters and be able to guide them as objectively as possible. Demonstrating empathy is critical. Empathy is more than feeling your daughter's pain as your own.

Empathy shows understanding, while giving your daughter the space to be able to express her feelings. At this time, we don't want our daughters worrying about us.

Carrie says, "When Julia told me her husband, Peter, was leaving, I started to cry, which made Julia furious. She said, 'Mom, not you! Don't you think I have enough to deal with? This is no time for you to break down. I need your support, not your tears!' " Julia's anger with her mother demonstrates how your daughter needs you to stay strong when she is feeling overwhelmed. The best outlet for your pain is to rely on your husband, supportive family members, and friends. You need to express your own anxiety, anger, and sadness away from your daughter. Regardless of how sad you feel, no matter how overwhelmed you are, the divorce is your daughter's not yours.

Many parents become involved in their daughter's divorce because of their closeness and involvement in their lives. Daughters need their mothers for support during the upheaval and aftermath of divorce. They need us to withhold judgment, be active listeners, and keep our own emotions in check. Our grandchildren need to be reassured that they have not in any way caused the breakup of their family. We can defuse the situation by explaining that they are still part of a family, even though their parents no longer live together.

Family Album

The mother-daughter relationship goes through many stages and remains significant for the well-being of both of them. There are moms who talk to their daughters every day, others who speak on a weekly basis, some who spend lots of time together, and others who see each other less frequently. Whichever category you fit into, as your daughter becomes a wife and mother, renegotiating the relationship is required. You have to find a place for yourself and, for the most part, take your daughter's lead. Many factors are taken into consideration: where you live in relation to your daughter, her husband's family and/or his experience with family intimacy, divorce, and becoming grandparents—all influence connection and closeness.

The good news is that many daughters in our focus groups say how much they enjoy being with their moms. If they live in different cities, they report how much they look forward to having a week with their moms by themselves, how coming home still gives them comfort and familiarity and provides an escape from the stress of their lives, a time to be taken care of once again. These experiences both maintain and extend intimacy.

Katherine, 30, says, "I still love coming home and feeling taken care of and nurtured by my mom and grandmother. They fix me all my favorite foods and are such a comfort for me. I love our routines. On Saturday mornings we have breakfast together, and after my mom takes my grandma to the beauty parlor, we shop." We are still vital and can provide a comforting presence for our daughters. These routines and memories make our daughters want to come home or turn to us when they are feeling out of sorts.

For those mothers and daughters whose relationship is not as close, when a daughter marries, her spouse can help mediate some of the conflict between her and her mother. Your daughter's spouse can help your daughter gain a more objective perspective so she can see you through a new lens. There is always an adjustment, but your daughter's husband can make this easier, and better.

Mutual Interests

As a daughter transitions into motherhood, she may establish a new closeness with her mom, even if her previous relationship was negative. According to the Council of Contemporary Families, mothers are doing more paid work than they were forty years ago. They are doing less housework and are spending more time with their children than they did in the past. The impact of this is that mothers and fathers are spending less couple time together and less time with friends. As a result, many daughters look to their mothers for companionship as well as help, because their husbands may be working late hours and they have less time to reach out to their own friends, who are similarly occupied. Good friends are also having children at various times, so they find themselves at different life stages. A mother is a natural; she requires little explanation and is often happy to spend time with her daughter. Unlike even the best of friends, we remain with our daughters at every stage.

Companionship with our daughters and becoming grandmothers brings us lots of joy. Many mothers in our focus groups tell us how much they love the opportunity to be better grandparents than they were parents. Although we are engaged in our lives and our careers, we reserve time for our grandchildren, even when we feel exhausted. Suzanne, a grandmother of two young boys, says, "I have so much patience for my adorable boys, much more than I had for my own children." Being older and wiser allows for greater appreciation.

Grandmothers can become guiding forces in their grandchildren's lives. We pass on our family traditions, serve as trusted companions, and help to nurture our grandchildren. Erma Bombeck described this special relationship by saying, "A grandmother pretends she doesn't know who you are on Halloween." At the same time, grandchildren offer us a wonderful opportunity to connect with our daughters on many levels and receive validation and appreciation. Most daughters and mothers describe their relationships as gratifying despite reporting frustration and irritation as well; this is particularly true because of its intensity. However, as one daughter says, "Mom, I love you even though you make me nuts, and I couldn't imagine my life without you."

8

Boundaries: Staying Close Is Hard to Do

Good fences make good neighbors.

—Robert Frost

Statute of Limitations

Developing boundaries begins early, as the toddler starts to explore the world and her mother realizes that her child has a life of her own. This ah-ha moment reappears with spectacular clarity when our daughters become teenagers, close their bedroom doors, keep secrets, and challenge all limits. During this developmental stage, teachers, your daughter's friends' parents, and, yes, the local police department beer party squad may know more about your child's social life than you do!

This process takes another wide turn when your daughter goes off to college and you become more peripheral to her life. An episode of the television program *Gilmore Girls* vividly demonstrates how the relationship changes and how boundaries must be renegotiated.

Lorelai (the mother) wants to speak with her daughter, Rory, to get the details of her daughter's date with a boy Lorelai doesn't know. When Lorelai's friend, Luke, sees that she is checking to see if her daughter left her a message, he asks her why she thinks she needs to check up on Rory. Lorelai tells him she is anxious now that her daughter lives away from home. Lorelai says, "I need to be careful about what I say. She is not at home. I always had 'the mom card,' in my back pocket. I didn't have to use it very much, but she lived here. The worst she did was to go in her room, slam the door, and listen to music. But the next morning I had control over the bathroom and the Pop-Tarts. She had to deal with me."

Lorelai explains to Luke, now that Rory is, "on her own, making her own decisions, my mom card is looking flimsier. If she doesn't want to hear what I have to say, she doesn't have to. She doesn't have to call or come home." Now that Lorelai's daughter is becoming a young adult, Lorelai understands that their boundaries must be different from when Rory lived at home. While this is a struggle, she chooses to respect the new boundaries and, by doing so, allows herself to form a new kind of closeness with her daughter.

The mother-daughter relationship remains complex because the frequent flow of information creates more opportunities for crossing boundaries inadvertently. Deborah Tannen, in her book *You're Wearing That?*, explains that, because mothers and daughters talk a lot about personal topics, they may be close, but they often run the risk of intense misunderstandings.

Mothers strive to say the right things but often blurt out inappropriate and sometimes distancing comments, pushing all of the old mother-daughter buttons. The parent-child bond continues to dominate the relationship, even as you and your daughter grow older and form an adult relationship.

The parent-child relationship has significant boundaries that emanate from parental authority and from the conflict between the child's expectation of being cared for and the need to individuate. Although these boundaries evolve as the daughter grows up, they don't dissipate. Mothers instinctively protect their children from both external sources of harm and the mother's own fears and vulnerabilities. This confluence of boundaries creates inconsistencies that result in missed cues and violations. In contrast, adult women friends, while protective, encourage experimentation, risk taking, individuation, and growth. Friendships are less judgmental, more respectful, and less expectation/result oriented. In this chapter, we'll look at and question appropriate boundaries between mothers and adult daughters.

To be successful, boundary creation must be an ongoing, conscious, and mutual process. Both mothers and adult daughters must be clear about their expectations, needs, and limitations. In focus groups, mothers repeat this mantra over and over again, "I need to know the limits, not guess." Clear and honest communication and respect for one another are key to navigating the new relationship successfully, as they both move from the daughter's childhood into her adulthood. This is not a cakewalk. For example, sometimes your daughter's sense of entitlement collides with your inability to set limits.

Marlene, mother of 23-year-old Brooke, recalls, "When Brooke moved into an apartment, I automatically offered to help set her up. I had done previous apartments and every dorm room she had lived in. I just assumed this was my job. My problem is, Brooke assumed this as well. On moving day, I found myself on the floor scrubbing the grime off of the linoleum in cracks you don't want to know about. I didn't mind pitching in, but I really minded that while I was working like a dog she was organizing her CD collection and making plans for dinner. In the middle of my back-breaking Cinderella work, I stood up and decided I was finished, even though the work wasn't done.

"I realized that this wasn't my job anymore and that I contributed to Brooke's sitting on her rear while I was on my hands and knees. I had not set appropriate boundaries for me that reflected her new age. How was she ever going to learn to take care of herself, if I didn't stop doing for her?" Mothers need to be conscious of what works for them as well as what works for their daughters. This is a perfect example of where mothers must set boundaries for themselves that enable their daughters to be more self-reliant. Brooke will never have the opportunity to be independent or have empathy for her mother if she continues to be dependent on her mom for things she should be doing herself.

Adult children should be living independently and making their own way, while staying connected to their parents. This is a good time to begin thinking of others as well as deciding for themselves what they want out of life and going after it. Ruth tells us, "My daughter repeatedly asks me to do errands for her on weekdays because I work as a consultant and have more flexibility than she does. Last week she asked me to meet the carpet cleaner at her apartment and was surprised when I said that I couldn't do it. I get the sense that she thinks her commitments are more important than mine. Sometimes I find myself trying to convince her that I really am busy and it makes me very angry. From her perspective when she was growing up it probably seemed like she could wave a magic wand and I appeared to solve her problem or satisfy her need. Now that she's an adult, I wish she could reset her expectations for me." While mothers have a hard time setting boundaries, daughters are also unclear about limits. We contribute to this vague understanding with our own uncertainties. Sometimes we should follow Nancy Reagan's advice and "Just say no."

Frequently setting limits with adult daughters requires that mothers first get their own emotional houses in order and take care of themselves before addressing their daughters' needs. This is for their daughters' benefit as well as for their own. For example, if you have dinner plans on a Saturday night, and your daughter makes a last-minute call to ask you to babysit, your first reaction may be to say yes to avoid disappointing her. However, by sacrificing your plans, you also may feel a bit intruded on. If you are resentful, this feeling may emerge when you least expect it, sometimes inappropriately. Your discomfort with setting boundaries will convey to your daughter the message that you are always on call, which is not necessarily the message you want to give and certainly not the basis for an adult relationship.

It is permissible to say what you really need to feel comfortable. Mothers in our focus groups say that because they are no longer occupied with their own child-rearing their daughters think they have a lot of free time and should be available "on demand." This can work for some, but for many mothers it creates a problem, even bitterness. Although many mothers are happy to help out, there are times when they would rather tend to their own lives. Unlike mothers, friends are not expected to provide a rationale for how they spend their time. Making a statement that says your time matters enables your daughter to find other sources of support so your relationship with her can be more balanced.

With self-awareness, you can distinguish more readily between your own needs and those of your daughter. If you don't take the time to understand where you leave off and your daughter begins, you are much more likely to behave inconsistently. By demonstrating your confidence, your daughter will develop her own boundaries more easily.

The Fundamental Things Apply

Close friends have expectations of each other that are different from those in a mother-daughter relationship. If a friend crosses a boundary and hurts our feelings, we talk about it, and if it continues, we usually choose not to spend much time with that friend, perhaps even lose contact. In contrast, the character of the mother-daughter relationship makes it much more difficult to cut ties. To avoid the trauma of distance or disconnection, daughters must participate in boundary setting, which allows for both individuality and closeness. For example, a daughter might tell her mother, "If you start commenting on my weight, I'm going to leave." Since a mother often sees her daughter as a mirror of herself, she can be quick to point out her daughter's flaws, which in turn can damage her daughter's self-esteem. The intense intimacy shared by a mother and her daughter also has a downside, for example, the freedom with which each of them says whatever she wants without constraints.

Sharon, mother of Talia, says, "I think when you feel you have the freedom to express whatever is on your mind, you risk saying things that may be hurtful. When I cross that line with Talia, she makes it clear to me that she is perfectly capable of handling the situation on her own." A mother should respect her daughter's need to individuate, which includes having her own way of doing things, creating her own style, and being in control of her own person.

The mother-daughter relationship also may involve shaming, which may occur during both public and private moments. An apparently innocuous example is when, during Thanksgiving dinner in front of the family, a mother says her daughter's makeup looks good in a tone that implies this is unusual. The daughter hears the compliment as a statement that expresses, "It must not have looked good before."

Shaming is a two-player sport. For example, in private, a daughter may lower her eyes and ask her mother, "Is that jacket hanging over there for me or for you?" When her mother answers, "For me, how do you like it?" Her daughter spits out, "Trendy" as if her mother has made the fashion faux pas from hell. Mothers and daughters can hurt each other with a single word or glance. Unlike with best friends, mothers must learn when and how to bite their tongues, and daughters need to learn to laugh to defuse the tension. We often take it for granted that someone we are close to won't be easily insulted. Boundaries are healthy because they protect our feelings.

Confidential

As our daughters get older they may begin to withhold certain information, especially if they decide our opinions will be different from what they want to hear. This separation is not necessarily negative or certain to lead to a poor relationship. The tendency to withhold may be a sign of maturity. We want our daughters to evolve into adults who are capable of making their own decisions. Part of this process is learning to keep one's own counsel and remain private about certain aspects of life. We want adult daughters to be integrated members of our family, but not subsumed by us to such an extent that they fail to develop their own sense of self. Privacy, as opposed to withdrawal, can be a good thing.

Melanie, mother of Tara says, "Tara came home from hiking in Alaska. She never told me that she was going deep into Denali National Park. If she had, I would have advised her against going there. After Tara returned home, she told me about her close encounter with being mauled by a bear! She said while she was hiking, she came across a bear with its cub. Tara came within ten feet of the bear and was petrified that the mother bear might attack her to protect her cub. She thought she was going to die. Thankfully, Tara stood still while the bear blew itself up twice her size, growled, and turned in the other direction to follow her baby. She tells me the whole story. I'm thinking, you know, some daughters keep secrets from their mothers. This story is not something I need to know!" Creating a little bit of distance from the family to find oneself is not incompatible with retaining close ties as an adult.

Trapped Door

Another important characteristic of an adult relationship is one based on mutual respect. This quality includes being mindful of what to say and when to say it. Indeed, one of the most important things we can do for our adult daughter is to listen. We need to listen to her worries, fears, and successes without making judgments. The parental role becomes one of listening more and of telling and instructing less. Advice is appropriate, but only when requested. This transition requires a lot of work and intentional behavior. Our daughter doesn't need us to take action, nor should we deliver our opinions without being asked for them. We aren't responsible for fixing her problems, and by stepping back, we're telling her we think she can handle things on her own.

Even when mothers know they should keep their mouths shut and stay out of their daughters' business, they often fail to self-edit. As one mother says, "I try, but I just can't stop myself when I see my daughter spending money she doesn't have." Mothers may think that everything in their daughters' lives is their business and responsibility. It is not.

One friend of Lana's relays the following story: "Lana's daughter had just made an 'exclusive commitment' with her boyfriend. They were at the stage of their relationship where they were comfortable discussing how they felt about each other when they first met. Lana's daughter, Stephanie, called her mom to talk about this very significant conversation. She said, 'Mom, I asked Jason what he thought of me when we first met.' Lana asked, 'What did Jason say?' Stephanie responded, 'Mom, that's my business, some things are private between me and Jason.' Lana asked again, hoping Stephanie would change her mind, but Stephanie held her ground. Lana acquiesced and said, 'You're right, honey, that is your business.'" Sometimes it takes our daughters to remind us about the importance of privacy. Small boundaries like this one can reap big rewards and alleviate some of the tension between mothers and adult daughters.

Confidentiality goes both ways. While the boundaries are more permeable between today's mothers and adult daughters, there are some parts of both a daughter's and a mom's life that shouldn't be shared. Joanne, mother of 34-year-old Kate, says, "I was thrilled to be included in Kate's bachelorette party the week before her wedding. But when the toasts began and one of her bridesmaids recounted the intimate details of her sexual escapades before she met her fiancé, I wished I wasn't there. There are many intimate details about Kate's life that I could live my whole life without knowing. I sat there with all of her friends wanting to disappear. In that moment it was crystal clear that I am not her friend, I am her mother."

Another mother echoes the same sentiment: "My daughter told me how her boyfriend prefers her to be bikini waxed. Yucch! Why did she think I was interested?" While mothers don't mind their daughters confiding in them about emotions, problems, or finances, when it comes to more intimate issues like sex, the line is clear to many of them. Most agree these topics should be discussed on a need-to-know basis only. Most mothers say, no matter how close they are with their daughters, they do not share more sensitive and intimate personal issues in their own lives, such as marriage, sex, or financial worries. A mother can demonstrate respect for her daughter's maturity by permitting her to express her opinions freely and by showing consideration for her privacy. This respect should go both ways.

Handy Mom

Many daughters expect their mothers to fix things for them, and we have to be ready to set appropriate boundaries. Our daughters see us as competent women who have resources, networks, and the ability to make life run smoothly. At this stage of our daughters' lives, setting limits is especially important because they need to become more independent and self-reliant.

It is in the best interest of both mothers and daughters to set boundaries, even if your daughter is struggling. As one mother tells us, "I lost many nights' sleep until I gave up the notion that I had control. It's not my responsibility to fix Jenna's problems. Since I've stepped back, we get along much better."

Adult daughters often regress when they need comfort. Ellen says, "I get a call on my way to work from my daughter, who lives in Portland. I pull over before I get to my office building because the signal cuts off in the underground garage. Melanie is moaning over the phone, 'Mom. My tooth cracked and it's throbbing.' I respond, 'Melanie, did you call the dentist?' 'No, because I don't want to get a crown,' she answers. I respond, frustrated, 'Melanie, what do you want from me?'

"I was so frustrated that she hadn't tried to figure out how to help herself and chose to call me instead of calling her dentist. I said, 'I have to go to my meeting now, people are waiting for me.' Melanie repeats, 'But my mouth is killing me.' 'Melanie, what do you want me to do from here? I'm eight hundred miles away from you and can't drag you to the dentist myself. Why did you call me before the dentist?' Melanie answers in a voice a decade younger than her age, 'Because you're my mom.' 'That's fine,' I say, 'but if you don't feel well, call the dentist.' "

Close friends don't demand to be saved and don't regress emotionally when rescue is unavailable. Because of the history and comfort level between most mothers and daughters, many daughters turn to their mothers to be soothed when they are feeling overwhelmed and stressed. The hard part is that sometimes this is okay, and sometimes it impedes a daughter's maturity and her ability to take care of herself. A daughter's job is to become incrementally self-sufficient; a mother's job is to make sure appropriate boundaries are set so she is able to do this.

Mistaken Identities

Because of the gender similarities, mothers have an opportunity to develop a relationship that can be mistaken for a "best" friendship. Many mothers are staying invested long past the time when their adult daughters should be making more decisions on their own, often blurring the boundary where their life ends and their adult daughter's life begins. While planning for her daughter's wedding, Pat, Lauren's mother, says, "I know I should hold my tongue, mostly because when I talk to Lauren about marriage, she keeps reminding me that I'm describing my marriage, not hers. I tell her that while I believe marriage is wonderful, it's a plot to destroy the self. This appropriately enrages her and she says, 'Stop it, Mom! I don't see it that way. That's about you, not me. I will never lose my individuality. You lost yourself. I plan on working really hard to avoid the mistakes you made.' "

Lynn, mother of 28-year-old Rachel, says she worries about Rachel's choice of a boyfriend. She is dating a perfectly nice 30-year-old man who is working as a middle-school teacher. Rachel is happy, and Lynn admits he is both very attentive to her daughter and treats her with loving respect. However, Lynn has always worried about money. She said that her insecurities stem from knowing how hard her parents worked to provide for her and her sisters. But her daughter's relationship with money is very different because Lynn and her husband were able to provide her with a comfortable life.

While Rachel doesn't share her mother's insecurities, her mother can't keep her fear to herself. Lynn admits that on many occasions she asks Rachel, "If you marry Matt, how are you going to be able to pay for luxuries like your gym membership and pedicures?" Lynn's concern is really her projection of her own insecurities. At this age, you usually have one opportunity to react and say, "I am worried about . . ." After you give your daughter one "I" message to let her know it's your own concern and may not be hers, you have to move on. If she doesn't respond, it doesn't mean she doesn't hear you. In this case, Rachel is making her own choice, which should be respected.

Daughters also can experience the same identity confusion. Christiana, 32, says, "It is hard to know where my mom ends and I begin. In fact, it takes a lot of effort. I often ask myself, 'So why am I doing this?' Why am I buying the conservative black pants instead of the edgy, fashionable ones? Am I doing it because I want to, or because my mom always said, 'High fashion is stupid. Before you know it, you'll be giving those pants away in a Hefty bag.' "

Another daughter talks about this same struggle with her mom: "I spent a lot of my twenties wanting to be different from my mom. In college, I wore Obsession perfume and my boyfriend loved it and I told my mom about it. That was it, she started using Obsession perfume, and I was thinking, eech, this is my perfume and my boyfriend really likes it and what are you doing wearing my perfume? She still wears it. She carries it around in a travel bottle." It's never a good idea to blur identities. While imitation is said to be "the sincerest form of flattery," a daughter can experience a Mini-Mother or Alpha Mother as smothering.

Separation of identities is more complicated in the parent-child relationship than it is in the best friend relationship. In a best friend relationship, imitation is more likely to be viewed as affirmation. In the parent-child relationship, imitation is more likely to be viewed as a denial of individualization. The key to healthy boundaries is whether the mother or daughter is comfortable making the same choices. If one or the other is not comfortable, then each should accept this expression of differentiation without feeling guilty. You also want to give your daughter the message that she doesn't need to be a "Mini-Me" to stay connected.

At Her Service

Without clear boundaries, mothers and daughters often clash over different expectations for each other. Some mothers find their daughters expect that they will take care of their grandchildren "at the drop of a hat." Jody, mother of two daughters, discussed this issue in one of our focus groups. She told the other mothers that her daughter asked her to babysit the next morning for her grandson, Will, while her daughter, Robin, volunteered at her toddler's preschool. Jody had a meeting scheduled at work and told Robin she couldn't watch Will. Then the meeting at work was cancelled and she said, while she really needed to use the time to do some errands for herself, she felt guilty not telling her daughter that she was available.

The other mothers in the focus group, while understanding Jody's effort to be a very involved grandmother and a supportive mother to her daughter, suggested that she complete her errands and let Robin find an alternative sitter. The group agreed that this was the perfect opportunity to set a boundary so that her daughter could view Jody's life as separate, which would sometimes compete with Robin's needs. They also gave Jody permission to help her daughter if her need to help is stronger than her need to get things done, given her tight schedule. Jody appreciated the group's support, which encouraged her to make independent choices, with an understanding of the difference between "selfishness" and "good boundaries."

Certainly, we should support our daughters when they have a valid need they cannot address readily. The goal is to find the balance between being the "chore completer" and a supportive ally. Knowing the difference is precisely why setting limits is so difficult. Susan, mother of Caroline, says, "Caroline works very long hours as an accountant. When she has to prepare financial statements, she often asks me to be her backup. I don't want to provide this kind of service on a constant basis. Caroline's husband is helpful, but they both really need 'a wife' and, believe me, that is not going to be me."

Nina, recently remarried, says, "I'm a newlywed and getting my Ph.D., I'm working, and I have two married daughters with two children. I want to spend time with my husband, have time for myself, spend time with my children, and enjoy my grandchildren. Something has to give, and the only way I know is to forfeit the time I want for myself." Finding a balance and setting limits is tricky. Appropriate boundaries allow us to voice our wants and needs without self-reproach.

One mother shares the following story concerning her daughter and the changes in their relationship when her daughter became a mother. Linda tells us, "Rebecca has become more assertive now that she has a child. She asks me to stop insisting that Isabelle needs a pacifier to sleep through the night, and she tells me when I've overstepped my bounds. Her decisiveness makes it easier for me to assert my needs as well. I don't have to worry about saying or doing too much. She lets me know when I've crossed the line. I only pick the battles that I think are important. I know Rebecca will respond honestly, and we are both careful to respect each other's wishes." A mother can guide her daughter by demonstrating appropriate limits and by showing respect for the boundaries her daughter requires.

Best of Both Worlds

It is clear that a mother should not be enmeshed in the details of her adult daughter's life. Boundaries encourage maturation. A mother must give up control over the decisions her adult daughter makes. In our focus groups, daughters express frustration with mothers who give uninvited advice or commentary. A mother also has to give up thinking of her adult daughter as a little girl. Because mothers and daughters often project onto each other, they are more likely to have conversations that are loaded with intentional or inadvertent criticism than they are to have them with their friends. Christy, 27, says, "Every time my mother offers advice or some suggestion for improvement I tense up." While Christy hears her mother's suggestion as an implied criticism, her mother may see it as an expression of caring.

Developing mutual respect minimizes misunderstandings. Roberta says, "My daughter, Lexie, gave me her house key, but I never use it without telling her I'm coming over. I call her first. I believe she is entitled to the courtesy of a phone call and to tell me that it's not a good time before I come to visit." Adhering to boundaries gives your daughter the critical opportunity to mature and be comfortable with her own decisions.

Healthy boundaries help you to step back and separate your own experience from your daughter's experience. Certainly, there are times when you make suggestions that are fair and appropriate, even though your daughter may disagree. It is important for you to keep from imposing your own preferences when it doesn't respect your daughter's thoughts and feelings, and, instead, reflects what might be more appropriate for you. However, it's human for us to want our daughters to act in ways that are familiar to us. Respect for your daughter's opinions and choices gives her the space to grow into her own adulthood, and not become a Shrinky Dink of her mom. Further, by setting appropriate boundaries with your daughter, you are modeling what she can expect from herself in all of her other relationships. Boundaries help adult daughters to establish an independent life and set their own course.

9

Tyranny of Beauty: "Mirror, Mirror, on the Wall . . ."

I am tired of the tyranny of trying to defy the odds and look younger than I am. When do we get to retire from the unrealistic demands of our culture? When can I relax in *comfort*? I think your whole life shows in your face and you should be proud of that.

—**Lauren Bacall (2008)**

Beauty Is As Beauty Does

Why discuss beauty in a book about mother-daughter relationships? Because it remains one of the principal standards by which women are judged, regardless of their age. The media and our culture define what beauty means for our daughters and for us. The narrow standards for how women should look are pervasive, and mothers and daughters struggle to meet them. Of course, this is impossible, especially when we are expected to have bodies that nature never intended. This preoccupation with physical appearance creates an opportunity for a unique understanding, as well as tremendous conflict, between mothers and daughters.

Many daughters in our focus groups feel they don't quite measure up to their mother's expectations for looking "good," and this doesn't end when they enter adulthood. One daughter tells us, "I found out that my mother was taken to the hospital. Without thinking, I grabbed my daughter, packed a quick suitcase for her, left my clothes at home, and went to the car and drove to Pennsylvania from my home in Virginia. When I arrived at the hospital, I found my mother looking scared and ill. While her first reaction was that she was happy to see me, her second was, 'What happened to your hair? It looks awful.' Without a beat I started to explain how I had run out of the house the minute I heard she was in the hospital. Then, even after I stopped myself from defending my appearance, my mother went on to say that even my father had commented on my hair. At that point, I told my mother that my father couldn't care less, especially under these circumstances!"

Regardless of their weight or body type, virtually none of the women with whom we spoke was satisfied with her body. Notwithstanding positive trends toward healthy eating and exercise, the unattainable standards of beauty and youth dominate women's thoughts, self-assessments, and relationships, including those between mothers and daughters. The media, marketers, and popular culture promote this tyranny of beauty, which does not generally apply to men.

Appearance is one of the primary expressions of self in our culture. Because most girls and young women are unhappy with their bodies, they are dissatisfied with *themselves*. Because girls and young women view the image of the anorexic fashion model as exciting and tantalizing, it has the power to make them feel diminished, no matter how normal their bodies may be. This self-concept is not limited to the young; for many women this dissatisfaction continues throughout adulthood. A February 2008 *Oprah Winfrey Show* focused on women at war with their bodies. Women were tired of obsessing about their body size, and they expressed frustration with the tape in their head telling them their arms were "jiggly" and their butts were big. In today's society you are constantly reminded of your flaws. There's a cream for everything: lighten those stretch marks, reduce your wrinkles, zap that cellulite, take away those bags from under your eyes, spray on a tan, and, while you're at it, bleach your teeth!!

Other mothers discussed the pressure for their pregnant daughters to have the perfect baby bump. Janet says, "When I was pregnant with Marisa, I bought clothes that made me feel like I was hiding my body. I could have hidden a small army of kids under my tent-shaped tops. In contrast, Marisa wore a bikini seven months pregnant and she felt sexy." While it's a step forward for women to feel good about themselves while they are pregnant and to shed the infantile baby-doll pregnancy clothes of the 1950s and 1960s, our daughters are currently fed images of celebrity mothers at their prebaby weight at six weeks post-delivery.

In addition to celebrity mothers, we are bombarded with images of airbrushed celebrities and fashion models who condition us to feel inadequate. These images affect mothers just as much as they do their adult daughters. Amy, a 56-year-old mother of one adult daughter, says, "I was outraged when I saw a cover of AARP magazine promote an article entitled, 'Look Younger, Erase Ten Years (or more).' Cut us a break, it's not even safe to accept aging in the one magazine geared for women and men over fifty!"

Modern society has created more educational and career opportunities for our daughters. Along with these advances and opportunities, however, we are saddled with this unrealistic and unattainable ideal of the perfect female. Unfortunately, the emphasis is still on looks rather than character. One mom said she remembers events, weddings, and trips by how well she felt she fit into her clothes and looked in the photos. This preoccupation takes up too much space in the lives of women. This beauty ideal is so insidious—it is ironic that even those who write and lecture about this topic struggle constantly to break free of it.

Fixation on Perfection

During the twentieth century, women's notion of self shifted. Before the development of mass production technologies—daguerreotypes, photographs, etc.—women rarely saw images of idealized beauty except through the Church. In fact, before the 1830s, beauty was not deemed attainable for ordinary women. Fast forward to present day and contrast contemporary women and girls who are bombarded with media and marketing imagery that instructs them about beauty and what they have to do to attain it. These images not only tell a woman how to become an "American beauty," they almost demand it. Now "we see beautiful people as often as we see some of our own family members, making exceptional good looks seem real and attainable."

In the Victorian era, women focused on their inner selves and placed a high value on personal and moral character. Women judged other women who worried about their looks as vain and self-absorbed. Today, adolescent girls and women are obsessed with their appearance, manifested by their fixation on body size, shape, and tone. Mothers and adult daughters both subscribe to the unattainable standards created by airbrushed and touched-up photos of counterfeit perfection. According to the Media Awareness Network images of idealized women are everywhere, urging us to believe that if we could lose a few pounds we would have a perfect marriage, loving children, great sex, and a satisfying career.

Failing to achieve this perfect vision creates anxiety and insecurity, which fuels conflict between mothers and daughters. Rita, a 26-year-old daughter, tells us, "I notice whenever I enter the room, my mother literally looks me up and down. I know she is doing a review in her head about what I am wearing, my weight, my makeup, and whether or not I measure up." These images are internalized, and when most women compare themselves to the standards we see in the media, we fall short.

Mothers need as much insight about themselves as possible. The messages girls and young women get from our culture are powerful and pervasive, and threats to their ability to be satisfied with themselves are found everywhere. These threats are much more painful and damaging when your daughter hears them from you.

Valerie Frankel, author of *Thin Is the New Happy*, tells a story about how her own mother's obsession with thinness impacted her. "As a plumpish child . . . Ms. Frankel was badgered by her mother to lose weight and bullied with cries of 'Put down that Twinkie' and 'Give me that Ring Ding,' while her skinny sister and brother snacked to their hearts' contents . . . At age eleven, she was put on a diet, and she remained on one diet or another for the next thirty years."

Your approval is important, and your judgments can cause damage to your daughter and conflict in your relationship. To be helpful, you must demonstrate that you can deal with these issues for yourself. So be careful how you express your own body image problems and other related anxieties. If you have trouble doing so, try talking to friends instead, out of your daughter's hearing.

Mixed Messages Persist

We face an assault on aging. Middle-aged women get a mixed message about their self-worth. While we are supposed to celebrate our acquired wisdom, we are bombarded with exhortations to eradicate our body changes, including the laugh lines, age spots, and wrinkles that come with this wisdom. We are encouraged to smooth our faces with fillers and paralyze our expressions with botulism. The advertisement for Botox, alone, can make you crazy, insisting that it offers us "freedom of expression," when ironically it "freezes your expressions." According to journalist Natasha Singer, author of "Skin Deep: Is Looking Your Age Now Taboo," we now have "Newer, less invasive treatments—including Botox injections to temporarily paralyze muscles beneath frown lines, Restylane injections to fill out facial creases and updated lasers to eliminate surface layers of skin—

that are easily available and relatively safe, albeit still too expensive for most people of middle-class means. These cosmetic technologies are also changing the way pop culture perceives the aging face."

In our youth-obsessed culture, which doesn't tolerate aging, especially for women, Natasha Singer writes that Rush Limbaugh had the audacity to say the following on his radio show about presidential candidate Hillary Clinton: "Will Americans want to watch a woman get older before their eyes on a daily basis? And that woman, by the way, is not going to want to look like she's getting older, because it will impact poll numbers." While there was widespread criticism about his comments, he is still on the air, continuing to make demeaning comments about women. In fact, the Drudge Report estimated that he was rewarded with a $400 million contract. Rush Limbaugh's devaluation of Hillary Clinton's candidacy based on physical appearance without consequences for his crass depiction of a successful woman, underscores the continued existence of both ageism and sexism.

It takes a very grounded woman to cope with our culture's distaste for aging and obsession with youth. The beauty of an older woman is largely unappreciated, and our acquired wisdom doesn't protect us from feeling invisible. In another article, Natasha Singer observes, "Many women . . . said they are feeling caught between nature and an anti-aging climate. Many are involved in an internal debate—a negotiation, of sorts—about how much they are willing to intervene . . . One reason for the pressure is increasing life spans. As Americans live longer, middle age has shifted to 60 from 40, with 40 recast as a youthful stage. That leaves some women grappling with the idea of what 60 looks like." It's no wonder that women feel the pressure they do to look young and attractive and struggle with the inevitability of aging.

Looking good for your age is getting harder. While many women say they just want to look good for their age, our new version of 60 requires a commitment of time and money. Today, looking good for your age means looking good for someone 10 years younger, especially if 60 is the new 50 or 40. Approval of our outside appearance is so powerful that many women who look fabulous in a size 10 are starving themselves and running on empty. The pressure to look good has increased because we are becoming more accustomed to seeing faces plumped up and smoothed over.

To be a good role model for your daughter regarding aging, a mother needs to take care of herself from the inside out. Beauty is multifaceted; it includes a healthy lifestyle, an inquiring and curious mind, and finding peace with how you look. Susan, 61, says, "I thought we had a lock on youth and we'd never age. What a shock when I filled out a survey for the Gap and had to check the last category, sixty-plus. Right now I'm wearing a tank top and cargo shorts, but the survey made me feel like I shouldn't be shopping at the Gap."

Mixed messages also persist because mothers of adult daughters are children of the 1960s or early 1970s. Aging presents a paradox for this generation of mothers because America focused on and celebrated our youth during the 1960s and 1970s. This celebration of youth, along with sayings such as, "Don't trust anyone over thirty," makes it more difficult for us to accept the fact that we are not forever young. The reality is that our daughters are now at the age we both connect with and romanticize.

Many of us feel ambivalent when we see our daughter's youthful beauty. The reality of our age creates dissonance when we look in the mirror and see a disconnect between how we think we look and how we actually appear.

Caught in the Crow's Feet

Age differences between mothers and daughters produce anxieties. We see in our daughters what we used to see in ourselves, a lifetime of endless possibilities. Many mothers talk about how they feel invisible when they walk down the street with their adult daughters. As daughters become their most beautiful selves, mothers, often in midlife, observe them as reminders of their own diminishing youth. One mother says, "No matter how fit I am, it's only about damage control. I am pushing back time. On the other hand, my daughter is in her prime. She is my younger, more beautiful, more sexual self. It's hard to be middle-aged in a world that idealizes youth." Existential angst over aging produces a natural separation between mothers and daughters.

In various ways, some mothers respond to their diminishing youth by engaging in an unspoken competition. Mothers and daughters often fail to recognize and/or discuss this competition. In the modern age of worshiping youth, it's hard not to feel marginalized as we age. Talking with close friends helps us to face the effects of aging on our self-esteem.

Margie, mother of Lisa and Emily, tells us, "I no longer feel like eyes are on me when I enter a room; I have become invisible. Last month my family vacationed in Wyoming. When I was on a horse, nobody talked to or noticed me. The horse wranglers talked to my husband, Peter, about riding technique and flirted with the girls. I felt like I was unseen. Thankfully, I talked with my girlfriends, and they knew exactly how I felt. We discussed how we no longer have to get outraged at men whistling and jeering at us on the street, because it doesn't happen anymore. My friends knew too well exactly what I was feeling." Discussing this issue with friends reminds you that you're not alone and that aging gracefully is easier to believe than to implement.

Aging forces you to see yourself as a separate person from your daughter. One way of seeing that separation is when you notice your daughter's youthfulness contrasted with your aging. She reminds you of your age; you are no longer the center of attention. This separation is healthy because you have to recognize that you are the older person, the mother; accepting this is one of the adjustments we have to make, not as a best friend, but as a mother.

Barbara, 55-year-old mother of twin adult daughters, says, "My daughters dress like hippies. They wear peasant blouses and bell bottoms. I feel kind of jaded when I tell them I've been there and done that. The fact that it is not fresh and new for me forces me to confront my age and represents something that is gone along with my youth. Somewhat cynically I've told them, 'Girls, each fashion craze should be experienced once in your lifetime. If it comes around again, like bell bottoms or hot pants, you're too old to wear it.' " Humor is a good communication tool to avoid the competitive sound of "Been there, done that."

It is damaging when you communicate your own unhappiness with and insecurity about your body to your daughter.

Twenty-nine-year-old Rebecca says, "My mother is always talking about losing weight. She hates her thighs and talks about getting liposuction. Her arms look normal to me, but she would never let the light of day shine on her upper arms. I feel bad because I'm struggling myself. How can I learn to accept myself, warts and all, when my own mother can't relax about her body?" According to Joan Brumberg's *The Body Project*, many young women ask the same question. It becomes particularly difficult to nurture a daughter's confidence in her appearance when her own mother is struggling with negative feelings about her own body.

In addition to our feelings about the size of our body, mothers have to face the changes in how our older body functions. Jill says, "Yesterday, I did Pilates with my daughter, Anna, and I have to readjust my expectations. Positions I do now in my workout hurt me. I'm not unhappy; I just need to be realistic about what I can do. Anna, on the other hand, is like a pretzel. She bent in positions I used to assume, but no more. Of course, I'm happy she's so agile, but her flexibility puts my limitations in high relief."

Nora Ephron writes about her struggle with her futile efforts to keep age at bay in her book, *I Feel Bad About My Neck*. Many women stare at the mirror endlessly checking themselves from different angles. Toni says, "I miss being someone who has the vitality imbued in my skin and hair. Now I feel faded. No matter what I do, I can't reclaim this vitality." Adds Claudia, "My daughter has that natural, fresh-scrubbed look. I can't get away with natural anymore. My face disappears without lipstick." And from Stacie, "I've always had the body of a young person. Unlike my friends, I've been comfortable with my body. But now that

I'm fifty-seven, I have to adjust to the changes and learn to stay comfortable." Toni's, Claudia's, and Stacie's struggle with feeling faded or invisible is echoed by many other mothers in our focus groups. We need to support each other, both young and old. The more we exude wisdom and grace, the more beautiful we are. We have to keep reminding ourselves that this is true!

A mother can also be sensitive to the changes in her adult daughter's appearance. "My daughter is living in New York City and feeling insecure. While walking with her in Chelsea, she said, 'Oh, my god, Mom, look around. My body's crappy and everyone is so beautiful and thin.' I struggled with my response, because my first impulse was to tell my daughter that she was letting herself get out of shape. But then I thought this judgment was my issue and I needed to support her. Instead, I said, 'Honey, how do you want to look?' and while I wanted to suggest she join a gym, I just listened to her. I am proud that I was able to suppress my own discomfort about how she looks and be supportive of her instead."

Mothers need to be sensitive to how their behavior impacts their daughters. A mother's inappropriate behavior can often create distance. Nikki, who has a thin mother, created an uncomfortable contrast to her own body. She says, "My mother and I have different body types. She is short and lean with no hips and I'm short and curvy. I always felt bigger than life next to her. By the time I was thirteen years old, I couldn't fit into her clothes. I always hated feeling bigger than my mom. I tried to take up as little space as possible, and now that I'm older, I understand that I couldn't look like my mother unless I ate cotton balls and gave up food entirely." Nikki says that her mom was always supportive about how she was built. Yet she still compared herself with her mother. Regardless of whether her mom was accepting of her, Nikki couldn't avoid unfavorable comparisons.

A New Kind of Beauty

Unlike best friends, a mother's perspective can help her daughter to realize how fleeting youthful beauty is for all of us. Debra, mother of 24-year-old Lisa, says, "Sometimes I'm comforted when I look at my niece who is eighteen years younger than me. I see her laugh lines and I'm reminded how youth is only a momentary blip in our life."

Even though we know that avoiding aging is like holding back the ocean with our hands, women experience a conflict between external and internal beauty. Women age 50 and older are at war with aging—the same women sit on both sides of this conflict. On the one hand, these women express security with aging and embrace it; on the other, they yearn to be considered younger and acknowledged in a society where aging is often hidden rather than celebrated. As we get older, we should be gratified by our accomplishments, intelligence, generosity of spirit, and abilities as caregivers. Instead, we often feel inadequate.

Consistent with cultural expectations, we are obsessed with physical perfection. Most of us are still driven by our desire to be appealing, especially to men. Unlike our daughters' best friends who are usually their peers, we have the perspective to see that they are in the early stages of becoming victims of these same false expectations. To assist them in countering the tyranny of beauty, mothers—and fathers—need to help their daughters to understand that to be truly happy and fulfilled they must try to define themselves by who they are as a person and what they are doing with their lives and not only by their physical appearance.

We have to teach our daughters that their bodies are not the primary expression of self, despite the countless seductive messages society concocts to sell goods and products. Lin, the mother of Molly, says, "I am happy that Molly has always been surrounded by women my age and older who have remained productive in their middle-age years. She will benefit from having many more role models than me. I hope that when she reaches her fifties, sixties, and seventies she will have many of these examples to call upon when she struggles with how to approach aging with grace and inner beauty." Lin adds, "I am looking for the same thing myself. I love when I see an interesting, feisty, and vibrant woman in her eighties. I use her as my muse."

We need to stop referring to our age in degrading terms. No more jokes about being over the hill and no more lying about our age. We suggest that we create a "no complaint zone" with our women friends and our daughters. We believe we can reframe middle age and older by modeling our own version of beautiful, which includes elegance, grace, style, strength, power, and dignity. When we reframe our experience of aging with enthusiasm and stand happily as adults in our own world, we provide more positive role models and an alternate reality for our daughters.

10

Lessons Learned: Close Encounters . . . of the Mothering Kind

Like Persephone, the daughter too must return in cycles to her house of stories, for it is through these stories that she will create her own.

—Suzanna Danuta Walters, *Lives Together, Worlds Apart*

Why Not Best Friends?

Mother-daughter relationships are possibly the most agonizing and the most satisfying relationships women share. This primary relationship runs the gamut of emotions and feelings, from the tremendous pride a mother can feel in her daughter's accomplishments to the genuine disappointment a daughter might feel if her mother can't respond immediately to a need. Just as we needed validation from our mothers, our daughters need validation from us. This need exists in the best and the worst of mother-daughter relationships. And though a remark such as, "You act more like your mother every day," might upset the mother or the daughter, or both, a mother is both the anchor that holds the relationship in place and the lighthouse that warns her daughter of risk.

This generation is closely connected to family and is taking longer to become adults. Our job is to advise them when asked and be patient with their incremental steps toward adulthood. One daughter describes the shift as her mother *asking* her what she needs instead of *telling* her what she needs. For adult daughters, this shift in our parenting is vital to their well-being and development. For mothers, for this shift to occur, we must create a supportive and safe environment for our daughters without putting up obstacles to their developing a self-directed life.

The most important question to ask yourself is: What can I do to empower my daughter to take care of herself, encourage a sense of well-being, and, simultaneously, sustain a positive relationship based on respectful interdependence? The intimate and unique relationship between a mother and her adult daughter is an evolving, lifetime process and is substantively different from a best friendship. Monica Pradhan, in her book about the relationship between mothers and daughters, *The Hindi-Bindi Club*, discusses this difference. Saroj, mother of 29-year-old, Preity, says, "A daughter can have any number of friends . . . she has only one mother. A mother can't forget she serves a different, *higher* purpose than a mere friend. Maybe it's the way I was brought up, but that's how I see it. I wasn't raised to be a best friend to my daughter; I was raised to present her a role model."

The Ties That Bind

The transition to adulthood is not simply a biological one; social, historical, and cultural constructs also affect this developmental stage. Understanding the impact of these constructs on our daughters helps us to empathize better with their experience. Our generation had a clear picture, a prescribed program for becoming an adult. In the past, the pressure to comply with society's expectations directed young women into a narrower range of acceptable options and life choices. Many married shortly after college or earlier and often had their first child by age 25. It was not uncommon for girls in the early 1960s to anticipate graduating with their "Mrs." degree. One mother recalls her older sister saying to her, after she became engaged during the second semester of her senior year in college, "Sherry, you just made it under the wire." Prolonged adolescence and dependence were not an option for earlier generations.

Another mother says she felt she only had two career choices, teacher or dental hygienist. Today, women have a broad range of life choices and career options—a full buffet versus just a continental breakfast. It should come as no surprise that many young women are having difficulties making choices. Many of them feel unsure about who they want to be or what they want to do.

Colleges today complain that parents are asking whether they can take class notes for their child if he or she is sick. Employers are seeing job applicants with fewer problem-solving skills, and mental health professionals are treating more and more twenty-somethings who are stressed about whether they can take care of themselves. In this uncertain environment, many adult daughters accept their parents' assistance.

Guardian Angel Mother Barbara shares the following story: The morning of her daughter, Sarah's, first post-college job interview, Barbara called to make sure was up on time. Her involvement didn't stop there. Later in the day she called Sarah to get a full report of the interview and advised her to follow up with a thank-you note. By the third interview, Barbara felt frustrated that Sarah didn't seem to be prepared to function independently in her own job search. She was surprised that Sarah seemed a beat behind, always waiting for her mother's cue.

But how could it be any different? Barbara had enabled this behavior. She searched for Sarah's job opportunities, helped her to write her resumé, Googled the company after the interview was scheduled, and acted as her human alarm clock. Her extensive intervention in Sarah's life has prevented Sarah from learning how to be responsible for herself. Thus far, Barbara has not taught Sarah the necessary adult life skills that would enable Sarah to take better care of herself. These missed "teachable moments" deny her daughter the opportunity to learn personal responsibility and maintain appropriate boundaries, two of the contemporary characteristics of adulthood. This symbiotic type of relationship may appear to be a friendship, but it is merely excessive and counterproductive parenting. Many mothers are struggling with setting boundaries and finding balance.

Access has given our daughters the sense that we are instantly available to meet their every need; this is not friendship. Even if daughters feel comfortable enough to ask their mothers for help, as adults, they may want to consider asking themselves, "Is this something I should ask my mother to do?" We believe it is okay to provide our daughters with support but it is more important to model and teach them self-reliance and for daughters to assume more and more personal responsibility.

Enabling dependent behavior may cause adult children to feel guilty and resentful, even when they ask for our help. Every time a parent rescues a daughter who doesn't need to be rescued, that parent gives her the message that he or she doesn't believe their daughter can survive without their help. We don't want our daughters to feel this way and they don't want to be dependant any longer than they have to.

Support, which is different from enabling behavior, should be given without conditions. Whether it is emotional or financial, there should be no strings attached. At the same time, you must allow yourself to withhold support when you are uncomfortable giving it, especially when it requires you to make a sacrifice to subsidize something you think is unnecessary. Given the economic conditions, parents have to be more careful about their resources. Once support is offered, adult daughters should expect it to be given freely, based on understood and agreed-to terms. Whether your daughter is living at home or living on her own, individual family expectations should be considered.

Today's parents of adult daughters can no longer count on turning that unused bedroom into a guest room. When adult children return home, mothers find themselves, once again, struggling with problems such as stocking the refrigerator with food, planning family dinners, waiting up for a daughter to arrive home in the early morning hours, sharing a bathroom with a daughter who may take over her beauty products, and finding her favorite cashmere sweater in her daughter's overnight bag or underneath the sofa. If your daughter returns with a husband and child, things are very different. In addition to the new family members she has brought with her, she likely will arrive with equipment that fills the entire house, dirty laundry and child-friendly detergent, and, sometimes, a freezer filled with breast milk. Both parents and adult daughters must learn to make adjustments quickly, establish new rules, and negotiate responsibilities.

Great Adaptations

We had so much invested in having our kid be the best. We believed that, with enough effort, we could make anything happen. We were so good at everything, including working and maintaining the family and fixing everything—even serving as private tutors. This expectation persists in our adult daughters. Even as many of them have become mothers themselves, we have continued to be mothers, rather than taking on the more traditional grandmother role. Because women value affiliation over self-enhancement, mothers make substantial sacrifices for their children. Full-time working mothers reduce their work schedules to help their daughters juggle the competing demands of work and home. Grandmothers in the majority culture are now also raising and/or caring for their grandchildren, as is the norm in other cultures.

Daughters often look to their mothers for help with their

children. It is harder with children today because they have less freedom and can't play outside as we did. Play dates have to be arranged, carpooling has to be scheduled, and babysitters can cost $10 an hour and more. All of these stressors bring daughters closer to their mothers, especially if they live in the same city. Even when they don't live in the same city, mothers are expected to pitch in.

Arlene says, "When Zoe has the baby, she's going to be as clueless as I was. She and Ben have no idea of the overwhelming feeling of parenthood. Zoe expects me to move in with them when the baby's born. Two weeks is plenty for me. My daughter is due in four weeks, and I plan to fly to San Francisco to be with them. I offered to help my son-in-law with planting bulbs in the garden. He has been nesting by planting and fixing up the outdoors. Ben says, 'Oh, no. We need you to be with the baby 24/7.' I kept my mouth shut, but thought, 'Oh, my god, I am really expected to be the baby nurse.'" By having these expectations, Zoe and Ben are casting Arlene in the role of a Guardian Angel Mother, without her permission and against her better judgment.

Regardless of taking on child care responsibilities, grandparenting is a joy. Virtually every grandmother in our focus groups says that she now knows why full-time parenting is for the young, and, while they adore being with their grandchildren, they also relish saying good-bye, shutting the door behind them, kicking off their shoes, and having a glass of wine. Many grandmothers can enjoy their grandchildren because they are free of the day-to-day anxieties of decisions, discipline, planning playdates, and making school choices. It's no longer your job to micromanage their world. Your job is to enjoy your grandchildren and indulge them. Grandchildren keep us young because we get to see the world through their eyes. How else would you know *Hannah Montana*, *High School Musical*, or Wii Fit? Even though we have a more limited role than parents do, many grandparents are the ones who can make a child feel really special.

According to author Naomi Lowinski in her book *Stories From the Motherline*, women in middle age have the opportunity of knowing themselves as an adult daughter, mother of an adult daughter, and grandmother. Therefore we understand and experience the struggle of separating from our own mother while wanting closeness with our daughter. This allows a mother the potential for knowing herself across generational life-cycle transitions. Middle age puts us smack in the middle of our past, present, and future.

Mothers are the touchstone for their family. We are the institutional memory for our family rituals and cultural imperatives, and a repository for the evolution of the role of women. In a stressful time, mothers can provide a safe harbor. As mothers, we can provide a foundation on which our daughters (and sons) can build a future. We can provide them with knowledge, skills, and opportunities to build their self-confidence. All of these are tasks for parents, not best friends.

Benefit of the Doubt

As we are completing the book, the lessons learned are brought into high relief by our own experiences as well as those of the mothers we interviewed. One mother, Jodi, tells us that, as she was reviewing the draft of this book, her daughter was considering moving across the country. She raised her daughter with the understanding that she could be anything and do anything as long as she had the will, perseverance, and skills. Much to Jodi's surprise, her daughter, Mia, is going to move across country. Mia keeps telling her mom that the only thing preventing her from doing this is her relationship with her parents. But Mia's husband, Ben, is from San Jose, California, and wants to move back to the West Coast. Mia has been living in Boston, and Jodi lives in Providence, which was close enough to be able to visit for a day. This mother is concerned because visiting her grandchild more than twice a year won't be possible.

For a mother, this is where "the rubber hits the road." Jodi has to deal with boundary issues, giving advice only when asked, accepting her daughter's ability to make decisions for herself, and biting her tongue about her desire for her daughter to live closer. She did slip and tell her daughter that California is prime for a major earthquake in the next thirty years, and she went on to say that there is a 99 percent chance of such a quake! The lesson here, albeit not an easy one, is that it's her daughter's life, and Mia is entitled to go where she wants to go without a heavy heart. For both mother and daughter, the distance doesn't mean they can't have a close relationship, it's just harder. Keeping in touch has to be a priority for both of them.

Distance isn't the only challenge for mothers and adult daughters. Another mother, Betsy, told us of an opposite experience. Her daughter, Sarah, lives close to her family. Sarah assumes that, when she has a hard day, she can call her mother, who will drop whatever she is doing and help out. This can be ideal as long as there is mutual respect and not a sense of entitlement. When you live in close proximity, it becomes vitally important to have boundaries that permit a mother to say no and have her own life without suffering pangs of guilt.

A mother-daughter relationship is a work in progress. A positive adult relationship gives one another the benefit of the doubt, has empathy, and allows for differences of opinion. These factors in a mother-daughter relationship obviously apply to friendships as well. However, unlike friendships, mother-daughter relationships have a strong emotional and psychological component as well as a built-in hierarchy.

Many of our parenting decisions are made in reaction to something uncomfortable we experienced as the daughter of an Alpha Mother. Kathleen, daughter of an Alpha Mother and mother of Stella, says, "When I was a new mother, of course, I wasn't sleeping, and when I'm sleep-deprived it is all I can think about. When I complained about the exhaustion to my mother, she said very offhandedly, 'Kathleen, nobody ever died from lack of sleep.' Although I know her comments weren't mean-spirited, what I was looking for was a little empathy. All she had to say was, 'It's hard to be tired.' I wasn't really looking for anything else but an opportunity to express myself and be understood.

"My mother would constantly offer what I'm sure she felt was useful advice to improve my child-rearing. For example, 'Kathleen, you really shouldn't be giving Stella a snack; it's too close to dinner,' or 'Put long pants on her when she rides her bicycle.' Although my mother felt her advice was helpful, I heard it as judgmental and critical. Over time I had more insight, and my relationship with my mother improved. I experienced her 'constructive criticism' as less hurtful."

Kathleen continues, "My experience with my own mother has taught me many things. First, I learned to be careful not to misinterpret complaining and to be more respectful when my daughter expresses her discomforts. Second, to be aware that advice is not necessarily heard as positive and constructive." Kathleen learned to validate her daughter's feelings by paying attention to her past and changing some behavior that frustrated her as a daughter. Understanding the past provides you, as a mother, with knowledge and insights that enable you to be less reactive and to think before you speak. The truth is that there is no objective reality. What is important is that you understand how you felt as a daughter and adjust your parenting to maximize the positive feelings you experienced and minimize the negative ones. As we see from Kathleen's story, for many mothers, their experience as daughters informs their experience as mothers. Mothers in our focus groups tell us how the lessons learned from their more challenged relationships with their own mothers taught them how to do it differently. Best friends do not have to deal with this dynamic.

The mother-daughter relationship has some attributes of friendship, but it is not a best friendship. Mothers and daughters are never at the same stage of life at the same time. Mothers will always have experienced more years than their daughters. One mother refers to this divide as the "wisdom gap." Alternatively, mothers and daughters share so many common experiences. These common threads provide our generation of mothers and daughters with many opportunities to develop a satisfying adult relationship, one that isn't static, but, rather, is constantly evolving.

A mother's desire to be friends with her daughter often conflicts with her daughter's need to individuate. Conflict between these opposing objectives can cause hurt feelings for both. Most mothers and daughters want to have a meaningful, intimate relationship while maintaining their own identities and points of view. This is why interpersonal boundaries are so necessary to both their emotional well-being and their ability to develop a healthy and close adult relationship. This is also why boundaries between mothers and daughters are necessarily different from social boundaries between best friends. The lives of mothers and daughters are so entwined that the lines between them are often blurred. Between friends, communication is frequently less censored and emotionally loaded. Between best friends, boundaries are clearer and less burdened with issues of individuation and family ties.

All mature adults need to establish suitable boundaries for themselves and respect those of others. A mother who successfully raises her daughter to be independent will have an easier time accepting her daughter's choices. This is not an easy thing to do, even when you are acting intentionally to raise her to be her own person. In contrast, best friends can be engaged without feeling self-conscious and with much less risk of conflict.

Sometimes there is that seminal moment that teaches us a lesson and reminds us of this new relationship with our adult daughters. Nancy, mother of 30-year-old Carrie, tells us, "Carrie called me when she went into labor, and my husband and I rushed to the hospital for the birth of our first grandchild. When I got to the maternity floor I asked the nurse how Carrie was doing. The nurse said, 'I'm sorry but the HIPAA [Health Insurance Portability and Accountability Act] privacy rules prohibit me from giving you any information.' I said, 'But it's my daughter, not a stranger I'm asking about!' This was the first time my role as mother held no weight. I was surprised to have the hospital deny me information about my own child's well-being. I thought, how ironic, my daughter was giving birth to her child, and one day she would also be denied information about her child's well-being. The circle of life just smacked me in the face."

"I'll Be There"

There are mothers who describe their relationships with their daughters as special, but not as best friends. In many of our stories, daughters and mothers prefer that mothers stay mothers and daughters want them that way. Leslie, mother of a 26-year-old daughter, says, "My daughter and I are not 'best friends.' I will always be too protective of her to ever pour out the full contents of my heart, even if I thought she would be sympathetic. I'm sure she won't let me know everything that's troubling her. And no matter how close we are, she says I will always be her mother. My daughter tells me, 'My friends wouldn't badger me to wear sunscreen higher than SPF fifteen.' "

Adult daughters also report that, in their twenties and thirties, they share time with their mothers because they want to, not out of obligation. Heather, 23, tells us, "When I was younger I would be upset if I didn't have plans with friends over the weekend, but now it's fun to spend time with my mom. We have a lot in common." Lola, mother of 26-year-old Terri, says, "I'm not sure I'd say my daughter is my best friend, although I love to be with her. I think she needs 'best friends' that are her age that she can be free to talk with about anything. I've heard her say that I am her best friend. That's kind of scary for me; for whatever reason, I think she needs to separate from me in a way that allows us to be close, but not best friends."

Individuation is a delicate balancing act between establishing separation and having mutual respect. In a *New York Times* article about mothers and daughters, Stephanie Rosenbloom wrote, "When Nia Tyler, 24, moved from New York to Boston for a new job with a nonprofit organization that trains school principals . . . Nia said, 'My mother came up here to talk and just guide me through. My mom is my support.' Nia added that she and her mother discuss everything from the necessity of having food staples in the house to what it means to be a black woman in America. 'She's my eyes and ears when I can't see or hear things for myself.'"

A close mother-daughter relationship has the potential to be a great source of understanding and fulfillment for each of them. After all, who has more in common? They share biology, history, culture, religion, and the experience of being women, mothers, and workers. These commonalities provide a foundation for connection. As Dr. Lee Sharkey says, "No relationship is quite as primal as the one between a mother and her daughter."

"Making Pre–Betty Friedan Choices in a Post–Betty Friedan World"

Dr. Mudita Rastogi, Associate Professor of Psychology at Argosy University/Chicago, reports, "Past literature shows that the mother-daughter relationship is considered the most significant of all intergenerational relationships. The reasons why mothers and daughters become estranged can be varied and complex. Most of us are trapped in cultural expectations of our societal roles.

Society expects women to be good mothers; if they fail, they are considered 'bad women.' "

"Mothers, rather than fathers, are held responsible for good parenting," adds Dr. Karen Eriksen. "In some instances, women haven't been well-prepared for these parenting responsibilities." This is a burden women carry, regardless of culture.

As mothers, we have the privilege of owning our own history. This means that age provides us with the opportunity to acknowledge who we are, where we come from, what our limitations are, and what we can and can't do. That kind of honest assessment is so important to pass on to our daughters. This is something every mother can do for herself and her daughter. We have much to offer our daughters as they are coming of age in their twenties and thirties.

Mothers of today's daughters have fought to ensure that their daughters have many choices. Our task now is to assist our daughters to overcome the next hurdle, which is assessing their options rather than being overwhelmed by them. Sometimes our daughter's choice includes making a decision that is a departure from what is expected. In this instance, mothers don't do their daughters a favor by trying to insulate them from unpleasant experiences or intolerance, which, in any event, is impossible. The most a mother can do is to talk honestly about problems her daughter may face and give her a "heads-up" if she sees potential conflict. In contemporary society, our daughters accept racial, religious, and cultural differences more readily. Either we prepare ourselves to accept this new reality, or we set ourselves up to risk losing our daughters. This is our choice.

With enmeshed empathy for their daughters, mothers may

suffer not only their own, but also their child's, stress from conflict. Detached engagement is critical for us to stay close while maintaining some degree of objectivity, so we can give our daughters the message that we have confidence in their ability to take care of themselves. Words like "separation," "individuation," "autonomy," and "differentiation" lead us to be either "too much" mother or "too little" mother. We need to change this oversimplified perception. As Betty Frain and Eileen Clegg explain in *Becoming a Wise Parent for Your Grown Child*:

> *There is a fine line between sharing wisdom and meddling, and there are few guideposts for finding that line. Traditional rules that used to govern intergenerational relationships have changed. As a result, adult children need loving support from their parents more than ever in our increasingly complex society. Love is the beginning, but sometimes love isn't enough to sustain relationships when delicate moral issues arise, or when parents are troubled by the paths their children choose. It takes creativity, self-awareness, and often a saintlike tolerance for ambiguity if parents are to maintain healthy relationships with their grown kids.*

Maternal Truths

We need to listen to our daughters' complaints and frustration and validate their sense of reality. We need to acknowledge their points of view, even when we disagree. We also need to give them the message that we believe they are competent and able to take charge of their own lives. We need to encourage and teach them how to be considerate of us. We very well may be around into our nineties. As older women we desire to support our daughters by sharing the wisdom we have attained over the decades of our lives. At the same time, we need to trust our daughters' experiences and perspectives, which sometimes takes a leap of faith. They see the world through different eyes. If we offer our wisdom with humility, we can help guide our daughters while affirming their worth. Adrienne Rich says, "As the mother is conceived an agent in her own right, so the daughter can claim this agency for herself. The mother can expand her daughter's horizon, quite simply and quite difficultly, by expanding her own." That is, by modeling the woman she hopes her daughter can become. We must be intentional, maintain our sense of humor, and have perspective if we want a positive relationship with our daughters. Anything is possible, but only if we stay connected.

Much of the overindulgent parenting of the 1980s and 1990s has made the relationship between mothers and daughters more complicated. It's harder to individuate, harder for us to say no, and harder for our daughters to accept no. Our culture and our parenting have made our daughters fearful of making mistakes, which contributes to many of our daughters relying on old patterns of dependence rather than trying to manage adulthood themselves. Many of us continue to behave as if we have the ability to make our daughters perennially happy, sheltering them from frustration, disappointment, and failure.

The smaller generation gap encourages a new kind of interdependence and closeness, making it important to mothers that our daughters like us. This new expectation raises some difficulties for maintaining healthy boundaries. Nobody prepares us for this new stage of parenting; there is no blueprint. As one mother said, "You can't tell your twenty-five-year-old to go to her room."

Although we are less concerned with hierarchy and more focused on developing an adult relationship, closeness doesn't obliterate the distinctions between the mother and child roles. Popular culture sometimes confuses us by marketing the misconception that today's mothers and daughters are peers, implicitly suggesting that they can be best friends. As our daughter matures, a friendship can develop, but the role of *mother* always trumps the role of *friend*. Her maturity does not end your mentoring or caretaking roles. Unconditional love exists only in the parent-child relationship. It's simple; you can't be best friends with your daughter. You are her Perfectly Imperfect Mother.

11

Strategies: Strengthening Healthy Connections

I have found the best way to give advice to your children is to find out what they want, and then advise them to do it.

—Harry Truman

We believe mothers and their adult daughters can't be best friends, but they can develop a gratifying relationship. Turbulence happens when a mother can't accept her daughter as an adult. The basic question for mothers is: Do you trust your daughter to be an independent and self-sufficient woman? And can you support her in making choices and doing things differently from how you would do them? Control is elusive, even when your daughter is younger, and it certainly is less appropriate when she is an adult. One of the most important messages you can give to your daughter is your permission to let her be herself, and as she becomes an adult, you should expect that same acceptance from her.

We want to avoid some of the dysfunctional patterns that may have occurred when our daughters were younger. What we say to our daughter as an adult, she may still hear with the ears of her younger self. We have to be more cautious with adult daughters, because we want them to hear us with their adult selves. According to Jane Isay, author of *Walking on Eggshells: Navigating the Delicate Relationship Between Adult Children and Parents*, parents should "keep their mouths shut and their doors open."

All of us have to accept at this point in our child's development that we did the best we could, and we should not focus our attention on "what could have been," or be filled with regrets. Instead, we have to keep our focus on what's really important: maintaining a good relationship. We want to establish elements of a friendship, intimacy, mutual respect, respectful interdependence, and sharing the good and bad times, understanding that our primary role is that of mother, and not best friend. No one else can occupy that space. This should be payoff time, when you are still healthy and vital, and she is, finally, an adult.

Some Basic Principles for Parenting Adult Daughters

Based on our personal and professional experience, research, and the wisdom offered by mothers in our focus groups, we have developed some overarching principles to assist you in finding your own answers. These principles include:

- Address your adult daughter in a manner that encourages effective communication and respectful interdependence.
- Becoming an adult is a learning process, and so is developing a positive and nurturing new way of parenting your adult daughter; so give yourself a break.
- Be flexible in determining what is appropriate to meet your child's needs as well as your own.
- Make a decision based on the lessons you would like your adult daughter to learn, not on the results you may want.
- Be open to the choices your adult daughter makes, even when those choices may not be the ones you would make.
- Believe that your adult daughter is okay and can stand on her own, and let her know that.

To implement these principles, we have created the following strategies for your consideration. We believe these strategies can help guide you to developing and sustaining a positive and rewarding relationship with your adult daughter. As was the case when your daughter was younger, parenting is never linear. Realize that all relationships have downsides. A mother and daughter should focus on the positive aspects of their relationship. The most important advice is to hang in there and invest time and energy into your relationship. Encourage your daughter's sense of well-being, while also taking care of yourself. It is okay to take a breath and enjoy!

Strategies for Mothers: A Baker's Dozen

GIVE ADVICE ONLY WHEN ASKED.

- Communicate directly and in a straightforward manner.
- Keep your remarks to the present; try not to rehash things from when your daughter was a young girl.
- Refrain from hovering; such behavior is no longer appropriate for an adult daughter.
- Avoid giving unsolicited advice that may risk your daughter's pulling away from you.
- Be intentional about the way you offer advice; be careful to give advice without judgment. Begin with statements such as, "Have you ever considered?" Being less judgmental will mean your daughter will be more likely to listen to what you are saying.
- Be clear in your intentions. Saying "Don't call me" and then being upset because she doesn't call sends a mixed message.
- Provide real support when your daughter asks for advice by telling her the truth as you see it. She has to trust that you will give her an authentic reality check.
- Avoid discussing weight, clothing, and hairstyles unless she asks for your opinion.
- Avoid words like "should," "must," and "ought."

- Be positive and respectful of her feelings and accept that, although she may seek your advice, she may come to a different conclusion.

BE AN ACTIVE LISTENER.

- Talk to your daughter in a collaborative way by seeking her input and listening very closely to her.
- Ask your daughter if she wants to talk; let her talk through what she is feeling without rushing her.
- Refrain from fixing her pain and concentrate on expressing empathy with expressions such as, "I know how difficult this must be." Your goal is to listen to her, not to try to influence her.
- Anticipate that there will be disagreements, but this doesn't mean that either of you has to withdraw from the relationship or stop listening to the other. Trust and communication is a two-way street and takes vigilance.
- Discuss issues openly and stay engaged. Compromise is key.
- Be aware of your body language; remember that 95 percent of communication is nonverbal.
- Listen empathetically and validate your daughter's feelings.

DEVELOP AND MAINTAIN APPROPRIATE BOUNDARIES.

- Keep from imposing your own views when it doesn't respect your daughter's thoughts and feelings about what is good for her, rather than what may be more appropriate for you.

- Be clear; don't set boundaries for the wrong reasons, such as trying to manipulate your daughter. Don't allow grown children to manipulate you, nor should you manipulate them.
- Set boundaries about when you are willing to provide assistance without guilt.
- Try to be as consistent as possible about setting limits. Helping your daughter to set limits gives her an opportunity to develop and practice problem-solving skills.
- Be direct and phrase things as "I" messages, such as, "I would like to see you," rather than, "Why don't you ever visit me?" The goal is to express your need, not to make your daughter feel guilty for disappointing you and failing to meet your needs and expectations. The danger of delivering a message that creates guilt is that your daughter may stay away from you to avoid your disappointment, which prevents you from attaining the intimacy and connection you desire.
- Think through what your goals are. Sometimes you may want her to listen and value what you are saying, other times you may want her to change her behavior. You are always more effective if you know what you want.
- Avoid quid pro quo.
- Respect your daughter's privacy and expect her to have respect for your privacy as well.
- Don't overburden your daughter with your problems. There are some parts of your life that should be kept private, and

vice versa. For example, bedroom details. "My mom has no shame when it comes to sex," says Julia, 27 years old. "She tells me about her lingerie purchases or asks what moves my husband is up to. I like her in my life, but sharing that part grosses me out."

- Don't be too buddy-buddy: It's a rare mother and daughter that can be best friends because there will always be a generation gap, says Christiane Northrup in her book, *Mother-Daughter Wisdom*. And there are some parts of your life that you and your daughter just shouldn't discuss. Sure, you can tell her how much fun you had at a party last night, but do you really want to brag that you did three shots of tequila—while wearing a lampshade (and not much else)? Sharing that kind of info "crosses a boundary," says Northrup.
- Don't be a punching bag. Because you may be your daughter's safest and most available target, she may lash out at you. But remember, it's not your responsibility to manage your daughter's anger.
- Coach your daughter rather than do things for her.

ACCEPT YOUR DAUGHTER FOR WHO SHE IS.

- Give your daughter permission to be herself. She may not tell you this, but she still wants your approval.
- Be tolerant of change.
- Praise her effort, not the results.

- Listen to your daughter and tell her you respect and admire her for how she handles herself and the decisions she makes. Of course, this praise must be genuine.
- Acknowledge your daughter's sense of reality. If she says she doesn't have any friends, don't deny her reality by telling her she is wrong because she was invited to "so and so's" engagement party last year. Instead, strategize with her about how she can find ways to make some friends. If she tells you she's panicked about taking the GMATS, don't tell her not to worry—just mirror or reflect back to her so you don't discount her feelings.
- Create enough separation so you no longer take responsibility for her bad manners. As an adult, her behavior should no longer reflect on you. If she doesn't write thank-you notes, it's about her.
- Accept your daughter's timetable for doing things, even if it kills you. You have to accept that your daughter will do things differently from you. If she was sloppy as a teenager, she may be sloppy as an adult. Unless you want to keep cleaning up after her, you need to "turn the other cheek."
- Remember, you learned from your mistakes, and it's time for her to learn from hers as well.
- Don't take out your anger and disappointment for who she isn't on your daughter.
- Help her to understand that she has the power to make her own life choices and you want to encourage her to exercise that power.

ACCEPT BEING A PERFECTLY IMPERFECT MOTHER.

- Know yourself first and forgive your imperfections. If you forgive yourself for not being an ideal parent, you provide a much more powerful role model for your daughter. What more powerful way is there, after all, to communicate to your daughter that no matter what life brings her, when she stumbles and when she soars, she'll be acceptable not just to you, but to herself as well?
- Don't view your daughter's struggles or frustrations as proof that you aren't a good mother. You may recognize this as Winnicott's "good enough" mother who prepares her child perfectly for adulthood. She understands that by being imperfect, she is helping her daughter learn to face adversity while she is there to help her adjust, cope, and persevere. Don't try to be a perfect mother because that creates an impossible ideal, one that no daughter can emulate or live up to.
- Give your daughter the message that you want and expect her to be a moral and responsible person, to have the strength to make her own choices, and to appreciate her own abilities and talents.
- Understand that your daughter may make very different choices in life; don't interpret this as a rejection of yourself or evidence of bad mothering.
- Value your daughter's feelings and see them as an opportunity for intimacy.

- Work at tolerating your daughter's anger and frustrations and don't give her verbal and nonverbal messages that you are uncomfortable with these feelings. Remember, you only have to listen; you don't have to fix it.
- Don't dictate how your daughter should look or feel. For example, try not to say things such as, "Don't frown, you look prettier when you smile."
- Tell the truth.

STEP BACK, BUT DON'T DISENGAGE.

- To support your daughter, try a skill we call "engaged detachment." Engaged detachment requires close involvement, but with a sense of perspective. Engaged parenting includes being empathetic, acting as a sounding board, and providing objective coaching.
- Empathize rather than overly identify with your daughter. If you don't step back, it is easier to lose perspective.
- Check your emotional temperature. When you can think clearly, you are much more able to refrain from making things bigger than they are.
- Don't jump in to save your daughter from making mistakes. This allows her to experience the natural consequences of her decisions. Only a victim needs to be rescued.
- "Hold and guide" your daughter, which requires affection, understanding, and active listening rather than "doing for

her." This behavior gives your daughter the opportunity to solve problems on her own with appropriate support.

- Communicate via e-mail or in writing when things get really hard and you think you will say things that you will regret. Somehow, putting down one's thoughts on paper, and then editing and rewriting one's words can offer a calmer perspective and prevent impulsive and angry reactions. Visualize that what you write will be above the fold in the *New York Times*. In other words, allow some breathing space before continuing the conversation . . . or find another way to communicate without speaking directly.
- Bite your tongue or duct tape your mouth when necessary!
- Encourage your daughter to have her own voice, thoughts, and opinions. This is your time to step back.

TREAT YOUR DAUGHTER AS AN ADULT.

- Try to work problems out collaboratively.
- Value her advice.
- Respect her capabilities.
- Share more of what is going on in your life without burdening her.
- If you are feeling unappreciated, explain to your daughter how you want your relationship to change.
- Be clear in your intentions and continue to model the behavior you would like your daughter to emulate.

- Agree to disagree when resolution doesn't seem imminent to maintain communication.
- Accept that "mother doesn't always know best." Let her be.

HAVE FUN TOGETHER!

- Focus on the positive aspects of your relationship and invest time and energy in them.
- Plan activities to do together; conversations are much more casual and exchanging information is more likely.
- Develop mother and daughter traditions; it's never too late to begin new ones.
- Remember to use humor!

DEVELOP AND MAINTAIN RESPECTFUL INTERDEPENDENCE.

- Show appreciation and affection.
- Develop a balance between letting your daughter go and being a nurturing parent of an adult daughter.
- Build trust with your daughter, and she will be more receptive to your involvement in her life.
- Respect her autonomy; this is a critical component in building trust and mutual respect.
- If your adult daughter moves back home, model the kind of mutual respect adults should have for each other. Living

with an adult daughter can present opportunities and challenges in maintaining a close relationship. Basic courtesies should be expected and should go both ways. You are not running a hotel; it is your home. You should feel comfortable expressing your needs and expectations.

RESPECT YOUR DAUGHTER'S NEW FAMILY.

- Step back and give them time to develop their new identity as a couple.
- Allow her to establish the roots of her new marriage/commitment and understand that this is an important part of a healthy transition.
- Accept and enjoy your new status as the second, rather than the first, "go-to" person in your daughter's life.
- Don't get in the middle of arguments or disputes between your daughter and her spouse/partner.

BE THE GRANDMOTHER, NOT THE MOTHER.

- Encourage, support, and, once again, bite your tongue!
- Continue to nurture your daughter. Being a new mother is very stressful.
- Provide a comforting and friendly ear.
- Provide kind and reassuring attention.
- Assist and help when you can.

- Speak up if you see a threat to your grandchild's safety. At times your advice will be welcome. But you may have to remind yourself from time to time that you've had your turn!
- Enjoy your grandchildren!

DON'T PERSONALIZE YOUR DAUGHTER'S DISAPPOINTMENTS.

- Separate your own feelings when you interact with your daughter.
- Support your daughter without attaching blame. For example, no matter what you feel about the end of your daughter's marriage, this is not the time to attach blame. Her ex may be less than likeable, but you don't want to jeopardize any further relationship, because they may get back together and/or he may be the father of your grandchildren.
- Share your own feelings of disappointment with your spouse and/or friends.

MAINTAIN THE MOTHER-DAUGHTER BOND.

- Sustain your relationship with your adult daughter. In some ways it doesn't matter how you do it, it's just important that you do it.
- Be respectful of her schedule and lifestyle if you want to be included in her life.
- Say what you need and want. During this transition time, you can repair a broken relationship with your daughter or begin a new one.

- Let your daughter know you love her no matter what.
- Maintain your role as the mom. Mother trumps best friend every time.

Advice for Daughters

- Your mother wants to feel loved and appreciated for making you the wonderful adult you are. She wants you to call and sincerely say, "Mom, how was your day?"
- Your mother wants to be included in your life. If you don't have time to see her, try to say it nicely. It never hurts to be considerate and protect her feelings.
- Realize it's difficult for some mothers to stop seeing their adult daughters as younger daughters.
- Try to understand your mother's life circumstances, the choices she makes, and the challenges she faces, especially when you are engaged in minor conflicts.
- Learn to live within the consequences of your conduct and be prepared for your mother's disapproval when you make a decision with which she disagrees.
- Be clear in your intentions; you want to be talked to as an adult. Continue the dialogue even when the going gets tough.

Regardless of age, your children remain your children. Their increasing maturity does not bring an end to your caretaking role, it merely changes the ways in which you execute this role. Parenting adult daughters can be much more difficult than parenting children. There are no road maps or manuals on what to say or do, and you must proceed without knowing what lies ahead. The pattern of more than two decades has ended, and you and your daughter must adjust to new roles: her economic independence, her role as wife or partner, and her role as mother. Both mother and daughter have to adjust to a new order, where the relationship is more equitable. Maintaining the balance among caretaker, companion, and trusted confidant; guiding your child without taking charge; and helping your daughter to carry out her own solutions is your new role. Take a breath and enjoy, and, as the saying goes: "If you love something, let it go; if it comes back to you, it is yours forever."

NOTES

vii "If a girl never learns . . .": Morrison, Toni. *Lives Together/Worlds Apart: Mothers and Daughters in Popular Culture.* Suzanna Danuta Walters, ed. Berkeley: University of California Press, 1992, p. 234.

CHAPTER 1

7 " 'I want her to hold on to pieces of my vine . . .": Steinhauer, Jennifer. "In the Hospital, Mrs. Edwards Sets Campaign's Fate." *New York Times*, March 25, 2007.

10 "In 1960 only 40 percent . . .": Clark, Sandra Luckett, and Weismantle, Mia. *Employment Status: 2000.* Census 2000 Brief, U.S. Census Bureau. Washington, D.C.: U.S. Department of Education, 2002.

10 "Sixty percent of married women . . .": Kuo, Yu-Chen. "Fertility and Labor Prospects in the United States, 1960–2000." Ph.D. dissertation. Texas: A&M University, 2005.

10 "Mothers are still more likely . . .": Pew Research Center. (2007/7/12). "Fewer Mothers Prefer Full-time Work: From 1997–2007." See pewresearchcenter.org/pubs/536/working-women (accessed September 2, 2008).

10 "Wives now work for pay . . .": Lang, Molly Monahan, and Risman, Bar-

bara J. *A "Stalled" Revolution or a Still-Unfolding One? The Continuing Convergence of Men's and Women's Roles.* Discussion paper prepared for the 10th Anniversary Conference of the Council on Contemporary Families. Chicago: University of Chicago, May 4–5, 2007.

11 "Centers for Disease Control and Prevention . . .": Yabroff, Jennie. "The Feminine Mistakes." *Newsweek*, April 28, 2004. See http://www.newsweek.com/id/132891 (accessed May 29, 2008).

13 "A recent study of sixty public universities . . .": Robb, Amanda. "Look! Up in the Sky! It's a Bird! It's a Plane! It's . . . Supermom!" *O: The Oprah Magazine*, July 2008, p. 212.

14 "Some parents will go so far . . .": Robb, 212.

16 "We cannot tell one story of mothers . . .": Walters, Suzanne. *Lives Together Worlds Apart: Mothers and Daughters in Popular Culture.* Berkeley: University of California Press, 1992, p. 234.

17 "Today more than 60 percent . . .": Levine, Susan. "All Grown Up with No Place to Go." *Washington Post*, June 4, 2002, B1. *See also*: Paul, Pamela. *The Starter Marriage and the Future of Matrimony.* New York: Villard, 2002.

17 "Even President Barack Obama and First Lady Michelle . . .": Lee, Jennifer. "The Incredible Flying Grannies." *New York Times*, May 10, 2007.

18 "Women have these templates . . .": Yabroff, 2008.

CHAPTER 2

22 "Motherhood was perceived as a new expertise . . .": White, Barbara Anne. "The Lives of Nineteenth-Century American Women." *National Women's Studies Association Journal*, 15, no. 1 (Spring 2003): pp. 137–146.

23 "In the lifetime of girls . . .": Rosenwieg, Linda W. "The Anchor of My Life: Middle-Class American Mothers and College-Educated Daughters," 1880–1920. *Journal of Social History* 25, no. 1 (1991): pp. 5–25.

25 "As late as the 1960s . . .": Bridgman, Anne. *Early Childhood Edu-*

cation and Childcare. Arlington: American Association of School Superintendents, 1988. (Also in 1989 in chapter 2.)

28 "Linda smiled and reminded her . . .": Interview with Susan Shaffer, April 7, 2008.

28 "Women no longer would be confused . . .": Paul, Pamela. *The Starter Marriage and the Future of Matrimony.* New York: Villard, 2002, p. 19.

34 "The cultural vision of superwoman . . .": Snyderman, Nancy. *Girl in the Mirror.* New York: Hyperion, 2002, p. 50.

34 "Generational conflicts in the American past . . .": Pogrebin, Letty Cottin. *Family Politics: Love and Power on an Intimate Frontier.* New York: McGraw-Hill, 1983.

39 "It's like a little person.": Garreau, J. "Cell Biology Like the Bee, This Evolving Species Buzzes and Swarms." *Washington Post,* July 1, 2002, p. C1.

40 "Much of human life, . . .": Fraenkel, P. "Beeper in the Bedroom." *Psychotherapy Networker,* March–April 2001, p. 22.

CHAPTER 3

43 "The literature has shown . . .": Lifshin, Lyn, *Tangled Vines.* San Diego: Harcourt Brace, 1992.

44 "According to psychologist Janet Surrey . . .": Miller, Jean Baker. "The Development of Women's Sense of Self." In *Women's Growth in Connection: Writings from the Stone Center,* eds. J. Jordan, A. Kaplan, J. Miller, I. Stiver, and J. Surrey. New York: Guilford Press, 1991.

48 "Years after daughters are grown . . .": Fingerman, Karen L. *Aging Mothers and Adult Daughters: A Case of Mixed Emotions.* New York: Springer, 2001, p. 6.

54 "Women's sense of integrity . . .": Gilligan, Carol. *In a Different Voice.* Cambridge: Harvard University Press, 1982, p. 14.

54 "Many women feel that preserving relationships . . .": Jordan, Judith.

Women's Growth in Connection: Writings from the Stone Center. New York: Guilford Press, 1991, p. 26.

57 "All around me, in recent years . . .": Warner, Judith. *Perfect Madness: Motherhood in the Age of Anxiety.* New York: Riverhead Books, 2006, p. 102.

57 "Mothers tend to experience their daughters . . .": Gilligan, 1982, p. 7.

58 "All of our dreams—those we've realized . . .": Nancy Snyderman, *Girl in the Mirror.* New York: Hyperion, 2002, pp. 12-13.

60 "Our own mothers' words echo when we talk.": Snyderman, pp. 12–13.

65 "Dependence is a byproduct of attachment . . .": Barnett, Rosalind C., Kibria, N., Baruch, G. K., and Pleck, J. H. "Adult Daughter-Parent Relationships and Their Association with Daughters' Subjective Well-Being and Psychological Distress." *Journal of Marriage and the Family*, 53 (1991): pp. 29–42.

CHAPTER 4

68 "More than 60 percent of today's college graduates . . .": *Business Wire.* "Nearly 60% of College Graduates Boomerang Back Home . . ." Seehttp://findarticles.com/p/articles/mi_m0EIN/is_2006_August_15/ai_n2695807 (accessed August 30, 2008).

70 "For example, young adults are the least likely . . .": DeNavas-Walt, Carmine, Proctor, Bernadette D., Smith, J. "Income, Poverty, and Health Insurance Coverage in the United States: 2006." *Current Population Report.* See http://www.census.gov/prod/2007pubs/p60-223.pdf (accessed April 11, 2008).

74 "The first generation to have homework-helping, . . .": Quindlen, Anna. "Home Cooking." *Newsweek*, March 3, 2008, p. 56.

78 Young adults today may watch . . .": Palmer, Kimberly. "The New Parent Trap." *U.S. News and World Report*, December 12, 2007, p. 4.

78 "I generation . . . as in both Ipod and me, me, me.": Zak, Dan. "Me." *Washington Post*, March 2, 2008, p. N4.

79 "As a historian, I can tell you . . .": Palmer, p. 1.

84 "In 2003, 54.8 percent of 18- to 24-year-old males . . .": Bronson, P., and A. Merryman. The Factbook: Eye Opening Memos on Everything Family. http://www.pobronson.com/factbook/ (accessed August 19, 2008).

86 "In Britain, a poll showed that one in ten . . .": Cordon, J. "Youth Residential Independence and Autonomy: A Comparative Study." *Journal of Family Issues* 18 (1997): pp. 576–607; Levine, S. "All Grown Up With No Place to Go." *Washington Post*, June 4, 2002, p. B1.

87 "This support comes in many forms . . .": Lynch, Eleanor W., and Hanson, Marci. *Developing Cross-Cultural Competence.* (Baltimore: Eleanor W. Lynch, Marci J. Hanson, Paul H. Brookes Publishing), 1998.

CHAPTER 5

97 "Karen Fingerman . . . concludes that a best friendship . . .": Interview with Susan Shaffer and Linda Gordon, February 22, 2008.

99 "Lorelai knew more than anyone else that just one night . . .": Sherman-Palladino, Amy. "Casablanca; Date Night." *Gilmore Girls*, season 4, 2005.

100 "Our kids are probably more precious . . .": Hoffman, Jan. "Obama's Young Backers Get Chance to Twist Parents' Arms, and Succeed." *New York Times*, April 8, 2008, p. A18.

104 "Recent articles, such as . . .": Rosenbloom, Stephanie. "Mommy Is Truly Dearest." *New York Times*, June 3, 2007.

105 "Best Friends: Mothers and Daughters . . .": Carpenter, Mackenzie. "Best Friends: Mothers and Daughters with the Deepest Connection." See http://post-gazette.com/pg/06134/689413-51.stm.

105 "Social, demographic and technological changes . . .": Rosenbloom, 2007.

117 "Any relationship can be negotiated . . .": Gordon, Susan. See http://life.familyeducation.com.

118 "Parents are now more exponentially . . .": Hoffman, p. A18.

118 "By giving up the outmoded wish to control . . .": Jonas, Susan, and Nissenson, Marilyn. *Friends for Life: Enriching the Bond Between Mothers and Their Adult Daughters.* New York: William Morrow, 1997, p. 47.

CHAPTER 6

126 "If mother is the cornerstone . . .": Walters, Marianne B., Carter, B., Papp, P., and Silverstein, O. *The Invisible Web.* New York: Guilford Press, 1988, p. 34.

126 "Men bond around common interests . . .": Doherty, William. *The Intentional Family: How to Build Family Ties in Our Modern World.* New York: Addison-Wesley, 1997, p. 51.

127 "*Avoidant* adults are somewhat uncomfortable . . .": Ainsworth, M.D.S., Blehar, M. C., Waters, E., and Wall, S. *Patterns of Attachment: A Psychological Study of the Strange Situation.* (Hillsdale, NJ: Erlbaum), 1978).

128 "Whether a daughter feels secure . . .": Wallin, David J. *Attachment in Psychotherapy.* New York: Guilford Press, 2007.

138 "Everything I needed, they assumed . . .": Brown, Erin. "Modern Love: My Three Years as a Beloved Daughter." *New York Times*, September 30, 2007, p. 6.

143 "Velcro mother or Mini-Me Mother . . .": Harder, Arlene. *Letting Go of Our Adult Children.* See http://www.learningplaceonline.com/relationships/letgo/book-intro.htm, p.14.

151 "In other cultures . . .": Lynch and Hanson.

154 "'When I was on the *New York Times* best-seller list' . . .": Deborah Solomon interview of Amy Tan in *New York Times:* "The Good Daughter," on August 10, 2008, page 11.

157 "Similar to the benefits for daughters . . .": Walters.

CHAPTER 7

167 "Because of the scarcity of affordable . . .": Adrian, V. and Coontz, S. *CFF Mother's Day Fact Sheet on Day Care.* Chicago: Council of Contemporary Families, 2008.

179 "When a grandchild is born . . .": Kitzinger, Sheila. *Becoming a Grandmother: A Life Transition*, 1996, p. 45.

184 "Women in their sixties and seventies . . .": Kitzinger, p. 38.

185 "Most boomer grandparents work hard . . .": Zullo, Kathryn, and Zullo, Allan. *The Nanas and the Papas, A Boomer's Guide to Grandparenting* (Kansas City: Andrews McMeel), 1998, p. 18.

202 "Mothers are doing more paid work . . .": Coontz, Stephanie. See http://stephaniecoontz.com/books/marriage/review12.htm (accessed May 23, 2008).

CHAPTER 8

205 "While this is a struggle . . .": Sherman-Palladino.

CHAPTER 9

224 "We see beautiful people as often . . .": Rodin, Judith. *Body Traps.* New York: William Morrow, 1992, p. 24.

225 " 'As a plumpish child' . . .": Schillinger, L. "Yearning for the Lean Years." *New York Times*, September 14, 2008, p. 15.

227 "Will Americans want to watch . . .": Singer, N. "Skin Deep: Nice Resume. Have You Considered Botox?" *New York Times*, January 24, 2008, p. E3.

227 "In fact . . . he was rewarded with a $400 million . . .": Stelter, B. "A Lucrative Deal for Rush Limbaugh." *New York Times*, July 3, 2008. See http://www.nytimes.com/2008/07/03/business/media/03radio.html.

231 "Joan Brumberg's *The Body Project* . . .": Brumberg, Joan. *The Body Project: An Intimate History of American Girls*. New York: Random House, 1997.

234 "We have to teach our daughters . . .": Snyderman.

CHAPTER 10

236 "A daughter can have any number of friends . . .": Pradhan, Monica. *The Hindi-Bindi Club*. New York: Bantam, 2007, p.211.

248 "When Nia Tyler, 24 . . .": Rosenbloom.

248 "No relationship is quite as primal . . .": Shaw, G. "Women's Health." See http://health.discovery.com/centers/womens/daughter/daughter.html.

249 "Mothers, rather than fathers, are held responsible . . .": Eriksen, Karen. "Ideas for Strengthening the Mother-Daughter Bond." (2004). See http://www.pioneerthinking.com/ara-motherdaughter.html (accessed August 15, 2008).

250 "There is a fine line between sharing wisdom and meddling . . .": Frain, Betty and Eileen Clegg. *Becoming a Wise Parent for Your Grown Child*. Oakland: New Harbinger, 1997, p. 2.

251 "As the mother is conceived an agent . . .": Rich, Adrienne. *Of Woman Born: Motherhood as Experience and Institution*. New York: Norton, 1976, p. 71.

BIBLIOGRAPHY

"A Grandparent's Role in the Family," http://www.aarp.org/family/grandparenting/articles/grandparentsrole.html (accessed August 31, 2008).

Adrian, V., and S. Coontz. *CCF Mother's Day Fact Sheet on Day Care.* Chicago, IL: Council of Contemporary Families, 2008.

Ahrons, C. *The Good Divorce.* New York: Harper Paperbacks, 1995.

Ainsworth, M. D. S., S. M. Bell, and D. J. Stayton. "Infant-Mother Attachment and Social Development: 'Socialization' as a Product of Reciprocal Responsiveness to Signals." In *Becoming a Person*, ed. M. Woodhead, R. Carr, and P. Light, P. London: Routledge, 1991.

Ainsworth, M. D. S., M. C. Blehar, E. Waters, and S. Wall. *Patterns of Attachment: A Psychological Study of the Strange Situation.* Hillsdale, NJ: Erlbaum, 1978.

Apter, T. *Altered Loves: Mothers and Daughters During Adolescence*: New York: Ballantine Books, 1991.

Bacall, L., http://www.brainyquote.com/quotes/authors/l/lauren_bacall.html (accessed August 13, 2008).

Barnett, R. C., N. Kibria, G. K. Baruch, and J. H. Pleck. (1991). "Adult Daughter–Parent Relationships and Their Association with Daughters' Subjective Well-Being and Psychological Distress." *Journal of Marriage and the Family*, 53 (1991): 29–42.

Belsky, J., and T. Nezworski (Eds.) *Clinical Implications of Attachment.* Hillsdale, NJ: Erlbaum, 1988.

Bombeck, E. http://www.quotedb.com/quotes/3708 (accessed June 3, 2008).

Bowen, M. *Family Therapy in Clinical Practice*. New York: Jason Aronson, Inc., 1985.

Bowlby, B. *Attachment and Loss*. New York: Basic Books, 1980.

Bridgeman, A. *Early Childhood Education and Childcare*. Arlington, VA: American Association of School Superintendents, 1988 [1989 in chapter 2].

Bronson, P., and A. Merryman. *The Factbook: Eye-Opening Memos on Everything Family*. http://www.pobronson.com/factbook/ (accessed August 19, 2008).

Brown, E. "Modern Love: My Three Years as a Beloved Daughter." *New York Times*, September 30, 2007, [insert page # tk].

Brumberg, J. J. *The Body Project: An Intimate History of American Girls*. New York: Random House, 1997.

Bureau of Labor Statistics, 2000. http://www.bls.gov/data/home.htm (accessed June 23, 2008).

Business Wire. "Nearly 60% of College Graduates Boomerang Back Home After Living on Their Own; Experience, Inc.'s 2006 'Life After College' Survey Reveals Where Recent College Grads Live and How Often They Job Hop." http://findarticles.com/p/articles/mi_møEIN/is_2006_August_15/ai_n26958071 (accessed August 30, 2008).

Caplan, Paula. *Don't Blame Mother: Mending the Mother-Daughter Relationship*. New York: Harper Collins, 1989.

Carpenter, M. "Best Friends: Mothers and Daughters with the Deepest Connection." http://www.post-gazette.com/pg/06134/689413-51.stm, May 14, 2006, (accessed June 5, 2008).

Caruso, D. A. "Attachment and Exploration in Infancy: Research and Applied Issues." *Early Childhood Research Quarterly* 4 (1989): 117–132.

Centers for Disease Control and Prevention. "2001 Youth Risk Behavior Survey." www.cdc.gov (accessed April 7, 2008).

Chodorow, N. *The Reproduction of Mothering*. Berkeley, CA: University of California Press, 1978.

Claes, H. www.great-inspirational-quotes.com/daughter-quotes.html (accessed December 18, 2008).

Clark, S. L., and M. Weismantle. *Employment Status: 2000*. Census 2000 Brief, U. S. Census Bureau. Washington, DC: U. S. Department of Education, 2002.

Coontz, S. http://www.stephaniecoontz.com/books/marriage/review12.htm (accessed May 23, 2008).

Cordon, J. 1997. "Youth Residential Independence and Autonomy: A Comparative Study." *Journal of Family Issues* 18 (1997): 576–607.

Curtis, J. "Divorce and the Extended Family" (2004a) http://www.family2000.org.uk/divorce and the extended family.htm (accessed June 11, 2008).

Curtis, J. "Grandparents Feel the Hurt of Divorce, Too" (2004b). http://www.family2000.org.uk/grandparents%20hurt.htm (accessed August 15, 2008).

DeNavas-Walt, C., B. Proctor, and J. Smith, August 2007. "Income, Poverty, and Health Insurance Coverage in the United States: 2006. *Current Population Reports*. http://www.census.gov/prod/2007pubs/p60-233.pdf (accessed April 11, 2008).

Doherty, W. *The Intentional Family: How to Build Family Ties in Our Modern World*. New York: Addison-Wesley, 1997.

Edelman, H. *Motherless Daughter*. New York: Addison-Wesley, 1994.

Ehrensaft, D. "Kindercult." Paper presented at Council on Contemporary Families Conference, Fordham University, New York, April 26, 2002.

Ephron, N. *I Feel Bad About My Neck: And Other Thoughts On Being a Woman*. New York: Vintage, 2008.

Eriksen. K. ("Ideas for Strengthening the Mother-Daughter Bond," May 4, 2004. http://www.pioneerthinking.com/ara-motherdaughter.html (accessed August 15, 2008).

Fahlberg, V. *Fitting the Pieces Together*. London: British Agencies for Adoption & Fostering, 1988.

Faludi, S. *Backlash: The Undeclared War Against American Women*. New York: Three Rivers Press, 2006.

Fingerman, K. *Aging Mothers and Their Adult Daughters: A Case of Mixed Emotions*. New York: Springer, 2001.

Fingerman, K. *Mothers and Their Adult Daughters: Mixed Emotions, Enduring Bonds*. New York: Prometheus Books, 2002.

Fischer, L. R. *Linked Lives: Adult Daughters and Their Mothers*. New York: Harper Collins, 1987.

Fraenkel, P. "Beeper in the Bedroom." *Psychotherapy Networker* (March–April 2001): 22–30.

Fraiberg, S., E. Adelson, and V. Shapiro. "Ghosts in the Nursery: A Psychoanalytic Approach to the Problem of Impaired Mother-Infant Relationships." *Journal of the American Academy of Child Psychiatry* 14 (1995): 387–422.

Frain, B., and E. Clegg. *Becoming a Wise Parent for Your Grown Child*. Oakland, CA: New Harbinger, 1997.

Friedman, T. *The World Is Flat 3.0: A Brief History of the Twenty-first Century*. New York: Picador, 2007.

Gard, L. "Am I Going Through a Quarter-Life Crisis?" *Lifesmart Solutions Magazine*, January 20, 2002. www.lifesmartsolutions.com/features/quarterlife.asp.

Garreau, J. "Cell Biology Like the Bee, This Evolving Species Buzzes and Swarms." *Washington Post*, July 31, 2002, C1.

Gatlin, L. http://www.cwrl.utexas.edu/~ulrich/femhist/now (accessed August 8, 2003).

Gilligan, C. *In a Different Voice*. Cambridge, MA: Harvard University Press, 1982.

Goleman, D. *Emotional Intelligence: Why It Can Matter More than IQ*. New York: Bantam Books, 1995.

Gordon, L. P., and S. M. Shaffer. *Mom, Can I Move Back In With You?: A Mother's Guide to Twentysomethings*. New York: Tarcher/Putnam, 2004.

Gordon, S. http://life.familyeducation.com (accessed August 6, 2008).

Harder, A. "Letting Go of Our Adult Children (2002). http://www.learningplaceonline.com/relationships/letgo/book-intro.htm (accessed August 5, 2008).

Hardy, S. B. *Mother Nature: A History of Mothers, Infants and Natural Selection*. New York: Pantheon, 1999.

Hasseldine, R. "Lifting the Veil on Mothers and Daughters." *the f word*, March 14, 2007. http://www.thefword.org.uk/features/2007/03/uncovering_the (accessed February 7, 2008).

Hewlett, S. A. *Creating a Life: Professional Women and the Quest for Children*. New York: Miramax, 2004.

Hirsch, M. *The Mother/Daughter Plot: Narrative, Psychoanalysis, Feminism*. Bloomington: Indiana University Press, 1989.

Hoffmann, J. "Obama's Young Backers Get Chance to Twist Parents' Arms, and Succeed." *New York Times*, April, 8, 2008, A18.

Isay, J. *Walking on Eggshells*. New York: Flying Dolphin Press, 2008.

Jack, D. (1985). "Silencing the Self: The Power of Social Imperatives in Female Depression." In R. Formanek & A. Gurian (Eds.), *Women and Depression: A Lifespan Perspective* (pp. 161–181). New York: Springer.

Jonas, S., and M. Nissenson. *Friends for Life: Enriching the Bond Between Mothers and Their Adult Daughters*. New York: William Morrow, 1997.

Jordan, J. *Women's Growth in Connection: Writings from the Stone Center*. New York: Guilford Press, 1991.

Kitzinger, S. *Becoming a Grandmother: A Life Transition*. New York: Fireside, 1996.

Kohlberg, L. *The Philosophy of Moral Development*. San Francisco, CA: Harper and Row, 1981.

Kuo, Y. "Marriage, Fertility and Labor Market Prospects in the United States, 1960–2000." PhD dissertation, Texas A&M University, 2005.

Lang, M., and Risman, B. *A "Stalled" Revolution or a Still-Unfolding One? The Continuing Convergence of Men's and Women's Roles*. Discussion paper prepared for the 10th Anniversary Conference of the Council on Contemporary Families, May 4–5, 2007, University of Chicago.

Lee, J. "The Incredible Flying Granny Nannies." *New York Times*, May 10, 2007.

Levine, S. "All Grown Up With No Place to Go." *Washington Post*, June 4, 2002, B1.

Levy, P., (2007/5/2). "Running a Hospital," 2007, May 2. See http://runningahospital.blogspot.com/2007/05/for-students-helicopter-parents.html (accessed September 1, 2008).

Lifshin, L. (Ed.). *Tangled Vines*. San Diego: Harcourt Brace, 1992.

Lowinsky, N. *Stories From the Motherline: Reclaiming the Mother-Daughter Bond, Finding Our Female Souls*. Los Angeles, CA: Tarcher, 1992.

Lynch, E., and M. Hanson. *Developing Cross-Cultural Competence*. Baltimore, MD: Eleanor W. Lynch, Marci J. Hanson, Paul H. Brookes Publishing, 1998.

Mann, J. *The Difference: Growing Up Female in America*. New York: Warner Books, 1994.

Mead, M. See http://life.familyeducation.com (accessed August 6, 2008).

Media Awareness Network. "Beauty and Body Image in the Media." See http://www.media-awareness.ca (accessed March 30, 2009).

Miller, A. *The Drama of the Gifted Child: The Search for the True Self*. New York: Basic Books, 1996.

Miller, J. B. "The Development of Women's Sense of Self." In *Women's Growth in Connection: Writings from the Stone Center*, eds. J. Jordan,

A. Kaplan, J. Miller, I. Stiver, and J. Surrey. New York: Guilford Press, 1991.

Miller, J. B. *Toward a New Psychology of Women*. Boston: Beacon Press, 1976.

Miller, J. B., and I. P. Stiver. *Healing Connection: How Women Form Relationships in Therapy and in Life*. Boston: Beacon Press, 1997.

Mintz, S. *Huck's Raft: A History of American Childhood*. Cambridge, MA: Belknap Press, 2006.

Mogel, W. *The Blessing of a Skinned Knee: Using Jewish Teachings to Raise Self-Reliant Children*. New York: Penguin, 2001.

Mundy, L. "Maternal Truths." *The Washington Post Magazine*, May 4, 2008, 10–15, 27–30.

Nakao, A. "They Can (and Do) Go Home Again." *San Francisco Chronicle*, May 30, 2004, F1.

Navaro, M. "My Child's Divorce Is My Pain." *New York Times*, September 2, 2007. http://www.nytimes.com/2007/09/02/fashion/02parents.html (accessed October 20, 2007).

Northrup, C. *Mother-Daughter Wisdom*. New York: Bantam, 2006.

Palmer, K. "The New Parent Trap: More Boomers Help Adult Kids Out Financially." *U.S. News and World Report*, December 12, 2007: 4.

Paul, P. *The Starter Marriage and the Future of Matrimony*. New York: Villard, 2002.

Pew Research Center. (2007/7/12). "Fewer Mothers Prefer Full-time Work: From 1997–2007." pewresearch.org/pubs/536/working-women (accessed September 2, 2008).

Pogrebin, L. C. *Among Friends*. New York: McGraw-Hill, 1987.

Pogrebin, L. C. *Family Politics: Love and Power on an Intimate Frontier*. New York: McGraw-Hill, 1983.

Pradhan, M. *The Hindi-Bindi Club*. London: Bloomsbury, 2007.

Quindlen, A. "Home Cooking." *Newsweek*, March 3, 2008: 56.

Rastogi, M. "Ideas for Strengthening the Mother-Daughter Bond," May 4, 2005. http://www.pioneerthinking.com/ara-motherdaughter.html (accessed August 15, 2008).

Redford, G. "Erase Ten Years!" *AARP Magazine*, March 2007. http://www.aarpmagazine.org/health/skincare_erase_ten_years.html (accessed May 29, 2007).

Rich, A. *Of Woman Born: Motherhood as Experience and Institution*. New York: Norton, 1976.

Richards, A. *Opting In: Having a Child Without Losing Yourself.* New York: Farrar, Straus and Giroux, 2008.

Robb, A. "Look! Up in the Sky! It's a Bird! It's a Plane! It's . . . Supermom!" *O The Oprah Magazine*, July 2008: 212.

Rodin, J. *Body Traps.* New York: William Morrow, 1992.

Rosen, R., Family Education. "Can Mothers and Daughters Be True Friends, or Just Peers?" http://life.familyeducation.com/friendships/girls/54626.html (accessed June 7, 2008).

Rosenbloom, S. "Mommy Is Truly Dearest. *New York Times*, June 28, 2007.

Rosenzweig, L. W. (1991). "The Anchor of My Life: Middle-Class American Mothers and College-Educated Daughters," 1880–1920. *Journal of Social History* 25, no. 1 (1991): 5–25.

Rutter, M. "Attachment and the Development of Social Relationships." In *Scientific Foundations of Developmental Psychiatry*, ed. M. Rutter. London: Heineman, 1979.

Schillinger, L. "Yearning for the Lean Years." *New York Times*, September 14, 2008, 15.

Segell, M. (2008/4/28) "Still Advising Your Grown Kids? Time to Stop." (2008) http://www.msnbc.msn.com/id/24054514/ (accessed Sept. 12, 2008).

Shaw, G. "Our Mothers, Ourselves: Mother-Daughter Relationships," October 30, 2007. http://health.discovery.com/centers/womens/daughter/daughter.html (accessed August 15, 2008).

Sherman-Palladino, A. (Producer) (2005). "Casablanca; Date Night." *Gilmore Girls*, Season 4 [Video]. WGBH Boston.

Silverstein, S. *The Giving Tree*, New York: HarperCollins, 1964.

Singer, N. "SKIN DEEP: Is Looking Your Age Now Taboo?" *New York Times*, March 1, 2007. http://www.nytimes.com/2007/03/01/fashion/01skin.html March 1, 2007.

Singer, N. "SKIN DEEP: Nice Résumé. Have You Considered Botox?" *New York Times*, January 24, 2008, E3.

Snyderman, N. *Girl in the Mirror.* New York: Hyperion, 2002.

Solomon, D. "The Good Daughter." *New York Times Magazine*, August 10, 2008, p. 11.

Spock, B. *Dr. Spock's Baby and Child Care* (8th ed.) New York: Pocket, 2004.

Stelter, B. "A Lucrative Deal for Rush Limbaugh." *New York Times*, July 3, 2008. http://www.nytimes.com/2008/07/03/business/media/03radio.html.

Tannen, D. *That's Not What I Mean*! New York: Ballantine Books, 1992.
Tannen, D. *You're Wearing That? Understanding Mothers and Daughters in Conversation*. New York: Ballantine Books, 2006.
Tolstoy, L. (2008). BrainyQuote. http://www.brainyquote.com/quotes/authors/l/leo_tolstoy138670.html (accessed August 13, 2008).
U.S. Census Bureau (2000). http://factfinder.census.gov/ (accessed March 10, 2008).
U.S. Department of Labor (2000). http://www.dol.gov/ (accessed May 6, 2008).
U.S. Department of Labor. "A Labor Force Statistics From the Current Population Survey" (2003). www.dol.gov (accessed April 18, 2008).
Wallin, D. J. *Attachment in Psychotherapy*. New York: Guilford Press, 2007.
Walters, M., B. Carter, P. Papp, and O. Silverstein. *The Invisible Web*. New York: Guilford Press, 1988.
Walters, S. D. *Lives Together Worlds Apart: Mothers and Daughters in Popular Culture*. Berkeley, CA: University of California Press, 1992.
Warner, J. *Perfect Madness: Motherhood in the Age of Anxiety*. New York: Riverhead Books, 2005.
White, B. A. "The Lives of Nineteenth-Century American Women." *National Women's Studies Association Journal*, 15, no. 1 (Spring 2003): 137–146.
Winnicott, D. W. *Babies and Their Mothers*. Cambridge, MA: Da Capo, 1992.
Winnicott, D. W. *Playing and Reality*. London: Tavistock, 1971.
Wolf, N. *The Beauty Myth*. New York: Anchor Books, 1992.
Yabroff, J. "The Feminine Mistakes." *Newsweek*, April 28, 2004. http://www.newsweek.com/id/132891 (accessed May 29, 2008).
Zak, D. "Me." *Washington Post*, March 2, 2008, N4.
Zullo, K., and A. Zullo. *The Nanas and the Papas, A Boomers' Guide to Grandparenting*. Kansas City: Andrews McMeel, 1998.

INDEX

Page numbers in *italic* indicate illustrations.

AARP, 167, 223–224
accepting being a Perfectly Imperfect Mother (Baker's Dozen Strategy for Mothers), 261–262
accepting daughter for who she is (Baker's Dozen Strategy for Mothers), 259–260
accountability, supporting vs. enabling, 71–73
actions vs. words, supporting vs. enabling, 67–70
active listening (Baker's Dozen Strategy for Mothers), 257
adolescence, girls' vs. boys', 19, 49–50
adult, treating daughter as (Baker's Dozen Strategy for Mothers), 263–264
"adultescence," 91
adulthood journey
  catch and release, 5, 6, 9–11, 17
  lessons learned, 237–238
  supporting vs. enabling, 67–68
advice
  daughters, advice for, 267–268
  giving only when asked (Baker's Dozen Strategy for Mothers), 256–257
  knowing when to give, marriage, motherhood, and divorce, 173–175, 182–183
advocacy for children, overbearing, 73–76
African-American culture, 87, 149
African culture, 64–65
Aging Mothers and Adult Daughters: A Case of Mixed Emotions (Fingerman), 48
Ahrons, Constance, 195
Ainsworth, Mary, 127
Alpha Mother, 132–135, 141, 143, 174, 244
Altered Loves (Apter), 49
Among Friends (Pogrebin), 97
appropriate boundaries. *See also* boundaries
  developing and maintaining appropriate boundaries (Baker's Dozen Strategy for Mothers), 257–259
  New Adulthood characteristic, 6, 13, 82, 93, 116
appropriate type and amount of support, 80–83
Apter, Terri, 49
archetypes, 5, 122–163
Argosy University (Chicago), 149, 248
arranged relationships, 104–107
Asian-American culture, 87
Asian culture, 64–65
Asian-Indian culture, 149

INDEX

Attachment in Psychotherapy (Wallin), 46
attachment theory, 127–128
attachment vs. individuation, 19, 41–66, 248
avoidant vs. secure adults, 127

baby boomer parents, 24, 25–26, 27, 28, 35, 37
Bacall, Lauren, 221
baggage (our), recognizing and managing, 60–61
Baker's Dozen Strategies for Mothers, 6, 256–267
balance, finding
  attachment and individuation, 64–66
  supporting vs. enabling, 69–70
Barnett, Rosalind, 42, 65, 66
Bea, Aunt, 32
beauty, tyranny of, 221–234
Becoming a Grandmother: A Life Transition (Kitzinger), 179
Becoming a Wise Parent for Your Grown Child (Frain and Clegg), 250
being in a relationship, attachment vs. individuation, 47–48
Belgium culture, 86
"Best Friends: Mothers and Daughters with the Deepest Connection" (Carpenter), 105
best friends, mothers as. *See also* mother-daughter relationships
  archetypes vs., 5
  financial support and, 79
  healthy friendships vs., 96–102, 103–104, 109, 110, 118
  mothers vs., 3–4, 8–9, 235–236
  selflessness preventing, 64
Beth Israel Hospital (Boston), 13
Blessings of a Skinned Knee: Using Jewish Teachings to Raise Self-Reliant Children, The (Mogel), 129–130
body image, 222–223, 230–231, 234
Body Project, The (Brumberg), 231
Bombeck, Erma, 203
bond (mother-daughter)
  attachment vs. individuation, 44–45
  catch and release, 7–9
  defining relationship with, 4–5
  maintaining mother-daughter bond (Baker's Dozen Strategy for Mothers), 266–267
Botox, 226
boundaries, 204–220
  creating boundaries, 204–209, 238–239, 246
  developing and maintaining appropriate boundaries (Baker's Dozen Strategy for Mothers), 257–259
  marriage, motherhood, and divorce, 169–172
  New Adulthood characteristic, 6, 13, 82, 93, 116
Bowen, Murray, 139
boys' vs. girls' adolescence, 19, 49–50
Brady, Mrs., 32
"broken family," 195
Brown, Erin, 138
Brumberg, Joan, 231
Bureau of Labor Statistics, 10
Business Wire, 68

career (work) impacts, 9–10, 18, 101–102, 237
Carpenter, Mackenzie, 105
catch and release, 7–19
cell phones, 38–39, 40
Census Bureau, 167
Centers of Disease Control and Prevention, 11
Chameleon Mother, 146–149
changing relationships, 1–4
Chinese culture, 65
Chodorow, Nancy, 48, 57
choices, daughters making different, 175–179
Claes, Helen, 7
Cleaver, June, 32
Clegg, Eileen, 250
Clinton, Hillary, 24, 227
close friendships vs. best friends, 96–102, 103–104, 109, 110, 118. *See also* best friends, mothers as
comforting daughters, 24–25
common ground, 15–16
communication. *See also* connection
  connection and, 21, 22, 24, 128
  underlying conversation and, 52–53, 107–110

INDEX

companionship, 35–36, 103–104, 202–203
confidentiality (privacy) and boundaries, 211–213
conflicts and archetypes, 126–128
"connected" people, 48–49
connection. *See also* communication
attachment as groundwork for, 44–45
communication and, 21, 22, 24, 128
opportunities for, 20, 21, 38–40, 100, 238
consistency in caregiver's response and security, 46
Cookie Monster, 186
Coontz, Stephanie, 79, 193–194
Council on Contemporary Families, 79, 202
Creating a Life: Professional Women and the Quest for Children (Hewlett), 18
creating boundaries, 204–209, 238–239, 246
cultural competence (New Adulthood characteristic), 93
cultural impacts
attachment vs. individuation, 64–65
beauty, tyranny of, 221–224, 225, 227, 233
catch and release, 8, 15–16, 16–17
supporting vs. enabling, 86–88
Curtis, Jill, 199

daughters. *See also* adulthood journey; best friends, mothers as; independent vs. dependent daughters; mother-daughter relationships
accepting daughter for who she is (Baker's Dozen Strategy for Mothers), 259–260
advice for, 267–268
choices, daughters making different, 175–179
don't personalize daughter's disappointments (Baker's Dozen Strategy for Mothers), 266
entitlement, daughters' sense of, 74, 78
failure, shielding daughters from, 74–75
father-daughter relationships, 19, 249
flashpoints between mothers and daughters, 123
motherhood (daughters'), 167, 179–193
past, daughter's connection to the, 115–117
principles for parenting adult daughters, 254–255
respecting daughter's new family (Baker's Dozen Strategy for Mothers), 265
self-sufficiency of daughters, 18–19
setting boundaries, daughter's participation in, 209–210, 239
treating daughter as adult (Baker's Dozen Strategy for Mothers), 263–264
delayed rewards, little patience with, 40
dependent vs. independent daughters. *See* independent vs. dependent daughters
"deselfed," 139
detachment, engaged (Baker's Dozen Strategy for Mothers), 262–263
developing and maintaining
appropriate boundaries (Baker's Dozen Strategy for Mothers), 257–259
respectful interdependence (Baker's Dozen Strategy for Mothers), 264–265
disappointments of daughter, avoiding personalizing (Baker's Dozen Strategy for Mothers), 266
disengaging (not), stepping back (Baker's Dozen Strategy for Mothers), 262–263
divorce, 193–200
Doherty, William, 126
don't personalize daughter's disappointments (Baker's Dozen Strategy for Mothers), 266
Dr. Spock's Baby and Childcare (Spock), 24
Drudge Report, 227

Edelman, Hope, 55
education experiences, 26
Edwards, Elizabeth, Cate, and John, 7
Ehrensaft, Diane, 88
Emotional Intelligence (Goleman), 91
emotional support, 72
empathy
importance of, 124, 199–200
New Adulthood characteristic, 92–93
empty nesters, 68, 69
emulation vs. separation, identity constructed by, 49–51

enabling, 71–72, 73, 238, 239. *See also* supporting vs. enabling
engaged detachment (Baker's Dozen Strategy for Mothers), 262–263
engaging in mature relationships (New Adulthood characteristic), 93
entitlement, daughters' sense of, 74, 78
environmental context, understanding (New Adulthood characteristic), 93–94
Ephron, Nora, 231
Eriksen, Karen, 249
European-American culture, 87–88, 149
expectations
  boundaries and, 217–219
  supporting vs. enabling, 89–90

Facebook, 40
failure, shielding daughters from, 74–75
false sense of reality, 89
families, marriage, motherhood, and divorce, 164–168
family of daughter, respecting (Baker's Dozen Strategy for Mothers), 265
Family Politics (Pogrebin), 20
Family Therapy in Clinical Practice (Bowen), 139
Family Therapy Practice Center, The, 126
father-daughter relationships, 19, 249
fault lines and archetypes, 126–128
feminist movement, 27–31
financial responsibility (New Adulthood characteristic), 92
financial support, 71–72, 76–77, 78, 79–80
Fingerman, Karen, 10–11, 48, 97
Fischer, Lucy Rose, 99–100
"five-second rule," 36
flashpoints between mothers and daughters, 123
Fraenkel, Peter, 40
Frain, Betty, 250
Frankel, Valerie, 225–226
Friedman, Thomas, 154
Friends for Life: Enriching the Bond Between Mothers and Their Daughters (Jonas and Nissenson), 118–119
"friendship breakers," 111
friendship characteristics, 96–121. *See also* best friends, mothers as
Frost, Robert, 204
fun, having together (Baker's Dozen Strategy for Mothers), 264
Furstenberg, Frank, 78
future, mom's connection to the, 115–117

gender equality, 27–31
generational conflicts, 23–24, 34–37
"generation overlap," 15–16
George Washington University, 51
German culture, 86
Gilligan, Carol, 53, 54
Gilmore Girls (TV show), 98–99, 204–205
Girl in the Mirror (Snyderman), 58
girls' vs. boys' adolescence, 19, 49–50
giving advice only when asked (Baker's Dozen Strategy for Mothers), 256–257
Giving Tree, The (Silverstein), 17
Golden Girls (TV show), 15
Goleman, Daniel, 91
"good divorce," 195
"good enough mother," 111–114, 261
Good Housekeeping, 23–24
Gordon, Linda Perlman, 84, 127
Gordon, Susan, 117
grandmothers, mothers, and daughters, 55–61, 113–115, 155
grandmother vs. mother, being (Baker's Dozen Strategy for Mothers), 265–266
grandparenting
  catch and release, 17–18
  lessons learned, 240–242
  marriage, motherhood, and divorce, 167, 179–186, 187–193, 196–198, 202–203
Grey's Anatomy (TV show), 36
Guardian Angel Mother, 127, 128–132, 139, 238, 241

Harder, Arlene, 143–144
Hardy, Sarah Blaffer, 96
Hasseldine, Rosjke, 139
having fun together (Baker's Dozen Strategy for Mothers), 264
Health Insurance Portability and Accountability Act (HIPAA), 246
healthy friendships vs. best friends,

96–102, 103–104, 109, 110, 118. *See also* best friends, mothers as
"helicopter parents" (hyperparenting), 13–15, 105, 128, 237–238
Hewlett, Sylvia Ann, 18
Hindi-Bindi Club, The (Pradhan), 236
HIPAA (Health Insurance Portability and Accountability Act), 246
historical context for lives, 21
Hoffman, Jan, 118
"hotel families," 86
humor (sense of) for parenting, 85–86
hyperparenting, 13–15, 105, 128, 237–238

identity confusion and boundaries, 215–217
identity constructed by emulation vs. separation, 49–51
I Feel Bad About My Neck (Ephron), 231
"I generation," 78–79
immigrants and parenting, 26, 34, 149–155
independence of mothers, 20–22
independent vs. dependent daughters
  attachment vs. individuation, 65–66
  lessons learned, 238–239
  paradigm shift, 25–27, 38
  supporting vs. enabling, 73–79
Indiana University, 16
Indian culture, 65
individuation vs. attachment, 19, 41–66, 248
interdependence. *See* respectful interdependence
interfering in divorce, avoiding, 198–199
internal vs. external beauty, 233
"invisible umbilical," 118–119
Isay, Jane, 254

Jack, Dana, 61
Japanese culture, 65
Jonas, S., 118–119
Jordan, Judith, 54
Joy Luck Club, The (Tan), 154
"just say no," boundaries, 208

"Kindercult" (Ehrensaft), 88
Kindlon, Dan, 100
Kitzinger, Sheila, 179, 184
Kohlberg, Lawrence, 53

Latino culture, 64–65, 87, 149, 167
legacy of divorce, 194–196
lessons learned, 235–252
Letting Go of Our Adult Children (Harder), 143
Levy, Paul, 13–14
life-cycle transitions, 6, 42–44, 110–111
life span, increase in, 11
Lifting the Veil on Mothers and Daughters (Hasseldine), 139
Limbaugh, Rush, 227
limits, setting. *See* boundaries
Linked Lives: Adult Daughters and Their Mothers (Fischer), 100
listening (active) (Baker's Dozen Strategy for Mothers), 257
Lives Together, Worlds Apart (Walters), 235
Long-Distance Mother, 135–139
long-term support, 73–79
Lost (TV show), 35
Lowinski, Naomi, 242

maintaining
  appropriate boundaries (Baker's Dozen Strategy for Mothers), 257–259
  respectful interdependence (Baker's Dozen Strategy for Mothers), 264–265
markers of New Adulthood, 90–95
marriage, motherhood, and divorce, 164–203
marriage impacts, 9, 10
Maryland State Department of Education, 28
"matrophobia," 102–103, 236
maturation encouraged by boundaries, 219–220
mature relationships, engaging in (New Adulthood characteristic), 93
Mead, Margaret, 67
Media Awareness Network, 225
"meta-messages," 107–108
midlife, mothers at, 5, 42–44
Miller, Jean Baker, 45
Mini-Me (Velcro) Mother, 143–145, 174, 217
mirrors, mothers as, 57–58, 60
Mogel, Wendy, 129–130

Mom, Can I Move Back In with You? A Survival Guide for Parents of Twentysomethings (Gordon and Shaffer), 84, 127
"Mommy Is Truly Dearest" (xx), 104–105
money, root of some evil, 79–80
moral development, attachment vs. individuation, 53–54
mother-daughter bond, maintaining (Baker's Dozen Strategy for Mothers), 266–267. *See also* bond (mother-daughter)
mother-daughter relationships, 1–6. *See also* adulthood journey; advice; best friends, mothers as; bond (mother-daughter); boundaries; communication; connection; cultural impacts; daughters; empathy; expectations; grandparenting; independent vs. dependent daughters; Perfectly Imperfect Mother; renegotiating relationships; respectful interdependence
  archetypes, 5, 122–163
  attachment vs. individuation, 19, 41–66, 248
  beauty, tyranny of, 221–234
  catch and release, 7–19
  friendship characteristics, 96–121
  lessons learned, 235–252
  marriage, motherhood, and divorce, 164–203
  paradigm shift, 20–40
  strategies: strengthening healthy connections, 253–268
  supporting vs. enabling, 67–95
  testaments about, 1, 2
Mother-Daughter Wisdom (Northrup), 259
motherhood (daughters'), 167, 179–193
Motherless Daughter (Edelman), 55
mother nature, 41–42
Mother Nature: A History of Mothers, Infants and Natural Selection (Hardy), 96
mothers (our) impact on mothering (our), 55–61, 113–115, 155
moving back home phenomenon, 17, 68–69, 83–88, 239–240
multitasking skills, 32
mutual interests, 202–203
mutual respect and boundaries, 12, 212–213, 220
"My Child's Divorce Is My Pain" (Navarro), 198

Nanas and the Papas, The (Zullo and Zullo), 185
Native American culture, 87
Navarro, Mireya, 198
"need" vs. "want," 76
Nelson, Harriet, 24, 32
New Adulthood characteristics, 90–95
New York Times, 105, 138, 198, 248
nineteenth-century parenting, 22–23
Nissenson, M., 118–119
Northrup, Christiane, 259
"not alikeness," 51
now and forever, archetypes, 155–157

Obama, Barack (President) and Michelle (First Lady), 17
open relationship between mother and child, 44–45
Oprah Winfrey Show (TV show), 223
Opting In: Having a Child Without Losing Yourself (Richards), 115
other focus to self-focus, attachment vs. individuation, 42–44
overprotective child-rearing practices, 36–37

painful truths, catch and release, 11–13
Palmer, Kimberly, 79
paradigm shift, 20–40
parallel universe, 37–38
parent-child bond, defining relationship, 4–5. *See also* bond (mother-daughter)
"parentified child," 140
parenting. *See* mother-daughter relationships
past, daughter's connection to the, 115–117
perfection fixation, beauty (tyranny of), 224–226, 233–234
Perfectly Imperfect Mother
  accepting being a Perfectly Imperfect Mother (Baker's Dozen Strategy for Mothers), 261–262
  archetype, 124–125, 155–156, 178, 252

Perfect Madness: Motherhood in the Age of Anxiety (Warner), 32–33, 57
perfect mom vs. Supermom, 32–34, 190
permalinks, 99–102
Persephone, 235
personalizing daughter's disappointments, avoiding (Baker's Dozen Strategy for Mothers), 266
personal responsibility (New Adulthood characteristic), 92
physical support, 72
Pittsburgh Post-Gazette, 105
Playing and Reality (Winnicott), 122
Pogrebin, Letty, 20, 97
Pradhan, Monica, 236
pregnancy and beauty (tyranny of), 223
principles for parenting adult daughters, 254–255
privacy (confidentiality) and boundaries, 211–213
private act of parenting, 70
Proactive Questions for Mothers to Ask Themselves, 157–163
protection (sense of) of mothers, 105–106, 109–110, 206
Psychotherapy Networker, 40
Purdue University, 10
"push/pull" nature of mother-daughter relationships, 49

Quindlen, Anna, 74

Rastogi, Mudita, 149–150, 248–249
Reagan, Nancy, 208
recognizing and managing our baggage, 60–61
reduced generation gap, 35–37
Reed, Donna, 24
"relational" people, 48–49
release, catch and, 7–19
renegotiating relationships
  archetypes and, 127
  attachment vs. individuation, 42
  boundaries, 205
  friendship characteristics, 117–118
  marriage, motherhood, and divorce, 178, 181, 200–202
  supporting vs. enabling, 67
rescuing daughters and boundaries, 214–215
respectful interdependence
  developing and maintaining respectful interdependence (Baker's Dozen Strategy for Mothers), 264–265
  New Adulthood characteristic, 48, 69, 92
respecting daughter's new family (Baker's Dozen Strategy for Mothers), 265
Restylane, 226
Rich, Adrienne, 251
Richards, Amy, 115
Robinson, Marian, 17–18
role model, mother as a, 22, 42
Rosenbloom, Stephanie, 248

safety net, mothers as, 70, 77–78
San Diego State University, 78
secure attachment, 46
secure vs. avoidant adults, 127
seizing the moment, catch and release, 9–11
self-awareness for setting boundaries, 208–209
self-editing, 107, 108–109, 166
self-esteem, supporting vs. enabling, 75, 81, 82, 88
"selfishness" vs. "good boundaries," 218
selflessness of mothers, 61–64
self-sufficiency of daughters, 18–19
self-worth mixed messages, 226–229
sense of
  humor for parenting, 85–86
  protection of mothers, 105–106, 109–110, 206
  self and attachment vs. individuation, 45, 48
separation vs. emulation, identity constructed by, 49–51
Sesame Street (TV show), 186
setting limits. *See* boundaries
sex-role expectations, 19, 53–55
Shadow Mother, 139–143
Shaffer, Susan Morris, 84, 127
Shakespeare, William, 41
shaming, 210
shared biology, attachment and individuation, 48–53
Sharkey, Lee, 248

Shevitz, Linda, 28
shielding daughters from life, 73–75
Silverstein, Shel, 17
Singer, Natasha, 226–227, 227–228
single to committed relationship transition, 164–169
sisterhood, power of, 27–31
"Skin Deep: Is Looking Your Age Now Taboo" (Singer), 226
Snyderman, Nancy, 34, 58, 60
Somers, Patricia, 13
Spock, Dr., 24, 25
"stealth parenting" (hyperparenting), 13–15, 105, 128, 237–238
Steinem, Gloria, 24
stepping back, but not disengaging (Baker's Dozen Strategy for Mothers), 262–263
Stone, Mrs., 32
Stone Center at Wellesley College, 54
Stories From the Motherline (Lowinski), 242
strategies: strengthening healthy connections, 253–268
Supermom vs. perfect mom, 32–34, 190
supporting vs. enabling, 67–95
Surrey, Janet, 44–45
Survey: Mother and Daughter Friendships, 119–121

talk, bedrock of women's relationships, 126
Tan, Amy, 154
Tannen, Deborah, 51–52, 53, 54, 107, 205–206
technological advances impacts, 20, 21, 38–40, 100, 238
temporary nature of support, 72
testaments about mother-daughter relationships, 1, 2
text messaging, 38, 39–40
That's Not What I Meant (Tannen), 107
Thin Is the New Happy (Frankel), 225
30 Rock (TV show), 36
time for friendships, 10–11
Title IX, 28
Tolstoy, Leo, 12
Transcultural Mother, 149–155
treating daughter as adult (Baker's Dozen Strategy for Mothers), 263–264
treating vs. supporting, 80–81
troubled relationships, 11–13
Truman, Harry (President), 253
Twain, Mark, 98
Twenge, Jean, 78
twentieth-century parenting, 22–27, 251
twenty-first-century parenting, 70, 91
Twitter, 40
Tyler, Nia, 248
tyranny of beauty, 221–234

understanding environmental context (New Adulthood characteristic), 93–94
University of Minnesota, 126
University of Pennsylvania, 78
University of Texas (Austin), 13
U.S. Bureau of Labor Statistics, 10
U.S. Census Bureau, 167
Velcro (Mini-Me) Mother, 143–145, 174, 217
Victorian mothers, 23, 24, 225
Vietnam/Watergate-era mothers, 24

Walking on Eggshells: Navigating the Delicate Relationship Between Adult Children and Parents (Isay), 254
Wallin, David, 46
Walters, Marianne, 126
Walters, Susan, 16
Walters, Suzanna Danuta, 235
Warner, Judith, 32–33, 57
Washington Post, 39
Wellesley College, 54
Winnicott, Donald, 111–112, 122, 261
"wisdom gap," 245
Women's Growth in Connection: Writings from the Stone Center (Jordan), 54
women's movement, 20, 27–31
working outside the home, 9–10, 18, 101–102
World War II and parenting changes, 24–25, 32

yin and yang of support, 88–90
You're Wearing That? Understanding Mothers and Daughters in Conversation (Tannen), 52, 205
youthfulness orientation, 37–38, 227–233, 234

Zak, Dan, 78
Zullo, Kathyrn and Allan, 185